AMERICAN COUNTRY
Scrap Quilts

Liz Porter and Marianne Fons

Rodale Press, Inc.
Emmaus, Pennsylvania

OUR MISSION

We publish books that empower people's lives.

RODALE BOOKS

If you have any questions or comments concerning this book, please write to:

Rodale Press, Inc.
Book Readers' Service
33 East Minor Street
Emmaus, PA 18098

Front Cover: The inner quilt is Scrap Star, page 42, and the outer quilt is Flock of Geese Medallion, page 22.

Back Cover: The inner quilt is African Lattice, page 164, and the outer quilt is Galaxy Star, page 176.

Many of the fabrics featured in photos throughout the book are courtesy of Piney Woods, from The Heritage Collection by Fons-Porter, and Fabri-Quilt Inc., from The Virginia Robertson Collection.

The photographs on pages xii–1, 68–69, 116–117, and 184–185 were taken at the Georgetown Manor, Ethan Allen Home Interiors, 5064 Hamilton Boulevard, Allentown, Pennsylvania.

AMERICAN COUNTRY SCRAP QUILTS EDITORIAL STAFF

Editors: **Ellen Pahl** and **Karen Soltys**

Interior and Cover Designer: **Carol Angstadt**

Illustrator: **Sandy Freeman**

Photographer: **Mitch Mandel**

Photo Stylist: **Marianne Grape Laubach**

Studio Manager: **Leslie Keefe**

Copy Editor: **Candace B. Levy**

Manufacturing Coordinator: **Melinda Rizzo**

Administrative Assistance: **Stephanie Wenner**

RODALE BOOKS

Editorial Director, Home and Garden:
Margaret Lydic Balitas

Managing Editor, Quilt Books: **Suzanne Nelson**

Art Director, Home and Garden: **Michael Mandarano**

Associate Art Director, Home and Garden:
Mary Ellen Fanelli

Copy Director, Home and Garden: **Dolores Plikaitis**

Office Manager, Home and Garden: **Karen Earl-Braymer**

Editor-in-Chief: **William Gottlieb**

Library of Congress Cataloging-in-Publication Data
Fons, Marianne.
    American country scrap quilts / Marianne Fons and Liz Porter.
        p.   cm.
    ISBN 0–87596–626–8 (hc : alk. paper)
    1. Patchwork—United States—Patterns.
2. Quilting—United States—Patterns. 3. Patchwork quilts—United States. I. Porter, Liz. II. Title
TT835.F63   1995
746.46—dc20   95–24009

Distributed in the book trade by St. Martin's Press
2 4 6 8 10 9 7 5 3   hardcover

Dedicated to

the makers of the

great American

scrap quilts of

yesterday and

today.

Contents

VINTAGE SCRAP QUILTS

SCRAP QUILTS FROM GRANDMA'S ATTIC

TODAY'S SCRAP QUILTS

ONE PATCH WONDERS

Acknowledgments

The authors would like to thank the following persons for the loan of their beautiful quilts: Kim Baird, *Crazy Cabins;* JoAnn Belling, *Color Rotation;* LaNelle Bentz, *Grandmother's Fan;* Kathy Corones, *October;* Marty Freed, *Flock of Geese Medallion;* Linda Fiedler, *Tulips in the Spring;* Nancy Granner, *Six-Pointed String Star;* Julie Hart, *Square in Square;* Marilyn Hein, *Centennial Baskets* and *Original Star;* Frieda Holt, *Snowball* and *Love Ring;* Mary Jo Kellog, *Homespun Bricks;* Wade and Jessica Kerrigan, *Zigzag Log Cabin;* Nadi Lane, *She Did the Best She Could;* Edith Leeper, *Rocky Road to Kansas;* Bev Munson, *Aunt Sukey's Choice, Feathered World without End,* and *Shooting Star;* Mabeth Oxenreider, *Galaxy Star;* Mary Radke, *Cosmos Garden, Plaid Nine Patch,* and *Sunbonnet Sue;* Jill Reber, *Kansas Twister;* Judy Roche, *Hourglass Charm Quilt;* Fern Stewart, *African Lattice Wall Quilt;* and Connie Tilman, *Scrap Star.* We would also like to thank Mary Ann Norville for her generosity.

Introduction

Women of the past did have actual scraps from which to fashion their quilts, and they used those scraps in wonderful ways that continue to inspire.

When we began making quilts in the mid-1970s, cotton fabrics were hard to find. We were young mothers then, with limited incomes, so it was probably just as well. We had to start out by designing and sewing quilts with as few as two and as many as eight or nine fabrics. Our limited palette of colors and prints resulted in rather formal designs, but we were hooked on quilting just the same. Our attention was focused on developing our sewing skills and understanding elements like drafting patterns, mitering borders, and putting a quilt in a frame.

By the early 1980s, the American fabric industry had started to catch up with what seemed to be an insatiable desire within every quilter for huge supplies of printed cotton fabric. Quilt shops had sprung up across the land, our kids were in school, and we set out in our cars to buy cloth. We didn't have bags of scraps like our foremothers did, but we knew where to get them.

As our stash of fabrics grew, so did our collection of books full of photographs of old quilts. Looking through these books, we discovered that the majority of quilts from the past were, in fact, scrap quilts. The frugality that has long been credited to the pioneer women of America was evidenced in quilt after quilt after quilt. Those wonderful, multifabric quilts had a spontaneity that was missing in our early, more formal projects.

In the mid-1980s, the rotary cutter made its entrance into the world of quilting. Now, not only did we have lots of fabrics but we could cut them up faster and more accurately than ever before! The stage was set for a scrap quilt revival that would last a long time. Indeed, American quilters have been producing fantastic scrap quilts for the past decade or so, sometimes turning to the past to reproduce the best of the nineteenth- and early twentieth-century styles, sometimes creating innovative masterpieces that could come only from our own time.

Today's quilters often struggle with the term *scrap quilt*, partly because nonquilters are always teasing us about buying our "scraps" at fabric stores! Like much of women's history, the exact process of quiltmaking in the nineteenth century was rarely recorded;

however, we do know that women sewed their own and all of their family's clothing, generally from cotton cloth. A woman's dress could easily require six yards of fabric! Leftover cuttings were saved for quilts. (Quiltmakers often kept two scrap bags, one for "lights" and one for "darks.") We also believe that as family clothing wore out, the still-usable parts were saved for patchwork. In other words, women of the past did have actual scraps from which to fashion their quilts, and they used those scraps in wonderful ways that continue to inspire.

Most women today do not produce cotton scraps. We tend to have jobs and purchase most of the clothing for ourselves and our families. This dilemma has caused a little awkwardness regarding our scrap quilts. The term *multifabric* was coined to replace the word *scrap* as a way for us quilters to own up to the fact that the fabric we use is not left over from anything, but brand new! Today, the term *scrap quilt* means a style of quilt that is made of dozens, scores, maybe even hundreds of different fabrics, rather than a quilt made of leftover bits of cloth.

In this book, we've collected wonderful scrap quilts from coast to coast. In "Vintage Scrap Quilts" and "Scrap Quilts from Grandma's Attic," you'll find beautiful representatives of a particular period in American quiltmaking history. You'll find antiques so charming you'll want to make them up in the reproduction fabrics readily available today. You'll find new quilts that draw heavily on the styles of the past. In "Today's Scrap Quilts," you'll find contemporary pieces that require the very latest fabrics from the trendiest quilt shops. In "One Patch Wonders," you'll find one patch examples that will inspire you to go on a scrap collector's quest.

From overflowing scrap baskets to stacks of neatly folded fat quarters, there's an outlet here for fabrics of all varieties.

We know everyone loves scrap quilts, and we hope you'll enjoy the scrap projects we've gathered in the following pages!

Happy sewing,

Marianne and Liz

Marianne and Liz

Today, the term *scrap quilt* means a style of quilt that is made of dozens, scores, maybe even hundreds of different fabrics, rather than a quilt made of leftover bits of cloth.

Using This Book

We've written this book with all levels of quilters in mind. For each project we have given a skill level rating from easy to challenging. Each "Fabrics and Supplies" list includes everything you'll need to make a quilt very much like the one in the photograph. When you choose one of the projects, you can create it in the colors shown if that is your preference. We encourage you to think of other options and be adventurous by selecting completely different colors.

Throughout the book, we've included "Scrap Recipes" to give you suggestions for alternate approaches to each quilt. To inspire you, we've even made up some of the blocks in color schemes that depart from the original.

Our instructions for all of the quilts incorporate the quick-cutting and sewing methods we love. For those who prefer traditional techniques, we've given instructions for making templates in "Quiltmaking Essentials," beginning on page 212.

The streamlined "Quick Cutting" charts include the following icons for many of the second and third cuts:

■ means to cut a square of the same dimension as the strip width.

◩ indicates that you should cut the square in half diagonally once.

◲ indicates that you should cut the square in half diagonally twice.

▬ includes the dimensions within the rectangular icon.

Fabric	First Cut		Second Cut		Third Cut	
BLOCKS	No. of Strips	Strip Width	No.	Shape	No.	Shape
Muslin	11	2¼"	31	2¼"×11"	—	—
Red print	7	2¼"	116	■	—	—
Dark scraps	5	2¼"	48	2¼"×4"	—	—
	4	2⅝"	48	■	96	◩
Shirtings	10	2¼"	96	2¼"×4"	—	—
Light scraps	2	4¼"	12	▢	48	◲
Medium scraps	3	2¼"	48	▢	—	—

QUICK CUTTING

Cut a square of the same dimension as the strip width

Cut the square in half diagonally once to make two triangles

Cut the square in half diagonally twice to make four triangles

Cut a rectangle with the dimensions indicated within the shape

No additional cutting

Vintage Scrap Quilts

Multitudes of
indigos were pro-
duced cheaply at
domestic printing
mills and incorpo-
rated into many
scrap quilts. Blue
shades range from
light cadets to
dark navys.

THE LOOK
OF VINTAGE QUILTS

The styles and patterns of quilts made in America during the years
that encompass the turn of the century (1875–1925) are ones many
quilt lovers, including us, consider the best of classic American design. It's satisfying to note that interior decorating falls back regularly
on the easy-to-live-with colors of this American folk art period.

Fabrics tended to be simple prints, rather than complex multicolored ones. A colored background might have only white or black
motifs. Multitudes of indigo blues, double pinks, yellow greens
(often called "poison"), and black-and-white shirting-style prints
were produced cheaply at domestic printing mills and incorporated
in multifabric quilts. Many "object prints," fabrics with small realistic
motifs such as horseshoes, anchors, or even insects printed on them,
were available during this time.

Quilt patterns were often simple, too, such as easily pieced stars,
nine patches, album squares, and baskets. Ladies' magazines became popular during the latter part of the century, and zealous editors established names for patterns. By 1900, nearly every woman
had a sewing machine, and she used it to speed up family garment
sewing and the piecing of quilt blocks.

Our favorite block characteristic of late nineteenth-century scrap
quilts is the presence of what we call "maverick" blocks. Mavericks
are blocks that don't fit the norm. Often they vary because of some
light/dark value placement incongruency. In a quilt that has mostly
light fabrics in the background areas, for example, there are always
a few blocks with the values switched or partly switched. You can
find mavericks in just about every quilt in this chapter. While we
may speculate that the quiltmakers of the past were making do with
fabrics at hand, who's to say that the mavericks weren't intentional,
as these blocks certainly enliven many quilts.

*Striped and plaid
fabrics, sometimes
printed, sometimes
woven, are found in
most patchwork
quilts of the turn of
the century.*

*Object prints, also called conversationals, are fabrics printed with
small realistic motifs. Various types of conversationals have been
popular throughout fabric history. Late nineteenth-century
quilters collected them for their patchwork and charm quilts.*

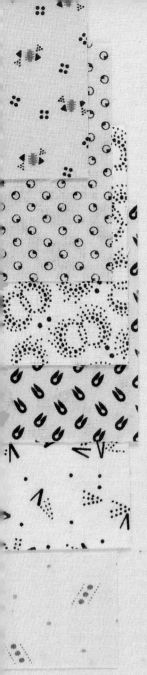

Settings for quilt blocks were straight or diagonal, rather than in the medallion format of the early nineteenth century. Blocks were generally joined either block to block or with sashing strips, which might be pieced. Zigzag sets almost always come from this historical period.

One way to achieve the look of the last century in your quilts is to use vintage fabric. Many quilters find a special joy in sewing with 100-year-old cloth. They hunt for mint-condition antique fabrics at quilt shows where antique dealers have booths, flea markets, garage sales, and at quilt shops that carry pieces of old fabric and antique blocks. Often, however, the quilter has to combine a limited amount of old (and expensive!) fabric with old-looking but newly made prints to have enough for a quilt.

Here are some additional hints for achieving this classic style in your own scrap quilts. We've noted which quilts in this book illustrate each characteristic.

- Combine plaids and stripes with prints when choosing fabrics (see Zigzag Log Cabin, Aunt Sukey's Choice, and Snowball).

- Use shirting prints for light fabrics (see Aunt Sukey's Choice).

- Select simple designs for patchwork blocks (see Centennial Baskets and Scrap Star).

- Make several "maverick blocks" for each quilt (see Centennial Baskets, She Did the Best She Could, and Cosmos Garden).

- Cut occasional plaids and stripes noticeably off grain (See She Did the Best She Could and Plaid Nine Patch).

- Use double pink, poison green, or black as your setting fabric (see Centennial Baskets, Scrap Star, and Rocky Road to Kansas).

- Use black, blue, red, brown, off-white, green, pink, gold, and purple prints together in your quilt (see Flock of Geese Medallion).

- Choose a zigzag set (see Zigzag Log Cabin).

Poison green, a green shade more yellow than blue-green, was popular for setting pieces.

Shirting prints are light-background fabrics with small, dark motifs scattered overall. Light backgrounds range from pure white to dirty white to cream.

Pink fabrics, especially double pinks, were a mainstay of patchwork quilts from 1875 to 1925. These bright prints added zip to neighboring dull colors in scrap quilts.

SKILL LEVEL: Easy

SIZE: Finished quilt is 66 × 84 inches

Finished block is 9 inches square

Number of blocks: 48

Quilt owners: Wade and Jessica Kerrigan

FABRICS AND SUPPLIES

- 4¼ yards *total* of medium and dark print fabrics for blocks and pieced border (leftover 1½-inch strips will do just fine)
- 2½ yards *total* of light and medium light fabrics for blocks
- ⅛ yard of red solid for block centers
- ⅝ yard of red print fabric for inner border
- ⅝ yard of fabric for binding
- 5 yards of fabric for quilt back
- Quilt batting, at least 72 × 90 inches
- Rotary cutter, ruler, and mat

Zigzag Log Cabin

Part of the fun Liz Porter had in making this Log

Cabin quilt was deciding how to set the blocks.

Zigzag was a popular setting for Log

Cabin blocks during the late 1800s,

although less common than Straight

Furrow, Sunshine and Shadow, or Lights

and Darks sets. The pieced border of narrow fabric

strips is one we like to call Joseph's Coat because, like

the biblical reference, it is made of many colors.

AMERICAN COUNTRY SCRAP QUILTS

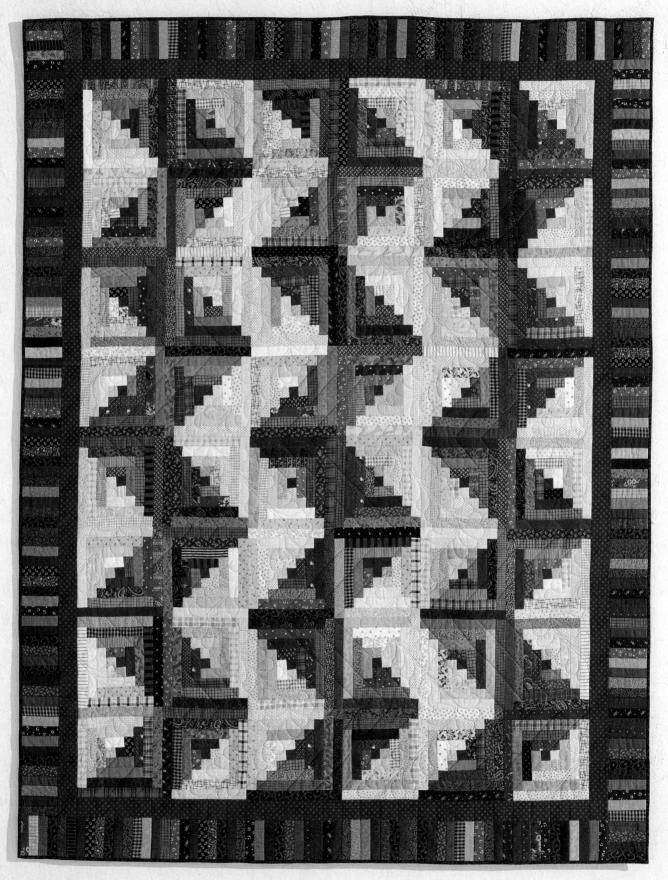

66 X 84 inches

SCRAP RECIPE

Log Cabin quilts are a great way to use even the smallest fabric scraps. Because these quilts use narrow pieces of fabric, they are part of a group of quilts called string quilts, which first became popular in the last quarter of the nineteenth century. Use leftover strips from previous projects to create your own twentieth-century version. In fact, the more scraps, the merrier.

When we make Log Cabin quilts, we try not to use the same fabric twice in any block. Using a variety of fabrics in the light half of the blocks creates interest and depth in these otherwise plain areas.

QUICK CUTTING				
Fabric	First Cut		Second Cut	
BLOCKS	No. of Strips	Strip Width	No.	Shape
Dark prints	60	1½"	48	2½" C logs
			48	3½" D logs
			48	4½" G logs
			48	5½" H logs
			48	6½" K logs
			48	7½" L logs
			48	8½" O logs
			48	9½" P logs
Light prints	48	1½"	48	1½" A logs
			48	2½" B logs
			48	3½" E logs
			48	4½" F logs
			48	5½" I logs
			48	6½" J logs
			48	7½" M logs
			48	8½" N logs
Red solid	2	1½"	48	■
BORDERS	No. of Strips	Strip Width	No.	Shape
Red print	7	2½"	—	—
Dark prints	32	1½"	—	—

QUICK CUTTING

The instructions for this quilt are for quick cutting the strips and logs for the Log Cabin blocks. Referring to the "Quick Cutting" chart, cut the number of strips needed from each fabric using a rotary cutter. Cut all strips across the fabric width unless directed otherwise. Measurements include ¼-inch seam allowances. If you are using scraps that are less than 42 inches wide, you will need to increase the number of strips you cut accordingly.

PIECING THE BLOCKS

The Log Cabin blocks are pieced from the center outward with pieces added clockwise around the center square in alphabetical order, as shown in the **Block Diagram.** As you add each piece, press the seam allowances away from the center square.

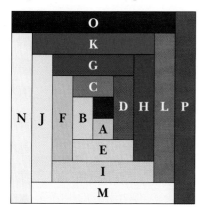

Block Diagram

STEP 1. Referring to **Diagram 1,** sew a light A square to a red center square. Continue feeding pairs of light and red squares through your

sewing machine until all 48 pairs have been stitched together. Clip the pairs apart. Open out the pieces and press.

Diagram 1

STEP 2. Place one of the units you just made on top of a B strip with right sides together. Stitch. Continue feeding the fabric pairs through your machine until you have 48 partial blocks that look like **Diagram 2.** Clip, open out the strips, and press.

Diagram 2

STEP 3. Rotate the partially completed blocks a quarter turn clockwise, and place each one on top of a C strip with right sides together. Stitch the seams, clip, open out the pieces, and press. Your unit should look like **Diagram 3.**

Diagram 3

STEP 4. Referring to the **Block Diagram,** continue adding pieces in alphabetical order in this assembly line manner, to complete 48 blocks.

Before cutting strips down to size, stack six strips on top of each other with long edges aligned. Cut through all layers to cut six pieces at one time. Sort the pieces by type and label them. We like to store cut strips in a new, large-size pizza box lined with a square of batting. The batting helps keep the pieces from sliding around. Stack the sets of pieces in the box and write the appropriate letter along the inner side of the box.

ASSEMBLING THE QUILT TOP

STEP 1. Referring to the **Quilt Diagram,** lay out the blocks in eight horizontal rows with six blocks in each row. Take care to turn each block so the shaded areas create the zigzag design.

STEP 2. Sew the blocks together into rows. Press seam allowances in alternate directions from row to row. Join the rows, and press the seam allowances to one side.

MAKING AND ATTACHING THE BORDERS

STEP 1. Measure the quilt length through the center. Join two sets of two red border strips, and trim each set to the length you just measured. Sew the two borders to the sides of quilt top. Press the seam allowances toward the borders.

STEP 2. Measure the quilt width through the center, including the side borders. Join the remaining three red border strips. From the long strip, cut two borders to your quilt width measurement. Sew the borders to the top and bottom edges of the quilt. Press the seam allowances toward the borders.

STEP 3. Referring to **Diagram 4,** join eight of the medium and dark strips together to make a strip set. Press the seam allowances to one side. Repeat to make four such strip sets. From the strip sets, cut 46 segments, each 4½ inches wide, for the pieced outer borders.

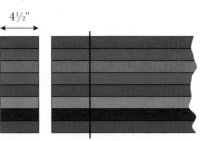

Diagram 4

STEP 4. For each side border, join ten segments together. Join eight segments together for each end border. Remove one strip from each of the end borders so they each have 62 strips. Press the seam allowances to one side.

STEP 5. Referring to the **Quilt Diagram,** pin the top border at the top left corner of the quilt top. Four

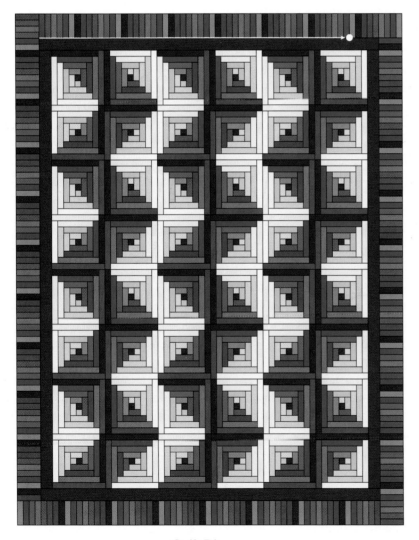

Quilt Diagram

strips should extend beyond the top right corner of the quilt top.

STEP 6. Stitch the border to the top of the quilt, beginning at the left corner. Make only a partial seam, leaving the last 6 inches of the border (indicated by the dot on the diagram) unsewn. This seam will be completed after the fourth border has been added. Press the seam allowances toward the red border.

STEP 7. Pin a side border to the left side of the quilt top and across the left end of the top border. Stitch the border to the quilt top and press the seam allowances toward the red border.

STEP 8. In a similar manner, add the bottom and right side borders to the quilt top.

STEP 9. Complete the seam on the top border, stitching across the top end of the side border.

QUILTING AND FINISHING

STEP 1. Mark quilting designs as desired, or see "Quilting Ideas" for suggestions.

STEP 2. To piece the quilt back, cut the backing fabric into two 2½-yard pieces. Cut one piece in half lengthwise. Trim the selvages, and sew a half panel to each side of the full panel. Press the seams toward the outer panels.

STEP 3. Layer the quilt back, batting, and quilt top. Baste the layers together. Trim the quilt back and batting so they are approximately 3 inches larger than the quilt top on all sides.

STEP 4. Hand or machine quilt as desired.

STEP 5. From the binding fabric, make approximately 320 inches of French-fold binding. See "Finishing" on page 223 for instructions on finishing the edges of your quilt.

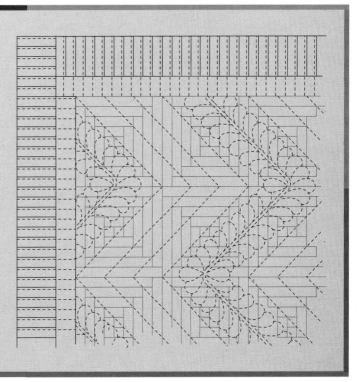

Quilting Ideas

This quilt was machine quilted in a straight line zigzag pattern through the dark areas and a feathered zigzag pattern through the light areas, as shown. Be sure to coordinate your thread colors to the areas you are quilting. Even if you choose to machine quilt with monofilament thread, choose clear for the light areas and dark clear for the darker areas.

Aunt Sukey's Choice

SKILL LEVEL: Easy

SIZE: Finished quilt is 38½ × 50¾ inches

Finished block is 10½ inches square

Number of blocks: 12

Hand quilted by Judy Trask

FABRICS AND SUPPLIES

- 1 yard of muslin for sashing strips
- ¾ yard *total* of assorted red prints for patchwork and sashing squares
- ½ yard *total* of assorted dark print scraps for patchwork
- 1 yard *total* of assorted shirting scraps for patchwork
- ½ yard *total* of assorted light prints for patchwork
- ¼ yard *total* of assorted medium prints for patchwork
- ½ yard of navy print for binding
- 1⅝ yards of fabric for quilt back
- Quilt batting, at least 45 × 57 inches
- Rotary cutter, ruler, and mat
- Template plastic (optional)

Michigan quiltmaker Bev Munson worked skillfully with antique patches believed to have belonged to her husband's grandmother, combining them with current fabrics from her own collection. The result is a cheery new lap quilt quite in keeping with the spirit of the past. This particular block pattern is not found in the standard reference books, giving this quilt a bit of extra mystique.

38½ × 50¾ inches

SCRAP RECIPE

At first glance, the most notable fabrics in this quilt are the red scraps set against a white background, and outlined in diamond shapes of dark navys and browns. You could chose only shades of reds, blues, and whites for a patriotic look or combine more colors as this quiltmaker did. The important point to remember is to separate your fabrics into lights (white-on-whites, beiges, light plaids), mediums (light blues, pinks, tans), and darks (navys, blacks, dark greens, browns). The reproduction fabrics available now will allow you to make a similar-looking quilt, but feel free to experiment with whatever you have on hand.

QUICK CUTTING						
Fabric	First Cut		Second Cut		Third Cut	
BLOCKS	No. of Strips	Strip Width	No.	Shape	No.	Shape
Muslin	11	2¼"	31	2¼"×11"	—	—
Red print	7	2¼"	116	■	—	—
Dark scraps	5	2¼"	48	2¼"×4"	—	—
	4	2⅝"	48	■	96	◩
Shirtings	10	2¼"	96	2¼"×4"	—	—
Light scraps	2	4¼"	12	☐	48	⊠
Medium scraps	3	2¼"	48	■	—	—

QUICK CUTTING

Referring to the "Quick Cutting" chart, cut the number of strips needed from each fabric using a rotary cutter. Cut all strips across the fabric width. All measurements include ¼-inch seam allowances. If you are using scraps that are less than 42 inches wide, you will need to increase the number of strips you cut accordingly.

We've included a special method called "Diagonal Seams" for piecing part of the blocks. For this method, you start with rectangles and trim them after stitching to avoid having to cut odd-shaped pieces. Follow the cutting instructions here.

PIECING THE BLOCKS

This quilt is made of 12 Aunt Sukey's Choice blocks, as shown in the **Block Diagram,** joined together with lattice strips.

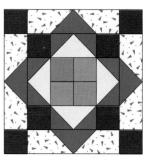

Block Diagram

STEP 1. Referring to **Diagram 1,** join four medium squares to make the four-patch block center. Make two rows of two squares per row. Press the seam allowances in opposite directions. Join the rows.

Diagram 1

STEP 2. Make four side units by sewing 2⅝-inch dark triangles to the short sides of the 4¼-inch light triangles, as shown in **Diagram 2.** Press the seam allowances toward the dark triangles.

Diagram 2

STEP 3. Sew the triangle units to two opposite sides of the four-patch block, as shown in **Diagram 3.** Press seam allowances toward the center four patch.

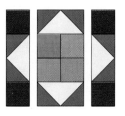

Diagram 3

STEP 4. Sew a red square to opposite ends of the remaining triangle units as shown. Press the seam allowances toward the red squares. Join the rows.

STEP 5. To make the outermost sides of the block, lay one shirting rectangle on top of a dark print rectangle, as shown in **Diagram 4.** Use a pencil to draw a 45 degree angle line on the shirting rectangle from the top inner corner to the outer edge as shown in the diagram. Stitch on the drawn line. Using a rotary cutter, trim off the excess corners $\frac{1}{4}$ inch from the stitching as shown. Press. Open out the shirting rectangle and press again. See **Diagram 5.**

Diagram 4

Diagram 5

STEP 6. Lay a matching shirting rectangle on the other end of the dark rectangle, as shown in **Diagram 6.** Draw a 45 degree angle line, stitch, trim, and press as you did for the other corner. **Diagram 7** shows the finished side unit. Repeat to make a total of 48 units.

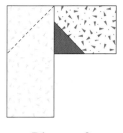

Diagram 6

Diagram 7

STEP 7. Referring to **Diagram 8,** sew two side units to two opposite

sides of the center unit. Press the seam allowances away from the center.

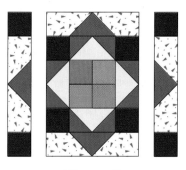

Diagram 8

STEP 8. Sew 2¼-inch red squares to opposite ends of the two remaining outer side units, as shown. Press seam allowances toward the shirting fabric. Sew the units to opposite sides of the block center. Press the seam allowances toward the outside of the block. Repeat to make a total of 12 blocks.

ASSEMBLING THE QUILT TOP

STEP 1. Referring to the **Quilt Diagram** on page 14, lay out the blocks, sashing strips, and red sashing squares in horizontal rows. Five of the rows will have four sashing squares and three sashing strips per row. Four of the rows will have four sashing strips and three pieced blocks per row.

STEP 2. Join the blocks and sashing pieces into rows. Press the seam allowances toward the sashing strips. Join the rows and press the seams to one side.

SEW WISE

This quilt is just the right size for a lap quilt or wallhanging. If you'd like to enlarge it for a twin-size or larger bed, just add more blocks. A five by seven-block quilt (including sashing) will measure $63 \times 87\frac{1}{2}$ inches. You'll need a total of 35 blocks . . . which of course means more fabric, more sewing, more fun!

Quilt Diagram

Quilting Ideas

This quilt was hand quilted, as shown. The simple lines of the quilting emphasize the piecing and the vintage feel of the quilt. The feather pattern used in the sashing strips is on the opposite page.

QUILTING AND FINISHING

STEP 1. Mark quilting designs as desired, or see "Quilting Ideas" for suggestions.

STEP 2. Layer the quilt back, batting, and quilt top. Baste the layers together. Trim the quilt back and batting so they are approximately 3 inches larger than the quilt top on all sides.

STEP 3. Hand or machine quilt as desired.

STEP 4. From the binding fabric, make approximately 194 inches of French-fold binding. See "Finishing" on page 223 for details on finishing the edges of your quilt.

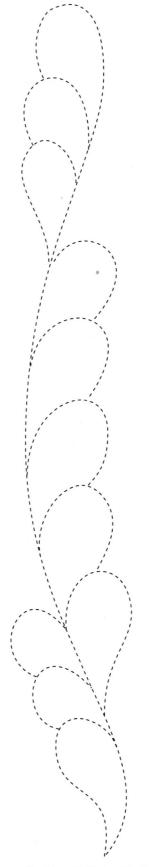

Sashing Quilting Design

Snowball

SKILL LEVEL: Easy

SIZE: Finished quilt is 72 × 80 inches
Finished block is 4 inches square

Number of blocks: 323

Quilt owner: Frieda Holt

FABRICS AND SUPPLIES

- 323 squares, *each* 4¹/₂ inches square, for the Snowballs

- 2¹/₄ yards of red solid fabric for the quick-piecing method *or* 1¹/₄ yards for the appliqué method

- ³/₄ yard of yellow-orange solid fabric for borders

- ⁵/₈ yard of fabric for binding

- 5 yards of fabric for quilt back

- Quilt batting, at least 78 × 86 inches

- Rotary cutter, ruler, and mat

Since the large octagonal pieces look almost round from a distance, this quilt pattern is often called Snowball. Although most of the "snowballs" are light-colored fabrics, the inclusion of indigo blue, red, black, and pink makes the quilt more interesting. The consistent use of red for the small squares unifies the design. The orange-yellow "Cheddar" colored border fabric was a popular color to include in quilts of this period. We've included two cutting and sewing methods for this quilt—quick machine piecing and hand appliqué. Hand appliqué is more time-consuming but gives a result more true to the original quilt.

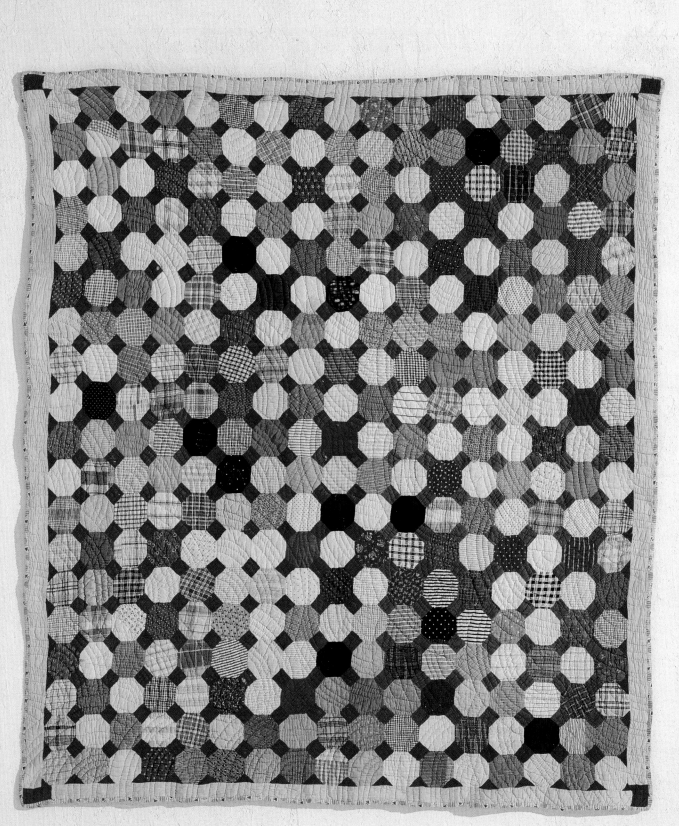

72 × 80 inches

SCRAP RECIPE

This pattern is also effective as a two-color quilt with all the Snowballs cut from a light fabric and the small squares from a dark fabric. You could use just two fabrics for a planned color scheme, or use many different fabrics in a two-color scheme. The small squares are a good place to use scraps. Here we've made a few Snowball blocks using plaids and stripes in soft shades of blue and tan.

QUICK CUTTING					
Fabric	**First Cut**		**Second Cut**		**From the red fabric, be sure to cut the strips for the piecing method you have chosen.*
BLOCKS	No. of Strips	Strip Width	No.	Shape	
Red*	For quick-piecing method				
	47	1½"	1,292	■	
	For appliqué method				
	18	2"	360	■	
BORDERS	No. of Strips	Strip Width	*†From the yellow-orange fabric, cut the border strips cross grain for efficient use of fabric; the result is that the borders will be pieced.*		
Yellow-orange†	8	2½"			
CORNER SQUARES	No.	Shape			
Red	4	2½" ■			

QUICK CUTTING

Read through the instructions to decide which method you plan to use and cut the red pieces accordingly. Cut all strips across the fabric width unless directed otherwise. All measurements include ¼-inch seam allowances. If you are using scraps that are less than 42 inches wide, you will need to increase the number of strips you cut accordingly.

MAKING THE BLOCKS AND ASSEMBLING THE QUILT

Quick-Piecing Method

STEP 1. Place a 1½-inch red square on top of a Snowball square, with right sides together, as shown in **Diagram 1.** Sew diagonally across the red square.

Diagram 1

STEP 2. Trim the Snowball and red fabric ¼ inch beyond the seam as shown in **Diagram 2.** Open out the red triangle and press so seam allowances are toward the triangle.

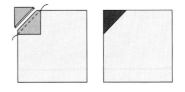

Diagram 2

STEP 3. In a similar manner, add a square to each remaining corner so your block looks like the **Block Diagram.**

Block Diagram

STEP 4. Repeat to make a total of 323 blocks.

STEP 5. Referring to the **Quilt Diagram,** lay out the blocks in 19 horizontal rows with 17 blocks in each row. Join the blocks into rows. Press the seam allowances in alternate directions from row to row.

STEP 6. Join the rows. Press the seam allowances to one side.

STEP 7. Join pairs of border strips to make four long borders. Measure the quilt through the middle to determine the length of the borders. Trim two borders to the measurement of the quilt width and two to the measurement of the quilt length.

STEP 8. Sew the shorter borders to the top and bottom edges. Press seam allowances toward the borders. Sew a border corner square to the ends of the two longer borders. Press seam allowances toward the borders. Sew these borders to the quilt sides. Press seam allowances toward the borders.

Appliqué Method

STEP 1. Press under ¼-inch seam allowances around all the 2-inch red squares.

STEP 2. Lay out the Snowball squares in 19 horizontal rows with 17 blocks in each row. Join the blocks into rows. Press the seam allowances in alternate directions from row to row. Label the rows by number so you can remember the order in which you want to assemble them.

STEP 3. Join the first three rows. Press the seam allowances to one side.

STEP 4. Appliqué a red square to each corner where the Snowball blocks meet as shown in **Diagram 3.** Use a red thread that matches the square.

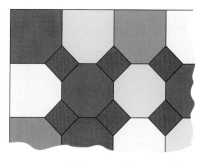

Diagram 3

STEP 5. Repeat to make five more sets of three rows of Snowball blocks with appliquéd red squares.

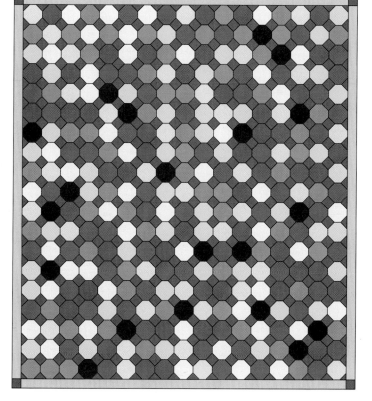

Quilt Diagram

SEW WISE

When pressing under the seam allowances of the red squares, a little spray starch will help hold them in place. Spray a small amount of starch into a small container, such as a plastic margarine tub. Use a cotton swab or small brush to paint the spray starch onto the seam allowance, concentrating it on the line where the actual turn will be. Press under the edges of the fabric with a medium hot iron. The starch will hold the seam allowance in place while you hand stitch the appliqué in position.

STEP 6. Join the six three-row groups. Add red squares to the corners created where the three-row groups meet. Add the final row and appliqué the squares in place.

STEP 7. Appliqué red squares around the outer perimeter of the quilt top. Trim excess red squares that extend beyond the edges of the quilt so they are even with the quilt edges, as shown in **Diagram 4.** The outer squares will now be triangles.

Appliqué red squares around the perimeter

Trim even with edges of quilt

Diagram 4

STEP 8. Refer to Steps 7 and 8 under "Quick-Piecing Method" on page 19 to make and add the borders.

QUILTING AND FINISHING

STEP 1. Mark quilting designs as desired, or see "Quilting Ideas" for suggestions.

STEP 2. To piece the quilt back, cut the backing fabric into two 2½-yard pieces. Cut one piece in half lengthwise. Trim the selvages, and sew a half panel to each long side of the full panel. Press the seam allowances toward the narrow panels.

STEP 3. Layer the quilt back, batting, and quilt top. Baste the layers together. Trim the quilt back and batting so they are approximately 3 inches larger than the quilt top on all sides.

STEP 4. Hand or machine quilt as desired.

STEP 5. Make approximately 320 inches of French-fold binding. See "Finishing" on page 223 for details on finishing the edges of your quilt.

Quilting Ideas

The Baptist Fan overall quilting design on page 41 was used on the quilt shown. You could quilt ¼ inch from all the seams or quilt a motif like the ones shown in the Snowball portion of the block and in the borders.

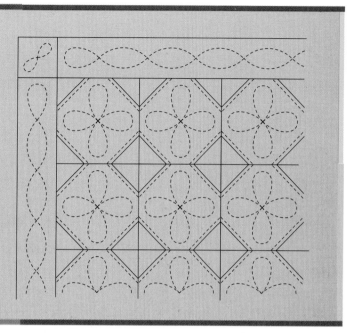

Flock of Geese Medallion

SKILL LEVEL: Easy

SIZE: Finished quilt is
76 × 92 inches

Finished block is 8 inches square

Number of blocks: 80

FABRICS AND SUPPLIES

- 5 yards total (1/8 to 1/4 yard *each*) of 40 medium and dark prints for blocks and borders

- 5 yards total (1/8 to 1/4 yard *each*) of 40 light prints for blocks and borders

- 2/3 yard of dark print fabric for binding

- 6 yards of fabric for quilt back

- Quilt batting, at least 82 × 98 inches

- Rotary cutter, ruler, and mat

Iowa quiltmaker Marty Freed achieved the look of the 1890s in a medallion format reminiscent of Barn Raising Log Cabin quilts. Marty used scores of print fabrics in colors popular during that era, successfully combining cadet and navy blues, bright reds, bubble gum pinks, poison and dark greens, golds, blacks, and browns with light-colored shirtings, prints, plaids, and stripes. While using more than 80 fabrics in one quilt may have the potential to cause chaos, the overriding visual effect in this quilt is one of light and dark, not a multitude of disparate fabrics.

76 × 92 inches

SCRAP RECIPE

Any colored scraps, whether they are reproduction prints or bright contemporary colors, will work well in this quilt. What's important is careful placement of light and dark *values*. And, for best results, make sure you have lots of fabrics—at least 40 different darks and 40 different lights.

QUICK CUTTING

Fabric	First Cut		Second Cut		Third Cut	
BLOCKS	No. of Strips	Strip Width	No.	Shape	No.	Shape
Medium/ dark prints	30	2⅞"	410	■	820	◩
Light prints	30	2⅞"	410	□	820	◪
Medium/ dark prints	10	4⅞"	80	■	160	◩
Light prints	10	4⅞"	80	□	160	◪
BORDERS*	No. of Strips	Strip Width	*For the borders,* the strips will be subcut into random lengths.			
Medium/ dark prints	8	2½"				
Light prints	8	2½"				

QUICK CUTTING

Referring to the "Quick Cutting" chart, cut the number of strips needed from each fabric using a rotary cutter and ruler. Cut all strips across the fabric width. All measurements include ¼-inch seam allowances. If you are using scraps that are less than 42 inches wide, you will need to increase the number of strips you cut accordingly. Layer three or four strips together for quicker cutting of the squares and triangles.

MAKING TRIANGLE SQUARES

This medallion-style quilt is made of 80 Flock of Geese blocks, which are composed entirely of large and small triangle squares, as shown in the **Block Diagram.**

Block Diagram

STEP 1. Referring to **Diagram 1,** join small light and dark triangles to make 820 triangle squares. You will need 640 triangle squares for the blocks and 180 for the border. Press the seam allowances toward the dark fabrics.

Diagram 1

STEP 2. Join large light and dark triangles to make 160 triangle squares. Press the seam allowances toward the dark fabrics.

PIECING THE BLOCKS

STEP 1. Referring to **Diagram 2,** lay out four small triangle squares, angling the seams as shown. Join the triangle squares in two rows of two units per row. Press the seam allowances in opposite directions. Join the rows. Repeat to make a total of 160 small triangle units.

Diagram 2

STEP 2. Referring to **Diagram 3,** lay out two small triangle units with two large triangle squares. Join the units into two rows. Press the seam allowances toward the large triangles. Join the rows to complete a Flock of Geese block. At this point, the block should measure 8½ inches square. Repeat to make a total of 80 Flock of Geese blocks.

Diagram 3

ASSEMBLING THE QUILT TOP

STEP 1. Referring to the **Quilt Diagram,** lay out the blocks in ten horizontal rows with eight blocks per row to form the Barn-Raising-style medallion. Pay careful attention to the angle of the seams and

Quilt Diagram

the placement of light and dark fabrics.

STEP 2. Stitch the blocks into rows. Press the seam allowances in opposite directions from row to row. Join the rows.

STEP 3. Cut the border strips into random lengths, and then piece lengths of different fabrics together to make two light borders and two dark borders each 64½ inches long for the end borders. In the same manner, piece two light borders

and two dark borders each 80½ inches long for the side borders.

STEP 4. Join the dark and light borders lengthwise so you have double borders for the top and bottom and for the sides of the quilt. Press the seam allowances toward the dark borders. Attach the long double side borders to the two sides of the quilt top, sewing the light strips to the edge of the quilt. Ease to fit if necessary, as described in "Sew Wise" on page 26. Press the seams toward the borders.

SEW WISE

If necessary, ease strip borders to fit the quilt. In order for the outer Sawtooth border to fit, the strip borders must be the exact size given in the text. If your quilt is longer or shorter than the border length, don't adjust the border length. Simply fold the border in half and crease lightly to find the midpoint. Match ends and midpoints of the quilt and borders and pin. Ease in any fullness and pin along the length of the quilt before stitching. Stitch with the larger piece (baggy side) down so the feed dogs on your sewing machine will aid the easing-in process.

STEP 5. Referring to **Diagram 2** on page 25, join four sets of four A small triangle squares to make four additional small triangle units for border corners. Sew the units to the ends of the top and bottom double borders. Then sew the borders to the top and bottom edges of the quilt, easing to fit if necessary, as described in "Sew Wise." Press the seam allowances toward the borders.

STEP 6. Referring to **Diagram 4,** join the remaining small triangle squares to make the Sawtooth border strips. Make two strips with 36 triangle squares each for the top and bottom borders and two strips with 46 triangle squares each for side borders. Note the placement of the dark and light fabrics in the border triangle squares; they change direction in the middle of each border strip.

Diagram 4

STEP 7. Sew the top and bottom borders to the quilt top. Press the seam allowances toward the middle border. Sew the side borders to the quilt. Press the seam allowances toward the middle border.

QUILTING AND FINISHING

STEP 1. Mark quilting designs as desired, or see "Quilting Ideas" for suggestions.

STEP 2. To piece the quilt back, cut the backing fabric into two 3-yard lengths. Cut one piece in half lengthwise. Trim the selvages, and sew a half panel to each side of the full panel. Press the seams toward the narrow panels.

STEP 3. Layer the quilt back, batting, and quilt top. Baste the layers together. Trim the quilt back and batting so they are approximately 3 inches larger than the quilt top on all sides.

STEP 4. Hand or machine quilt as desired.

STEP 5. From the binding fabric, make approximately 350 inches of French-fold binding by joining the binding strips with diagonal seams. See "Finishing" on page 223 for instructions on finishing the edges of your quilt.

Quilting Ideas

This quilt was machine quilted with a pattern of circles in the large light triangles. A wave pattern was quilted in the border. Use a teacup or small bowl to trace the circles on your quilt. It won't wear out as cardboard templates do!

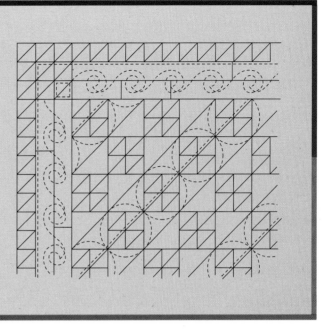

Rocky Road to Kansas

SKILL LEVEL: Intermediate to Advanced

SIZE: Finished quilt is 72 × 77 inches

Finished block is 11 inches square

Number of blocks: 42

Quilt owner: Edith Leeper

FABRICS AND SUPPLIES

- 3¼ yards of green print fabric for block background
- ¼ yard *each* of 10 to 20 assorted light fabrics for blocks
- ¼ yard *each* of 10 to 20 assorted medium to dark fabrics for blocks
- 4¾ yards of fabric for quilt back
- ¾ yard of fabric for binding
- Quilt batting, at least 78 × 85 inches
- Rotary cutter, ruler, and mat
- Template plastic
- Plastic-coated freezer paper

AMERICAN COUNTRY SCRAP QUILTS

Quilters in the latter part of the nineteenth century often used up their smallest scraps by making string quilts like Rocky Road to Kansas. They stitched their fabric strips onto paper foundation patterns often made from old newspapers or brown wrapping paper.

Finding antique blocks with old newspaper patterns still in place is a fun way to read about events from a century ago. We've streamlined the paper piecing technique and adapted it to today's methods—you sew strips together into strip sets and use freezer paper patterns to cut the string pieces.

72 × 77 inches

SCRAP RECIPE

Try using soft pastels on an off-white background. Another option is to use a black print for the A background pieces and bright jewel tone fabrics for the triangles and fabric strips as we've done in this alternate block. This creates a quilt with a very modern look.

QUICK CUTTING				
Fabric	First Cut		Second Cut	
BLOCKS	No.	Shape	No.	Shape
Green print	182	A pieces	—	—
Light prints*	42	3⅜"	84	
Medium and dark prints*	42	3⅜"	84	
STRIP SETS	No. of Strips	Strip Width	**For the light, medium, and dark prints, see "Sew Wise" before cutting.*	
Light, medium, and dark prints	48–96	1½"–2½"		

CUTTING

Make plastic templates for patterns A, B, and C on pages 33–35. Pattern A includes seam allowances. Seam allowances aren't needed on templates made from patterns B and C for the shortcut freezer paper technique we're using. See "Making and Using Templates" on page 215.

Referring to the "Quick Cutting" chart, cut the number of A pieces needed. Use a rotary cutter to quick cut the rest of the pieces as directed. Rotary-cut pieces include ¼-inch seam allowances. Cut all strips across the fabric width unless directed otherwise. If you are using scraps that are less than 42 inches wide, you will need to increase the number of strips you cut accordingly.

MAKING THE STRIP SETS AND STRING PIECES

STEP 1. Using the B and C templates, which do not include seam allowances, mark and cut 17 B, 14 C, and 14 C reverse pieces from freezer paper to use as patterns for cutting pieces from the strip sets. Freezer paper patterns should be finished size and should not include seam allowances.

STEP 2. Using the assorted width scrap fabric strips, make 12 strip sets that are approximately 7½ to 8 inches wide and 42 inches long. Choose a variety of light, medium, and dark strips for each strip set. Press seam allowances to one side.

STEP 3. Referring to **Diagram 1,** use your iron set at wool to press the shiny side of 17 freezer paper B patterns to the wrong side of a strip set. Space freezer paper patterns at least ½ inch apart to allow for seam allowances. Using a rotary cutter

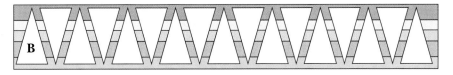

Diagram 1

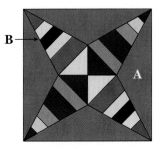

Block Diagram

and ruler, cut around the paper pieces adding ¼-inch seam allowances to all sides. After each piece is cut, remove the freezer paper to use again as a pattern. Replace paper patterns when they will no longer adhere to the fabric. Repeat to cut a total of 168 B pieces from ten strip sets.

STEP 4. Referring to **Diagram 2,** use freezer paper patterns to cut 14 C and 14 C reverse pieces for the side borders from the two remaining strip sets. Remember to add ¼-inch seam allowances around all pieces as you cut them from the strip sets.

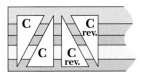

Diagram 2

PIECING THE BLOCKS

STEP 1. Choose two matching light and two matching medium or dark triangles. Referring to the **Block Diagram,** lay out the pieces for one block.

SEW WISE

You may want to wait until you are ready to sew before you cut each square in half diagonally into two triangles for the block centers. This will ensure that you don't lose the matching pieces.

STEP 2. Referring to **Diagram 3,** sew a center triangle to the short side of each B piece. Press seam allowances toward the triangles in the center. Join the four sections, leaving the seam allowances free at the beginning and ends of seams to allow for setting in of the A pieces. Backstitch to secure stitching at the beginning and end of the seams, but don't stitch into the seam allowances. See "Setting In Pieces" on page 217.

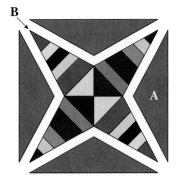

Diagram 3

STEP 3. Set the green print A pieces in to the openings around the block to form a square. Press seam allowances toward the A pieces.

STEP 4. Repeat to make a total of 42 blocks.

MAKING THE SIDE BORDERS

STEP 1. Referring to **Diagram 4,** sew a strip-pieced C and C reverse piece to an A piece. Press seam allowances toward the A piece. Make a total of 14 border units.

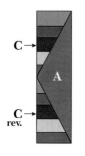

Diagram 4

STEP 2. Make two side borders by joining seven border units for each.

ASSEMBLING THE QUILT TOP

STEP 1. Referring to the **Quilt Diagram,** join the blocks in seven horizontal rows with six blocks in each row. Press the seam allowances in alternate directions from row to row. Join the rows. Press the seam allowances to one side.

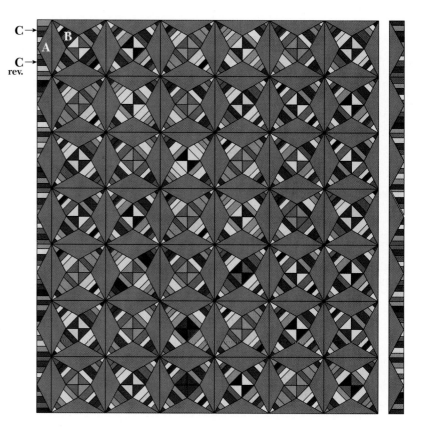

Quilt Diagram

STEP 2. Aligning the A pieces of the border with the center of the quilt, sew a border to opposite sides of the quilt top.

QUILTING AND FINISHING

STEP 1. Mark quilting designs as desired, or see "Quilting Ideas" for suggestions.

STEP 2. To piece the quilt back, cut the backing fabric into two 2⅜-yard pieces. Cut one piece in half lengthwise. Trim the selvages, and sew a half panel to each long side of the full panel. Press the seam allowances toward the narrow panels.

STEP 3. Layer the quilt back, batting, and quilt top. Baste the layers together. Trim the quilt back and batting so they are approximately 3 inches larger than the quilt top on all sides.

STEP 4. Hand or machine quilt as desired.

STEP 5. From the binding fabric, make approximately 320 inches of French-fold binding by joining the binding strips with diagonal seams. See "Finishing" on page 223 for details on finishing the edges of your quilt.

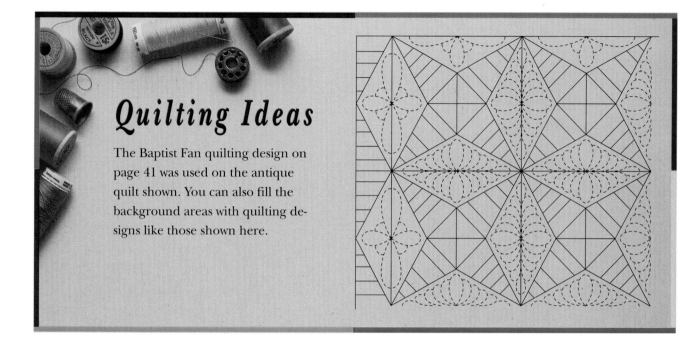

Quilting Ideas

The Baptist Fan quilting design on page 41 was used on the antique quilt shown. You can also fill the background areas with quilting designs like those shown here.

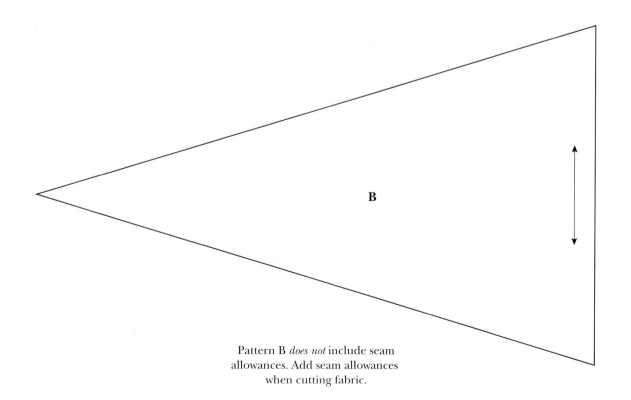

B

Pattern B *does not* include seam allowances. Add seam allowances when cutting fabric.

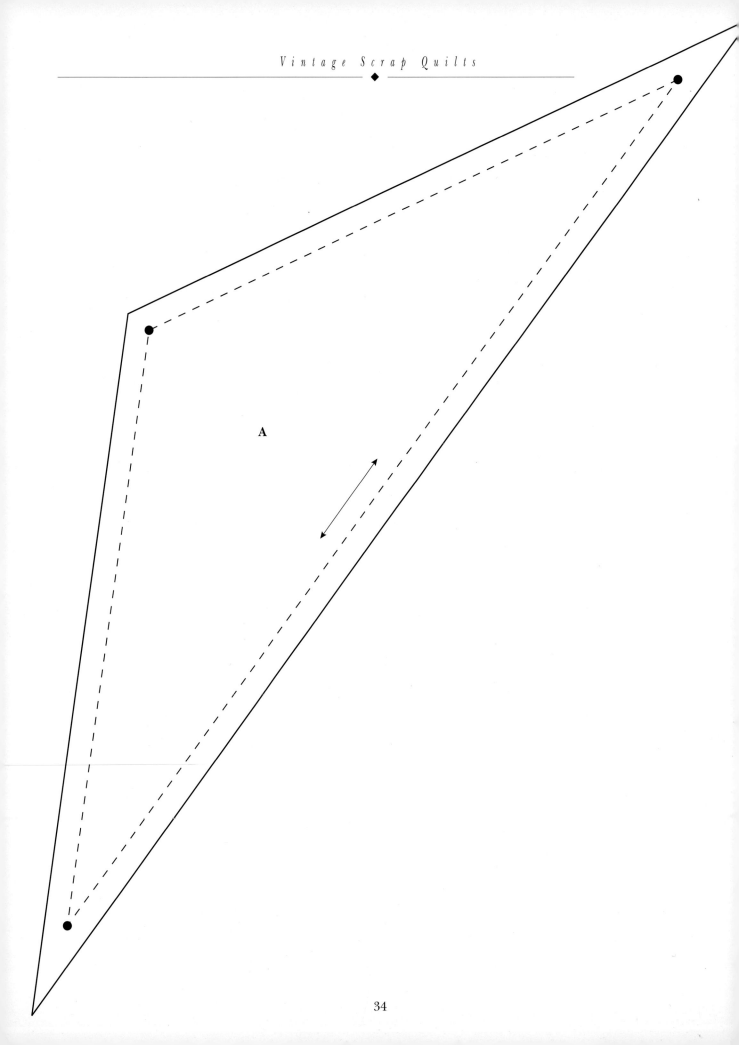

A

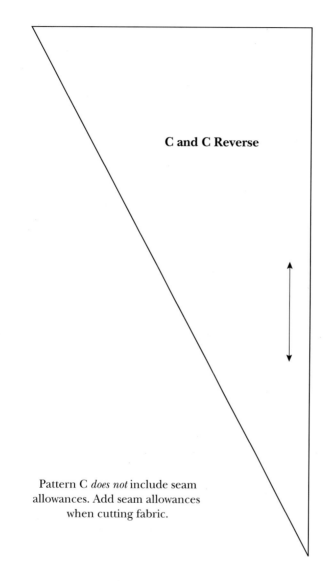

C and C Reverse

Pattern C *does not* include seam
allowances. Add seam allowances
when cutting fabric.

SKILL LEVEL: Easy

SIZE: Finished quilt is approximately 35¼ × 43¾ inches

Finished block is 5 inches square

Number of blocks: 32

FABRICS AND SUPPLIES

- ⅛ yard *each* or scraps of 12 different red plaid or stripe fabrics for sashing squares, blocks, and binding

- Six 10-inch squares of different medium value plaid fabrics for side and corner triangles

- ⅛ yard *each* or scraps of 30 different light value fabrics for sashing and blocks

- Scraps (at least 7 inches square) of approximately 20 different medium and dark value fabrics for blocks

- 1½ yards of fabric for quilt back

- Quilt batting, at least 41 × 50 inches

- Rotary cutter, ruler, and mat

She Did the Best She Could

Quiltmaking has long been credited as being a

frugal craft that uses leftover fabric pieces in a cre-

ative way. To pay tribute to this tradition,

quiltmaker Nadi Lane has made a

series of scrap quilts called She Did the

Best She Could. In this quilt, the third in the

series, Nadi intentionally created many "maverick"

blocks to help make her quilt look old. (For more

about maverick blocks, see page 2.) This pleasing

wall quilt combines lots of currently available woven

plaid and stripe fabrics in country colors.

35¼ X 43¾ inches

SCRAP RECIPE

To create a pleasing, scrappy effect, change the color, type (that is, stripe or plaid), or value (medium or dark) of fabrics used for the Churn Dash motifs in each of the blocks. Each block will look obviously different when the Churn Dashes are made from a variety of fabrics. Changing the light value background fabrics from block to block further enhances the overall scrappy feel.

This is the perfect quilt to benefit from a scrap swap with other quilting friends, since the pieces for the blocks and sashing are so small. Post signs at a local quilt shop, set one up at a monthly guild meeting, or join an on-line quilting group to organize a swap.

QUICK CUTTING						
Fabric	First Cut		Second Cut		Third Cut	
BLOCKS	No. of Strips	Strip Width	No.	Shape	No.	Shape
Lights	5	2⅞"	64	☐	128	A ◿
	6	1½"	160	B ☐	—	—
	No.	Shape	No.	Shape	*From the medium plaids, you will use only 14 of the setting triangles.*
Medium/ darks	64	2⅞" ▨	128	A ◿	
	128	1½" ▨	—	—	
SASHING	No.	Shape	No.	Shape	
Reds	49	1½" ■			
	No. of Strips	Strip Width	No.	Shape	
Lights	12	1½"	80	1½"×5½"	
SIDE & CORNER TRIANGLES	No.	Shape	No.	Shape	
Medium plaids	4	9¾" ■	16*	⊠	
	2	5⅞" ■	4	◩	

QUICK CUTTING

Referring to the "Quick Cutting" chart, cut the number of strips needed from each fabric using a rotary cutter. Cut all strips across the fabric width. All measurements include ¼-inch seam allowances. If you are using scraps that are less than 42 inches wide, you will need to increase the number of strips you cut accordingly. In some cases, since "Fabrics and Supplies" lists small squares of fabrics instead of standard-width yardage, there will be no strip cutting given.

As a general rule you will need to cut the following pieces for *each* Churn Dash block:

- Four matching A triangles from light fabric
- Four matching A triangles from medium/dark fabric
- Five matching B squares from light fabric
- Four matching B squares from medium/dark fabrics

Variations from this basic cutting plan will help you create "maverick" blocks, so be sure to stray from it for some of your blocks.

PIECING THE BLOCKS

STEP 1. Lay out the pieces for one Churn Dash block. Refer to the **Block Diagram** and **Maverick Block Diagram** for ideas on how to position light, medium, and dark pieces within the blocks. We've indicated just a few of the many maverick block variations. Study the photograph of the quilt to discover more possibilities, and use your creativity to invent some of your own.

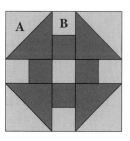

Block Diagram

 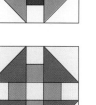 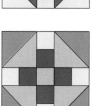

Maverick Block Diagram

STEP 2. Referring to **Diagram 1**, join pairs of light and dark A triangles to create a total of four triangle squares. Press seam allowances toward the dark fabric.

Diagram 1

STEP 3. Make four B units as shown in **Diagram 2**. Press seam allowances toward the dark fabric.

Diagram 2

STEP 4. Referring to **Diagram 3**, join the pieces together into three rows. Press seam allowances away from the center square in the middle row and away from the triangles in the outer rows. Join the rows, abutting pressed seams.

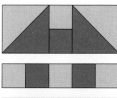
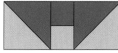

Diagram 3

STEP 5. Repeat Steps 1 through 4 to make a total of 32 Churn Dash blocks.

Getting set up for chain piecing can make assembling the triangle squares and B units a breeze. Set pairs of A triangles and pairs of B pieces, right sides together and ready to be stitched, next to your sewing machine. Pick up the first pair and run it through the machine. As the needle approaches the edge of the fabric, set the next pair in place so that the needle will continue sewing through that set. Continue adding pairs of squares and triangles, without stopping to clip the thread, until you have sewn all the units for one block. You'll end up with a long string of triangles and squares—just clip the threads and the individual units are ready to be pressed.

ASSEMBLING THE QUILT TOP

STEP 1. Referring to the **Quilt Diagram,** lay out the blocks, sashing strips, sashing squares, side triangles, and corner triangles in diagonal rows, as shown. As you lay out the components, work to achieve a pleasing color and value balance. For example, don't put all the red blocks in the same row.

STEP 2. Begin by joining the pieces, except the side and corner triangles, into diagonal rows. You are creating two different kinds of rows. In one, blocks are joined to sashing strips. In the other, sashing strips are joined to sashing squares to create a long, skinny row. (Do not add the side triangles yet.) Press seam allowances toward the sashing strips.

STEP 3. Join the sashing strip/square rows to the sashing strip/block rows. Use the row numbers in the **Quilt Diagram** to determine on which side the sashing is joined to the row of blocks. In Rows 1 through 4, the sashing goes on the right side. In Rows 5 through 8, the sashing goes on the left. NOTE: Do not join the center sashing strip to any row of blocks yet.

STEP 4. Following the **Quilt Diagram,** add side triangles to the ends of the rows.

STEP 5. Join the rows to complete the quilt top. Sew Rows 1 through 4 together, then add the center sashing strip/square row. Sew Rows 5 through 8 together, then add that

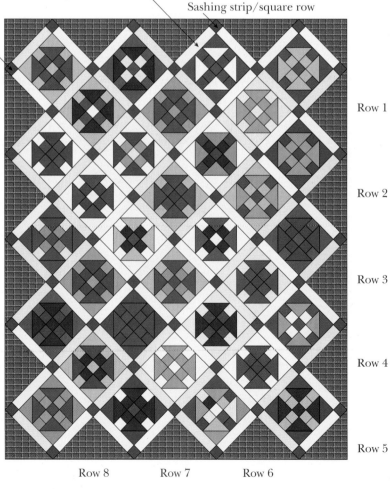

Sashing strip/block row

Sashing strip/square row

Center sashing strip/square row

Row 1

Row 2

Row 3

Row 4

Row 5

Row 8   Row 7   Row 6

Quilt Diagram

Quilting Ideas

Instead of having the quilting lines follow the geometric shapes within the blocks and sashing, an overall quilting design was used. The Baptist fan quilting design, shown here, flows across the surface of the quilt, creating an interesting secondary design that augments the lines and shapes created by the patchwork.

section to the other side of the center sashing strip/square row. Sew a corner triangle to each corner of the quilt top. Press the completed top.

QUILTING AND FINISHING

STEP 1. Mark quilting designs as desired, or see "Quilting Ideas" for suggestions.

STEP 2. Layer the quilt back, batting, and quilt top. Baste the layers together. Trim the quilt back and batting so they are approximately 3 inches larger than the quilt top on all sides.

STEP 3. Hand or machine quilt as desired.

STEP 4. From assorted red fabrics left over from blocks and setting squares, make approximately 175 inches of French-fold binding by joining the binding strips with diagonal seams. Using strips of different fabrics and of varying widths will create a pleasingly scrappy binding. In this quilt, all the fabrics used are red, so the differences in the binding fabrics are subtle; but that contrast adds a nice final touch. See "Finishing" on page 223 for details on finishing the edges of your quilt.

Scrap Star

SKILL LEVEL: Easy

SIZE: Finished quilt is
83½ × 96 inches

Finished block is 11 inches square

Number of blocks: 42

FABRICS AND SUPPLIES

- 3 yards of green fabric for sashing strips and borders

- Scraps *to total* 5½ yards of approximately 30 different medium, dark, and light value print fabrics for blocks and sashing squares

- ¾ yard of pink print fabric for sashing squares and binding

- 7½ yards of fabric for quilt back

- Quilt batting, at least 90 × 102 inches

- Rotary cutter, ruler, and mat

The way in which Virginia quiltmaker Connie Tilman used 30 different prints to make 42 Star blocks is typical of the way quilts were made a century ago. Though each block is a different fabric combination, only four prints appear in each block. In some of the blocks, the star contrasts well with the background fabric, but in many of them, the contrast between star and background is fairly low. A consistent level of contrast in blocks was often unimportant to the quiltmaker of the late 1800s.

83½ ✕ 96 inches

SCRAP RECIPE

◼️

If you want to create a quilt that looks as if it may have been made in the 1890s rather than in the 1990s, you can't go wrong with the poison green seaweed print for sashing and borders and the bubble gum pink sashing squares and binding, both from the Fons-Porter Heritage Collection of 1890s-style prints. But don't be afraid to dig into your scrap pile and pull out all sorts of fabrics you thought you'd never use again. You can tie together an unlimited amount of scraps in an effective scrap quilt, simply by purchasing one color for borders and sashing, and another contrasting color for sashing squares.

QUICK CUTTING						
Fabric	**First Cut**		**Second Cut**		**Third Cut**	
BLOCKS	No. of Strips	Strip Width	No.	Shape	No.	Shape
Assorted scraps*	28	3¼"	336	A ◼️	—	—
	16	3⅝"	168	◼️	336	B ◸
	7	6¾"	42	◼️	168	C �«⊠»
SASHING	No. of Strips	Strip Width	No.	Shape	No.	Shape
Green†	49	2"	97	2"×11½"	—	—
Light print scrap	3	1¼"		**From each assorted scrap, you will need four A squares and four C triangles that match for the block background.*		
Pink print‡	3	1¼"		*† From the green fabric, cut the border strips first from the lengthwise grain of fabric. Then cut the strips for the sashing crosswise from the remaining width of fabric.*		
BORDERS	No.	Shape				
Green†	4	4"×108" strips		*‡ From the pink print, reserve the remaining fabric for binding.*		

QUICK CUTTING

Referring to the "Quick Cutting" chart, cut the number of strips needed from each fabric using a rotary cutter. Cut all strips across the fabric width, except as noted. All measurements include ¼-inch seam allowances. If you are using scraps that are less than 42 inches wide, you will need to increase the number of strips you cut accordingly.

PIECING THE BLOCKS

STEP 1. Lay out the pieces for one Star block. You will need two pairs of matching A squares for the center four-patch unit, eight matching B triangles for the star points, and four A squares and four C triangles that match for the block background. The **Block Diagram** shows you several ways the dark, medium, and light value fabrics can be arranged.

STEP 2. Refer to **Diagram 1** for block construction. Join the central A squares in two rows of two squares per row. Press the seam allowances in opposite directions. Join the rows.

STEP 3. Make four star point units by sewing B triangles to the C triangles, as shown in **Diagram 1.** Press the seam allowances toward the small triangles.

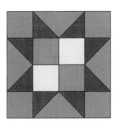

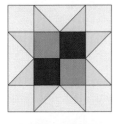

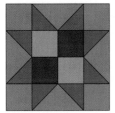

Block Diagram

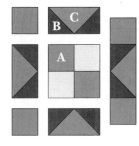

Diagram 1

STEP 5. Sew A squares to opposite ends of the remaining star point units to form the outer rows of the block. Press the seam allowances toward the squares. Join the rows to complete the block.

STEP 6. Repeat to make a total of 42 blocks.

MAKING THE SASHING SQUARES

STEP 1. Using the 1¼-inch-wide pink print strips and light print strips, make three strip sets as shown in **Diagram 2.** Press the seams toward the pink strips.

1¼"

Diagram 2

STEP 2. Cut the strip sets into 1¼-inch segments, as shown. You will need 112 segments.

STEP 3. Join segments, as shown in **Diagram 3,** to make 56 four-patch sashing square units.

Diagram 3

STEP 4. Sew the star point units to the top and bottom of the four-patch unit to form the center row of the block. Press the seams toward the four patch.

ASSEMBLING THE QUILT TOP

STEP 1. Referring to the **Quilt Diagram** on page 46, lay out the blocks, sashing strips, and four-patch sashing squares in horizontal

Quilt Diagram

and bottom of the quilt top. Press the seam allowances toward borders.

QUILTING AND FINISHING

STEP 1. Mark quilting designs as desired, or see "Quilting Ideas" for suggestions.

STEP 2. To piece the quilt back, cut the backing fabric crosswise into three approximately 87-inch lengths. Cut a 16-inch-wide lengthwise panel from one of the lengths. Sew the two wide panels and the narrow panel together.

STEP 3. Layer the quilt back, batting, and quilt top. The seams of the backing fabric will run parallel to the top and bottom edges of the quilt top. Baste the layers together. Trim the quilt back and batting so they are approximately 3 inches larger than the quilt top on all sides.

STEP 4. Hand or machine quilt as desired.

STEP 5. From the binding fabric, make approximately 380 inches of French-fold binding. See "Finishing" on page 223 for instructions on finishing the edges of your quilt.

rows. You will have eight rows of sashing strips and four-patch units, and seven rows of sashing strips and star blocks. Join the units to make the rows. Press seam allowances toward the sashing strips. Join the rows and press.

STEP 2. Measure the length of the quilt top through the middle. Trim

two of the border strips to this length. Sew the borders to the sides of the quilt top. Press the seam allowances toward borders.

STEP 3. Measure the width of the quilt top through the center, including the side borders. Trim the remaining border strips to this length. Sew the borders to the top

Quilting Ideas

This quilt was quilted in the ditch with heavy cotton thread and a long stitch along the seams of the star blocks and the sashing strips, extending into the borders, as shown.

When quilters of the past needed lots of quilts to keep their families warm, they used simple patterns and kept the quilting itself to a minimum. Connie Tilman developed her own method for "utility quilting," which not only helps her finish her quilts more quickly but at the same time adds a charming folk art element to her reproduction works.

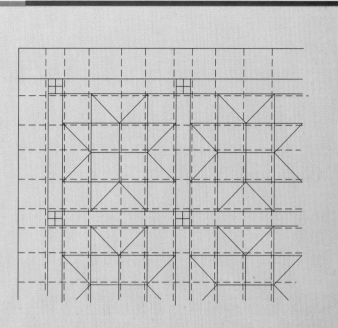

To do your own folk art quilting, use a no. 6 between needle to keep your stitches large and a single strand of no. 8 pearl cotton thread. Cotton crochet thread would also work. Layer the quilt and then quilt without a frame or hoop.

Plaid Nine Patch

SKILL LEVEL: Easy

SIZE: Finished quilt is 14³/₄ × 20 inches

Finished block is 4¹/₄ inches square

Number of blocks: 12

FABRICS AND SUPPLIES

- ¹/₄ yard of white with black shirting print for sashing strips

- ¹/₈ yard *each* or scraps of 12 medium to dark prints or plaids for setting triangles

- Scraps (8 inches long) of 15 medium to dark plaids and stripes for Nine Patches

- Scraps (8 inches long) of 12 light to medium plaids and stripes for Nine Patches

- Scrap (10 inches long) of navy print for sashing squares

- ¹/₈ yard of fabric for binding

- ³/₄ yard of fabric for quilt back

- Quilt batting, at least 21 × 26 inches

- Rotary cutter, ruler, and mat

- Six-inch (or larger) ruled plastic square

Illinois quilter Mary Radke enjoys presenting

lectures about American quilt history. She uses

small quilts that she has made to illus-

trate the characteristics of quilts from

each historic period that she discusses

in her talks. For this delightful little doll-

size quilt, Mary drew on her large collection of

plaid and striped fabrics and shirting prints to give

her project a late-nineteenth-century look.

AMERICAN COUNTRY SCRAP QUILTS

14¾ × 20 inches

SCRAP RECIPE

The blues, browns, beiges, and occasional pink and green in this quilt are typical of late 1800s fabrics. There are so many plaids and stripes available today that you can find these woven fabrics in virtually any color scheme you can imagine.

When working with directional fabrics such as plaids and stripes, you'll achieve a truer "vintage" look If you aren't too particular about grainline placement. Quilters in the 1890s didn't care a whit if their seams and the lines of their plaids were misaligned. Mary's conscious disregard for following the grain when cutting some of her setting triangles is part of what gives her quilt its nineteenth-century spontaneity.

QUICK CUTTING						
Fabric	**First Cut**		**Second Cut**		**Third Cut**	
BLOCKS & SETTING TRIANGLES	No. of Strips	Strip Width	No.	Shape	No.	Shape
Medium to dark prints or plaids	12	3¼"	24	▢	48	◩
Medium to dark plaids and stripes	15	1½"	15	1½"×7½"	—	—
Light to medium plaids and stripes	12	1½"	12	1½"×7½"	—	—
Navy print	1	1½"	6	▢	—	—
SASHING	No. of Strips	Strip Width	No.	Shape	No.	Shape
Shirting print	3	1½"	17	1½"×4¾"	—	—

QUICK CUTTING

Referring to the "Quick Cutting" chart, cut the number of strips needed from each fabric using a rotary cutter. Cut all strips across the fabric width. All measurements include ¼-inch seam allowances. If you are using scraps that are less than 42 inches wide, you will need to increase the number of strips you cut accordingly.

MAKING THE NINE-PATCH BLOCKS

This quilt is made of 12 Nine-Patch blocks, as shown in the **Block Diagram,** which are set on point with setting triangles.

Block Diagram

STEP 1. Referring to **Diagram 1** and the **Fabric Key,** make six A and three B strip sets. Press the seam allowances toward the darker fabrics.

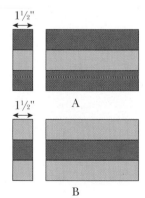

Diagram 1

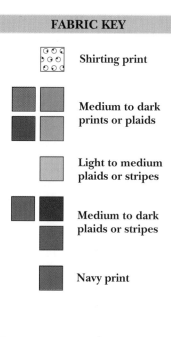

Shirting print

Medium to dark prints or plaids

Light to medium plaids or stripes

Medium to dark plaids or stripes

Navy print

STEP 2. Cut four 1½-inch-wide segments from each strip set.

STEP 3. Referring to **Diagram 2,** lay out two A and one B strip set segments to make one block. Join the segments, aligning pressed seam allowances, to make a Nine-Patch block as shown.

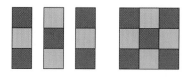

Diagram 2

STEP 4. Make a total of 12 Nine-Patch blocks.

STEP 5. Lay out one Nine-Patch block and four matching setting triangles. Referring to **Diagram 3,** center and sew the setting triangles to two opposite sides of the block as shown. Press the seam allowances toward the triangles.

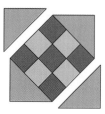

Diagram 3

STEP 6. Sew triangles to the remaining two sides of the block. Press seams toward the triangles.

STEP 7. Trim away excess from the setting triangles to make the block square. Position a ruled plastic square on top of the block and trim, making sure you leave a ¼-inch seam allowance at the corners of the Nine-Patch blocks. Squared-off blocks should measure 4¾ inches square.

ASSEMBLING THE QUILT TOP

STEP 1. Referring to the **Quilt Diagram** on page 52, join the blocks, sashing strips, and sashing squares into horizontal rows. Make four rows with Nine-Patch blocks and sashing strips and three rows with sashing strips and squares. Press the seam allowances toward sashing strips in all rows.

STEP 2. Join the rows. Press the seam allowances toward the sashing rows.

F or an even scrappier look, you could use four different fabrics for the setting triangles that square off each Nine-Patch block instead of four that match. For most of the blocks, cut triangles from four fabrics of similar value. For two or three of the blocks, throw in a squaring-off triangle that differs in value from the other three. This will give you "maverick" blocks, key elements in achieving a late-nineteenth-century look.

To cut the triangles, start with 3¼-inch squares and cut them in half diagonally just as indicated in the "Quick Cutting" chart. Mixing up the setting triangles will result in some leftover ones.

Quilt Diagram

QUILTING AND FINISHING

STEP 1. Mark quilting designs as desired, or see "Quilting Ideas" for suggestions.

STEP 2. Layer the quilt back, batting, and quilt top. Baste the layers together. Trim the quilt back and batting so they are approximately 3 inches larger than the quilt top on all sides.

STEP 3. Hand or machine quilt as desired.

STEP 4. Cut two crosswise binding strips from the binding fabric and join them with a diagonal seam to make one long strip. See "Finishing" on page 223 for details on finishing the edges of your quilt. If you plan to hang your quilt, see "Making a Hanging Sleeve for a Quilt" on page 226.

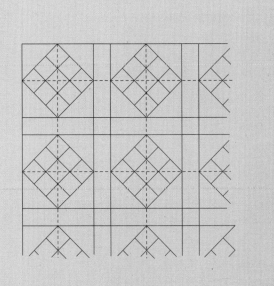

Quilting Ideas

This quilt was quilted with straight lines that intersect the center of each block. The result is a quilted X through each Nine-Patch block, as shown. If you'd like to add additional quilting, try outlining the sashing strips and squares.

Centennial Baskets

The Goose Chase sashing that separates the dainty

Basket blocks makes this baby quilt extra special.

Double pink fabrics, printed with two

shades of pink, were popular with

quilters during the last half of the nine-

teenth century. They have been called such

names as Merrimac pink, bubble gum pink, straw-

berry pink, and Pepto-Bismol pink. Twenty-eight of

the blocks are the same Centennial Basket structure,

but two are "maverick" blocks with a slightly dif-

ferent structure. Perhaps the woman who pieced these

blocks was just making do with her fabric, but we'll

never know for sure!

SKILL LEVEL: Intermediate

SIZE: Finished quilt is 46 × 54 inches

Finished block is 6 inches square

Number of blocks: 30

Quilt owner: Marilyn Hein

Hand quilted by Toni Fisher

FABRICS AND SUPPLIES

- 3⅝ yards of pink print fabric for border, quilt back, and binding

- 1¾ yards *total* of assorted pink print fabrics for Goose Chase sashing and basket handles

- 1¼ yards *total* of brown print fabric for background of Basket blocks

- 1¼ yards of muslin for Goose Chase sashing

- ¾ yard *total* of assorted light print fabrics for baskets

- ½ yard *total* of assorted medium and dark print fabrics for baskets

- Batting, at least 52 × 60 inches

- Rotary cutter, ruler, and mat

- Plastic-coated freezer paper

46 X 54 inches

Centennial Baskets

QUICK CUTTING						
Fabric	**First Cut**		**Second Cut**		**Third Cut**	
BLOCKS & SASHING	No. of Strips	Strip Width	No.	Shape	No.	Shape
Assorted pink prints	7	3¼"	84	◻	334	F ◨
	*	1⅜" bias	30	1⅜"×6"	—	—
Brown print	3	5⅜"	15	◼	30	C ◣
	5	2"	60	D 2"×3½"		—	—
	2	3⅞"	15	◼	30	E ◣
Muslin	16	1⅞"	334	◻	668	G ◿
Light prints	6	2⅜"	105	◻	210	A ◿
Medium and dark prints	2	2⅜"	30	◼	60	A ◿
	2	2"	30	B ◼	*From the assorted pink prints, cut as many 1⅜" bias strips as needed to obtain the thirty 6" basket handles.		
BORDERS	No. of Strips	Strip Width	No.	Shape		
Pink print	5	4"	—	—		
BACKING	No. of Pieces	Shape	No. of Pieces	Shape		
Pink print†	2	44"×51"	1	20"×51"		

†*From the pink print, cut the 51" pieces as directed. These are for the backing. From the remaining 22"-wide section, cut ten 2" × 22" strips for binding. Any extra pink fabric can be used for the Goose Chase sashing pieces or basket handles.*

SCRAP RECIPE

Double pinks were commonly combined with indigo prints, green prints, or brown prints as in the dainty little basket quilt shown. You may want to choose colors based on where and how the quilt will be used. Will it be a special gift for a new baby or a charming wallhanging for a family room? This would be a striking quilt done in Amish colors, as shown here.

QUICK CUTTING

Referring to the "Quick Cutting" chart, cut the number of strips and pieces needed from each fabric using a rotary cutter. Cut all strips across the fabric width. All measurements include ¼-inch seam allowances. If you are using scraps that are less than 42 inches wide, you will need to increase the number of strips you cut accordingly.

PIECING THE BLOCKS

There are 30 Basket blocks in the quilt shown; 28 of the blocks are Centennial Baskets and the remaining 2 are Variation Baskets as shown in the **Block Diagram** on page 56. The instructions are for making Centennial Baskets. To make the Variation Baskets, replace the B square with a triangle square made from a light A triangle sewn to a medium or dark A triangle. You will need to cut additional light and medium or dark A triangles for the number of Variation Baskets you wish to include.

Centennial Basket

Variation Basket

Block Diagram

STEP 1. Lay out the pieces for the block. Join the two dark A triangles to light A triangles to form triangle squares. Press seam allowances toward the dark triangles.

STEP 2. Sew the pieces together in rows as shown in **Diagram 1**. Press the seam allowances in opposite directions in alternate rows. Join the rows and press the seam allowances to one side.

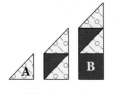

Diagram 1

Tips for Basket Handles

STEP 1. Use one 1⅜ × 6-inch bias strip for each basket handle.

STEP 2. To prepare a bias handle, fold one-third of the strip to the wrong side and press. Fold in the remaining long raw edge and press. Be sure the raw edge does not extend beyond the folded edge. The pressed strip should be approximately ⅜ inch wide.

STEP 3. Trace and cut the Handle Placement Guide on page 59 from plastic-coated freezer paper.

STEP 4. Fold a fabric triangle C in half and lightly crease to mark a center guideline. Fold the paper Handle Placement Guide in half and lightly crease to mark a center guideline.

STEP 5. Center the paper Handle Placement Guide with the shiny side facing the right side of the fabric triangle. Using a wool setting and no steam, press the paper to the fabric triangle as shown in the diagram.

STEP 6. Referring to the diagram, hand baste the inner edge of the folded bias strip along the edge of the Handle Placement Guide, allowing the bias strip to extend beyond the bottom raw edges of the fabric triangle. Remove the paper guide. The paper guide can be reused several times before you will need to replace it.

STEP 7. To reduce the possibility of stretching the bias edges of the triangle, join the patchwork pieces to complete the block before appliquéing the handle. Basting will hold the handle in place adequately until you join the sections. Then appliqué the handle, stitching the inner curve first, followed by the outer curve. Turn the block over and trim the extended ends of the handle even with the seam allowances.

STEP 3. Prepare a bias strip for the handle and baste it to the large C triangle as described in "Tips for Basket Handles."

STEP 4. Referring to **Diagram 2,** join the C triangle to the pieced triangle. Press the seam allowance toward the pieced triangle.

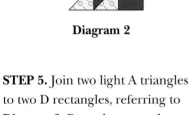

Diagram 2

STEP 5. Join two light A triangles to two D rectangles, referring to **Diagram 3.** Press the seam allowances toward the rectangles.

Diagram 3

STEP 6. Join the rectangle units to the sides of the block, referring to **Diagram 4.** Press the seam allowance toward the rectangle. Add an E triangle to the A triangles to complete the block. Press seam allowances toward the E triangle.

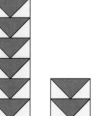

Diagram 4

STEP 7. Appliqué the basket handle in place.

STEP 8. Repeat to make a total of 30 Basket blocks.

MAKING THE GOOSE CHASE SASHING

STEP 1. Referring to **Diagram 5,** sew a muslin G triangle to both short sides of a pink F triangle. Press the seam allowances toward the muslin triangles.

Diagram 5

STEP 2. Repeat to make a total of 334 Goose Chase units.

STEP 3. Referring to **Diagram 6A,** join six Goose Chase units. Press the seam allowances toward the pink triangles. Repeat to make a total of 49 six-unit sections.

A   B

Diagram 6

STEP 4. Referring to **Diagram 6B,** join two Goose Chase units. Press seam allowances toward the pink triangles. Repeat to make a total of 20 two-unit sections.

The stitching lines of the Goose Chase unit will meet to form an X at the point. When sewing the Goose Chase units into sashing rows, have the point on top so that you'll be able to see exactly where to stitch to make sure your points come out nice and crisp. You should sew straight through the center of that X.

ASSEMBLING THE QUILT TOP

STEP 1. Referring to the **Quilt Diagram,** join five Basket blocks and four six-unit Goose Chase sections into a horizontal row. Make sure that the pink triangles are pointing downward in each Goose Chase unit. Press the seam allowances toward the blocks. Repeat to make a total of six rows.

STEP 2. To make a Goose Chase sashing row, lay out five six-unit sections and four two-unit sections, alternating types. Join the sections into a long strip that will have a total of 38 Goose Chase units. Press seam allowances toward the pink triangles. Repeat to make a total of five Goose Chase sashing rows.

STEP 3. Join the Basket block and sashing rows, alternating types. Press seam allowances toward the Basket block rows.

STEP 4. Measure the width of the quilt through the center, and trim two pink border strips to this size. Sew the borders to the top and bottom edges of quilt. Press the seam allowances toward the borders.

STEP 5. Cut one border strip in half and join a half strip to a full-length strip to make each side border.

STEP 6. Measure the length of the quilt through the center, including the top and bottom borders. Trim the two side borders to this length. Sew the side borders to the quilt top. Press the seam allowances toward the borders.

QUILTING AND FINISHING

STEP 1. Mark quilting designs as desired, or see "Quilting Ideas" for suggestions.

STEP 2. To piece the quilt back, join the two pink print backing pieces. Press seam allowances to one side.

STEP 3. Layer the quilt back, batting, and quilt top. Baste the layers together. Trim the quilt back and batting so they are approximately 3 inches larger than the quilt top on all sides.

STEP 4. Hand or machine quilt as desired.

STEP 5. From the binding fabric, make approximately 210 inches of French-fold binding by joining the binding strips with diagonal seams. See "Finishing" on page 223 for details on finishing the edges of your quilt.

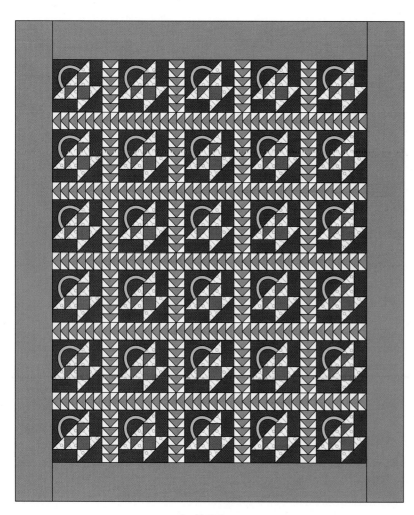

Quilt Diagram

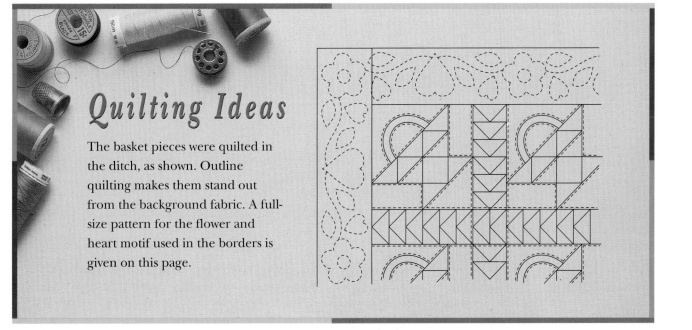

Quilting Ideas

The basket pieces were quilted in the ditch, as shown. Outline quilting makes them stand out from the background fabric. A full-size pattern for the flower and heart motif used in the borders is given on this page.

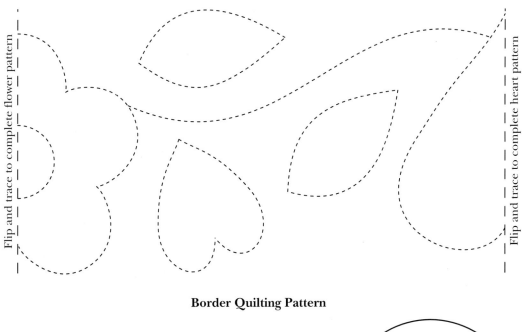

Flip and trace to complete flower pattern

Flip and trace to complete heart pattern

Border Quilting Pattern

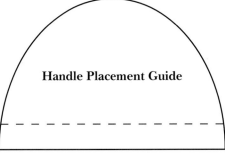

Handle Placement Guide

Align with raw edge

Cosmos Garden

SKILL LEVEL: Easy

SIZE: Finished quilt is
22 × 22 inches

Squared-off Four-Patch block is
approximately 2⅞ inches
square

Number of blocks: 25

FABRICS AND SUPPLIES

- ¼ yard of tan print
  fabric for wide
  border

- ¼ yard of dark blue print
  fabric for narrow border and
  binding

- ¼ yard *each* of two dark green
  print fabrics for leaves and bias
  vine

- Scraps, approximately 6 inches
  square, of approximately 30 different dark, medium, and light
  print fabrics for patchwork and
  appliqué

- 28 × 28-inch square of fabric for
  quilt back

- Quilt batting, at least 28 × 28
  inches

- Rotary cutter, ruler, and mat

- Template plastic

Quiltmaker Mary Radke achieved an old-fashioned look for her small quilt by utilizing reproduction fabrics and by keeping an overall dark look for the quilt. Mary's work shows a good understanding of the visual power of "maverick" blocks. Her placement of light, dark, and medium-value prints makes the Four Patch distinct in some blocks and virtually hidden in others. The combination of patchwork and appliqué has its roots in the early nineteenth century.

AMERICAN COUNTRY SCRAP QUILTS

22 × 22 inches

SCRAP RECIPE

Here's a place where you can mix and match fabrics to your heart's content, since this quilt lends itself to just about any scrap you have around. The random placement of lights and darks in the blocks gives it a spontaneity that matches the folk art flower appliqués in the border. Give yourself a challenge just for fun. Try using all stripes and plaids, or use just your oldest fabrics. You could even make it in all solids if you have an abundance of those.

QUICK CUTTING					
Fabric	**First Cut**		**Second Cut**		**From the assorted prints, you will need four matching triangles for each Four-Patch block. These triangles are cut larger than needed and will be trimmed after they are joined to the blocks.*
BLOCKS	No.	Shape	No.	Shape	
Assorted prints	50 pairs	1½" ▧	—	—	
	25 pairs	2½" ▧	100	⊠ *	
BORDERS	No.	Shape	*†From the dark green prints, you will need one 22"-long, one 16"-long, two 14"-long, two 12"-long, and two 10"-long pieces of bias for the vine appliqué. Cut strips a scant ¾" wide. See "Preparing Bias Strips for Appliqué Vines" on page 65 for pointers on cutting and preparing strips.*		
Tan print	2	4"×44"			
Dark blue print	2	1"×44"			
Dark green prints†	6	Large leaves			
	6	Small leaves			
Scraps	4	Large flowers			
	4	Small flowers			

CUTTING

Referring to the "Quick Cutting" chart, cut the number of strips needed from each fabric using a rotary cutter. Cut all strips across the fabric width. All measurements include ¼-inch seam allowances. If you are using scraps that are less than 42 inches wide, you will need to increase the number of strips you cut accordingly. Lengths given for the border strips are longer than needed. Borders will be trimmed to exact size before they are added to the quilt top. Make plastic templates for the two flower shapes, the large and small leaf shapes, and flower centers from the patterns on page 67. For the flower centers, you may want to use the method described in "Sew Wise" on page 64.

PIECING THE BLOCKS

STEP 1. Referring to **Diagram 1**, lay out two sets of two matching 1½-inch squares. Join the squares into two rows. Press seam allowances in opposite directions in the two rows. Join the rows to complete the Four-Patch block. Make a total of 25 blocks.

Diagram 1

STEP 2. To square off a Four-Patch block, begin by sewing matching triangles to two opposite sides of a block as shown in **Diagram 2**. Press seam allowances toward the triangles. Sew the remaining two matching triangles to the remaining two opposite sides of the block. Press as before.

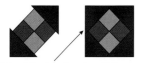

Trim block, allowing ¼" seam allowances at corners of Four Patch

Diagram 2

STEP 3. Using a rotary cutter and ruler, trim the triangles so that the block is squared off as shown in **Diagram 2**. Make sure to allow for ¼-inch seam allowances at the corners of the Four-Patch blocks as indicated on the diagram. The trimmed block will measure approximately 3⅜ inches, including seam allowances. In this manner, square off all 25 of the Four-Patch blocks.

ASSEMBLING THE INNER QUILT TOP

STEP 1. Lay out the squared-off blocks in five rows of five blocks per row as shown in **Diagram 3**.

STEP 2. Join the blocks to make the rows. Press seam allowances in opposite directions from row to row. Join the rows.

STEP 3. Measure the width of the quilt, measuring through the

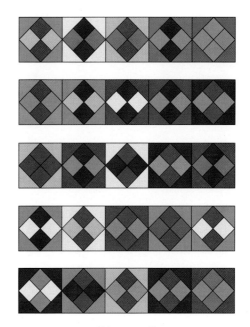

Diagram 3

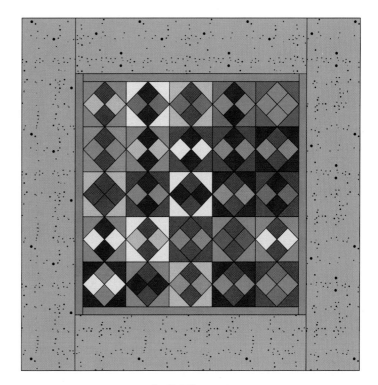

Quilt Diagram

middle. From the 1-inch-wide dark blue fabric strips, cut two borders the width of the quilt top. Sew the borders to the top and bottom of the quilt. Refer to the **Quilt Diagram.**

To make crisp, round appliquéd circles, make a plastic template (or use a spool or a coin). Trace around the template on the wrong side of the fabric. Cut out the fabric, adding a scant ¼-inch seam allowance. Use the same template and cut a circle of index card–weight paper.

Baste around the fabric circle between the drawn line and the raw edge. Position the paper template on the wrong side of the fabric circle. Pull on the basting thread to gather the fabric over the template. Tighten, then make a few stitches to secure the gathers.

Appliqué the circle in place. From the wrong side, make a cut in the background fabric, and remove the paper template.

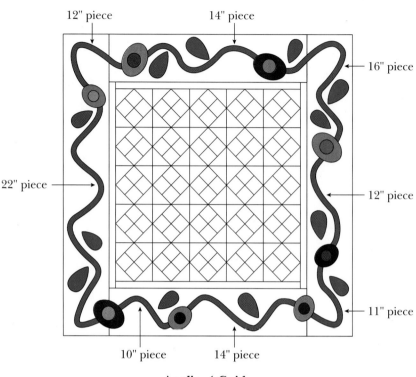

Appliqué Guide

STEP 4. Measure the quilt top in the opposite direction. Trim and add blue borders to the remaining two sides of the quilt top.

STEP 5. In the same manner, measure, trim, and add the wide tan fabric borders to the quilt top.

ADDING THE APPLIQUÉ

STEP 1. Prepare the bias strips for the vines as directed in "Preparing Bias Strips for Appliqué Vines."

STEP 2. Referring to the photograph of the quilt on page 61 and the **Appliqué Guide,** baste the prepared bias vine in place on the outer border. Plan the placement of the beginning and ending of each vine piece so that a flower will conceal them. You may want to trim the ends if they overlap. You can follow our placement guide for the vines and flowers or place them randomly any way you like.

STEP 3. Appliqué the vine in place using thread that matches the fabric.

STEP 4. Position and appliqué the flowers and leaves in place. See "Tips on Appliqué" on page 219. Add the flower centers.

Preparing Bias Strips for Appliqué Vines

Floral designs often include appliqué stems or vines. For the Cosmos Garden quilt, folded bias-cut strips form the pretty vine that travels around the outer border of the quilt, interrupted every so often by oval flower shapes. Follow these steps to prepare bias strips for appliqué.

Cut strips a scant $3/4$ inch wide. To cut with a rotary cutter, place your ruler across the fabric at a 45 degree angle and cut strips, making parallel cuts, as shown. You will need one 22-inch piece, one 16-inch piece, two 14-inch pieces, two 12-inch pieces, one 11-inch piece, and one 10-inch piece.

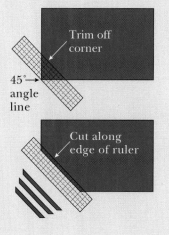

Trim off corner

45° angle line

Cut along edge of ruler

STEP 1. Place the bias strip wrong side up on the ironing board.

STEP 2. Use the tip of the iron to fold over the first third of the fabric, as shown.

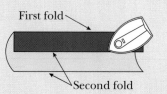

First fold

Second fold

STEP 3. Fold over the other raw edge and press, making sure it does not extend beyond the first fold.

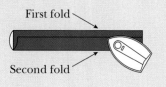

First fold

Second fold

STEP 4. Turn strip over to the right side and press once more.

STEP 5. Baste the prepared strip in position and appliqué it in place, stitching along both folds. Appliqué the inner curves first.

Another Option

Narrow bias strips can be made using bias bars or Celtic bars (available in quilt shops and mail-order catalogs). Cut a fabric strip wide enough to wrap around the bar and to allow for the $1/8$-inch seams. Fold the strip in half lengthwise with wrong sides facing. Sew the long raw edges of the strip together using a $1/8$-inch seam allowance. Insert the bar into the tube. Center the seam along the bar and press. Slide the bar along the tube, pressing as you go. Remove the bar and press the strip again.

QUILTING AND FINISHING

STEP 1. Mark quilting designs as desired, or see "Quilting Ideas" for suggestions.

STEP 2. Layer the quilt back, batting, and quilt top. Baste the layers together.

STEP 3. Hand or machine quilt as desired.

STEP 4. From the binding fabric, make approximately 95 inches of French-fold binding. See "Finishing" on page 223 for details on finishing the edges of your quilt.

Quilting Ideas

This quilt has outline quilting around the appliqué pieces. Quilt across the blocks, as shown.

Appliqué Patterns

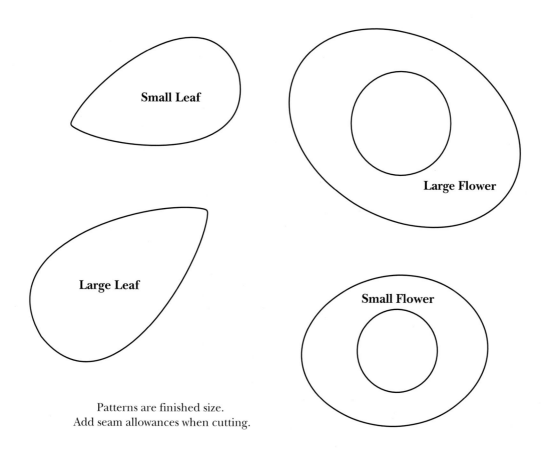

Small Leaf

Large Flower

Large Leaf

Small Flower

Patterns are finished size.
Add seam allowances when cutting.

Scrap Quilts from Grandma's Attic

THE LOOK OF QUILTS FROM GRANDMA'S ATTIC

During the years of the Great Depression, fabrics and quiltmaking underwent changes that make the quilts of this time period (1925–1940) very easy to identify. Improved synthetic dying made colors more permanent and bright colors available. Though times were financially bleak, quilts from the 1930s are light and floral.

Scrap quilts from this time period contain scads of multicolored, medium- to large-scale prints. Off-white solid fabric or muslin was generally the background choice for either patchwork or appliqué. The medium pink, yellow, lavender, green, and blue solid fabrics that we associate with this quiltmaking era were often incorporated into scrap quilts along with printed fabrics. The use of feed-, seed-, and flour-sack fabrics for quilts is the characteristic of 1930s quilts that even nonquilters know about. Many an adult today remembers waiting in the general store while Mother or Grandma personally selected the sacks of household staples so she would have enough printed cloth for her current quilt or for a dress.

Though women owned sewing machines, quiltmakers developed a penchant for making challenging patterns that required hand piecing. Perhaps they hand pieced to save on electricity. Ladies' magazines and newspapers published patterns on a monthly or daily basis, and the editors of these

Clear colors, strong light/dark contrast, and floral patterns were in vogue in the 1930s.

Muslin was often the primary or only light-value fabric in quilts made in the Depression years. Quilters also used other solids with their prints.

Check fabrics, both large and small scale, often found their way into Depression era patchwork. They contribute to the wholesome, informal flavor of many 1930s quilts.

The simple object prints of the earlier part of the century were replaced by more detailed novelty prints.

periodicals exerted a strong influence on pattern popularity. Double Wedding Rings, Flower Gardens, and intricate stars were the patchwork order of the day. Elaborate appliqué designs, sometimes created by professional quilt artists, were popular, too.

Quilt kits available by mail order led to more homogeneous, less personal appliqué styles. Kits for appliqué quilts were often medallion format. Kits for patchwork patterns like Trip around the World, Lone Star, and other designs contained precut, color-coordinated patches.

Here are some hints for achieving a Depression era look for your own scrap quilts. We've noted which quilts in this book illustrate each characteristic.

- Choose multicolored, high-contrast, medium-scale prints (see Original Star and Kansas Twister).

- Incorporate solid fabrics in patchwork or as setting pieces (see Kansas Twister, Six-Pointed String Star, and Grandmother's Fan).

- Use muslin for background or setting pieces to "calm down" busy print fabrics (see Original Star, Love Ring, and Sunbonnet Sue).

- Select "hard" patterns with set-in pieces (see Original Star and Six-Pointed String Star).

- Use black thread for blanket stitch appliqué (see Sunbonnet Sue).

- Use unusual edge finishes such as "prairie points" or scallops instead of ordinary binding (see Original Star).

Depression era scrap quilts contain lots of multicolored medium- to large-scale prints.

Original Star

SKILL LEVEL: Challenging

SIZE: Finished quilt is approximately 88 × 88 inches

Finished block is 10 inches square

Number of blocks: 64

Quilt owner: Marilyn Hein

Hand quilted by Toni Fisher

FABRICS AND SUPPLIES

- 4¹/₂ yards of muslin for background

- ¹/₄ yards *each* of 24 to 26 multicolored floral fabrics (at least 6 yards total) for blocks

- 8 yards of fabric for quilt back

- Quilt batting, at least 94 inches square

- Rotary cutter, ruler, and mat

- Template plastic (optional)

We named this quilt Original Star because the block was not identified in any of our pattern source books.

Although it's one of a kind, the palette of fabrics is certainly in keeping with typical 1930s style of multicolored prints combined with muslin. This quilt also reflects the passion in the 1930s for complicated patterns and challenging borders. Our quick-cutting and quick-piecing instructions will let you make this quilt much more easily than the methods used by the original quilt's maker!

88 × 88 inches

SCRAP RECIPE

Pastels, clear colors, blacks, and brights all work together successfully, even though most of the fabrics are busy floral prints, because large amounts of all the colors were used and because breathing space is provided by the muslin. This design would also be well suited to using reproduction fabrics as we have in this block.

Or try shades of blue on a white background. The key to blending fabrics, whether you use lots of colors or just one, is to use a large quantity of different prints, including florals, geometrics, and pictorials.

QUICK CUTTING						
Fabric	**First Cut**		**Second Cut**		**Third Cut**	
BLOCKS & BORDERS	No. of Strips	Strip Width	No.	Shape	No.	Shape
Muslin	16	2½"	256	A ▢	—	—
	26	3⅞"	256	▢	512	D ◸
Assorted prints	11	2⅞"	128	▢	256	B ◩
	8	5¼"	64	▢	256	C ⊠
	64	2"	—	—	—	—

QUICK CUTTING

Referring to the "Quick Cutting" chart, cut the number of strips needed from each fabric using a rotary cutter. Cut all strips across the fabric width. All measurements include ¼-inch seam allowances. If you are using scraps that are less than 42 inches wide, you will need to increase the number of strips you cut accordingly. Our quick-cutting instructions call for cutting triangles for the D pieces, rather than the odd-shaped D and D reverse pieces, which require a template. The triangles are trimmed after they are sewn to A/B/C units during piecing. For the B/E units, you will make strip sets and then use a special template to quick cut units from the sets.

If you prefer to use traditional cutting methods, make finished-size templates for a 2-inch A square, a 2-inch B right triangle, and a 2⅞-inch right triangle as well as for pattern pieces D, D reverse, and E on page 78. See "Making and Using Templates" on page 215.

PIECING THE STAR BLOCKS

Each block is made of four quadrants, which in turn are made from triangles cut from strips sets as well as the triangles you've already cut. The muslin triangles will be trimmed during the construction process, eliminating the need to make an odd-shaped template. See the **Block Diagram.**

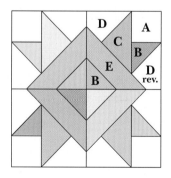

Block Diagram

Making the Strip Sets

STEP 1. Sew the 2-inch print strips together in sets of two, for a total of 32 strip sets. Press the seams to one side.

STEP 2. Make a Strip Set Triangle template for the E/B units, using

the pattern on page 78. Include the placement line on your template.

STEP 3. Referring to **Diagram 1,** place the template on the wrong side of a strip set, aligning the placement line on the template with the seam. Trace around the template to mark 11 triangles, then cut out the triangles using a rotary cutter and ruler.

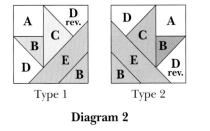

Diagram 1

STEP 4. Repeat, marking and cutting 11 triangles from each strip set, to make a total of 352 strip-pieced triangles. You will use 256 for the Original Star blocks and 96 for the quilt edges.

Piecing the Blocks

The Original Star block is pieced in four quadrants. There are two types of quadrants—Type 1 and Type 2—in the block, as shown in **Diagram 2.**

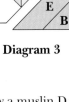

Type 1   Type 2

Diagram 2

STEP 1. Referring to the diagram, lay out the pieces for one Type 1 quadrant. The muslin D triangles will be trimmed later.

STEP 2. Diagram 3 shows the piecing order of the Type 1 quadrant pieces. First, sew a print B triangle to the muslin A square. Press the seam allowances toward the triangle. Join a print C triangle to the right-hand side of the A/B unit. Press the seam toward the C triangle.

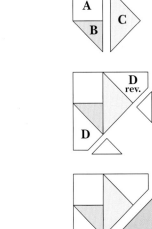

Diagram 3

STEP 3. Sew a muslin D triangle to the two opposite sides of the unit. The triangle points will extend beyond the unit. Press the seam allowances toward the muslin triangles. After pressing, trim the triangles even with the bottom of the print triangle, as shown.

STEP 4. Sew a strip-pieced E/B triangle made earlier to the long side of the partially completed quadrant. Press the seam allowances toward the strips.

STEP 5. Repeat to make a total of 128 Type 1 quadrants.

STEP 6. Referring to **Diagram 4,** make a total of 128 Type 2 quadrants in the same manner as you did for Type 1 quadrants. Pay careful attention to the diagram so that your finished Type 2 quadrants are mirror images of the Type 1 quadrants.

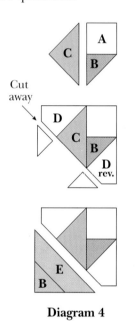

Diagram 4

STEP 7. Referring to the **Block Diagram** on page 74, lay out two Type 1 quadrants and two Type 2 quadrants. Join the quadrants in two rows of two quadrants. Press the seam allowances in opposite directions. Join the two rows to complete the block.

STEP 8. Repeat to make a total of 64 blocks.

ASSEMBLING THE QUILT TOP

STEP 1. Lay out the completed blocks in eight horizontal rows of eight blocks each, as shown in the **Quilt Diagram.** Join the blocks into rows. Press the seams in opposite directions from row to row. Join the rows.

STEP 2. Join the remaining E/B strip-pieced triangles in pairs, as shown in **Diagram 5,** to make a total of 48 border triangles.

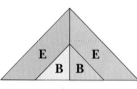

Diagram 5

STEP 3. Trim 40 border triangles, as shown in **Diagram 6.** To trim, measure and mark each triangle 3¾ inches in each direction from the center seam. Trim off the corners perpendicular to the long side of triangle, as shown. On four border triangles, trim the excess from the right side only. Trim only the left side on the remaining four triangles. The pieces with just one side trimmed will be used on the ends of the borders.

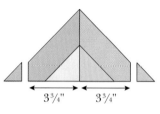

Diagram 6

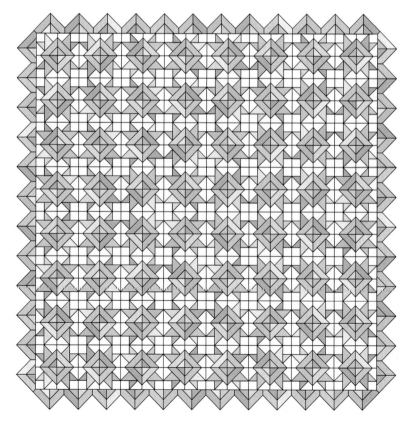

Quilt Diagram

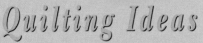Quilting Ideas

This quilt was outline quilted by hand, ¼ inch inside each muslin and printed patch. The border triangles were quilted with a double row of peaks in each strip, as shown.

STEP 4. To make each of the four borders, join 10 border triangles and two end triangles, with the untrimmed edge at the ends of the borders.

STEP 5. Center and sew a pieced border strip to each side of the quilt, stopping your stitching ¼ inch from the corner at each end of the quilt top. Backstitch, without sewing into the seam allowance.

STEP 6. Miter the border corner seams and trim off the excess border corners, leaving ¼-inch seam allowances.

QUILTING AND FINISHING

STEP 1. Mark quilting designs as desired, or see "Quilting Ideas" for suggestions.

STEP 2. To piece the quilt back, cut the backing fabric into three equal lengths, each about 96 inches. Trim the selvages, and join the three panels along the long edges. Press the seams away from the center panel.

STEP 3. Layer the quilt back, batting, and quilt top. Baste the layers together. Trim the quilt back and batting so they are approximately 3 inches larger than the quilt top on all sides, including the pieced border. To stabilize the pieced border, baste around the outside edges, ½ inch from the raw edges.

STEP 4. Hand or machine quilt as desired.

STEP 5. Trim the excess batting and backing so they are even with the raw edges of the pieced border. Then trim an additional ¼ inch off the edges of the batting.

STEP 6. Fold in the raw edges of the quilt top and backing ¼ inch. Slip stitch the edges of quilt top and backing together to finish the quilt.

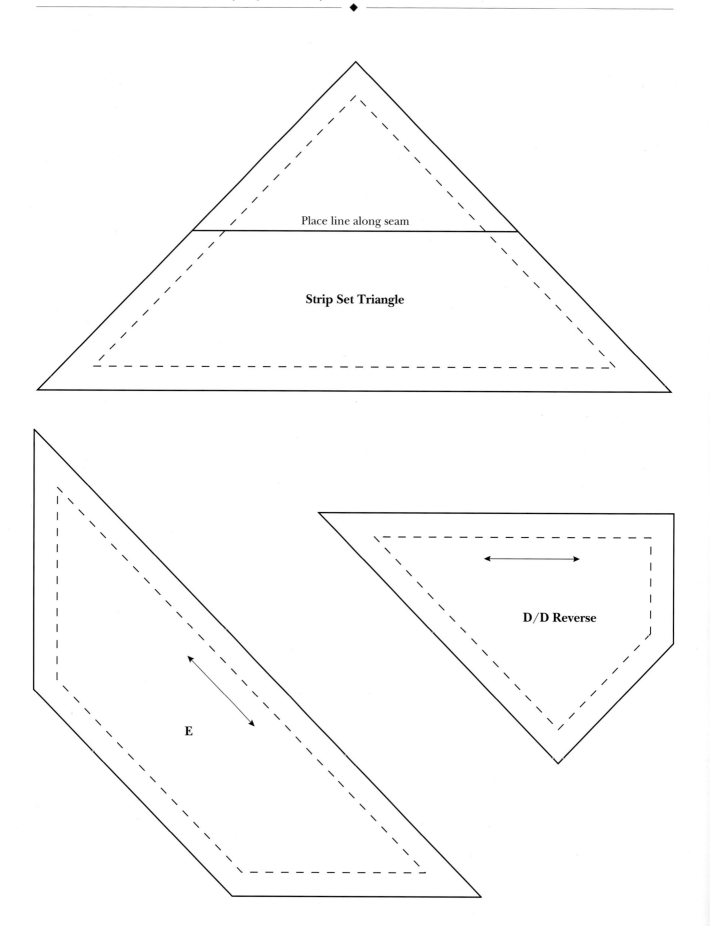

Place line along seam

Strip Set Triangle

D/D Reverse

E

Love Ring

This much-used but well-cared-for quilt from the

1930s is made from fan blocks arranged in a setting

that is more often used for Drunkard's Path

blocks. The setting, sometimes called Love

Ring, Nonesuch, Ozark Puzzle, or Chain

Link, is built from the center outward in con-

centric rings. For our instructions we've modified the

original fan block slightly to make the small wedges

easier to handle.

AMERICAN COUNTRY SCRAP QUILTS

SKILL LEVEL: Intermediate

SIZE: Finished quilt is
65 × 78 inches

Finished block is
6½ inches square

Number of blocks: 120

Quilt owner: Frieda Holt

FABRICS AND SUPPLIES

- 4½ yards of white fabric for block background

- Approximately ⅛ yard *each* of at least 40 different printed fabrics for fans

- 4 yards of fabric for quilt back

- ½ yard of medium green fabric for binding

- Quilt batting, at least 71 × 84 inches

- Rotary cutter, ruler, and mat

- Template plastic

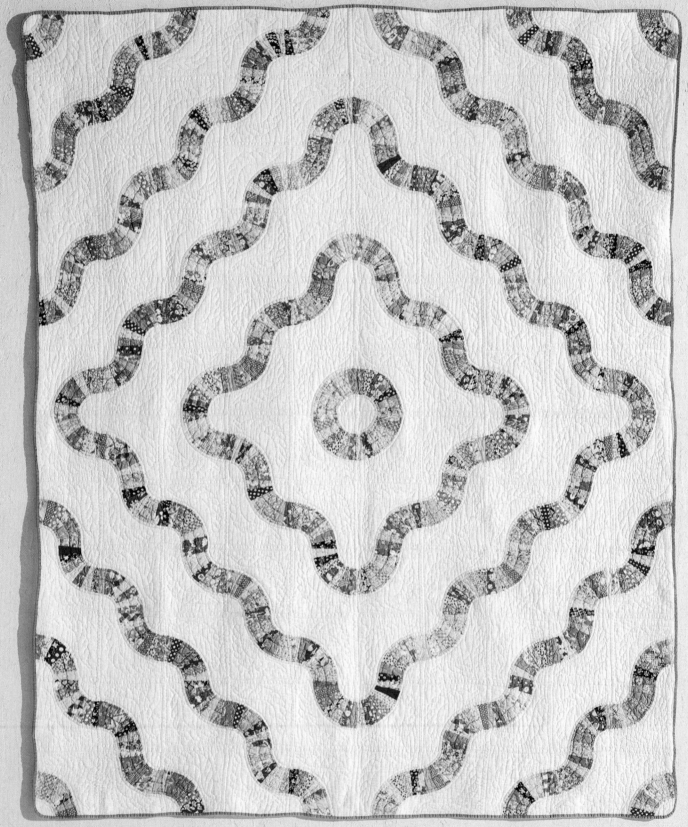

65 × 78 inches

Love Ring

QUICK CUTTING				
Fabric	**First Cut**		**Second Cut**	
BLOCKS	No. of Strips	Strip Width	No.	Shape
White	20	7"	120	☐
Prints*	No.	Shape	**From the prints,* cut 18 A pieces from each *of the 40 fabrics.*	
	720	A pieces		

SCRAP RECIPE

■

As with many Depression Era quilts, the Love Ring quilt shown was made of many medium-scale print scraps on a white background. For a quilt that looks totally different, try an Amish version. Use a variety of solid fabrics for the wedges and place them on a black background. You might also try a white background with jewel tone fabrics or shirting background with reproduction prints, as shown here.

CUTTING

Referring to the "Quick Cutting" chart, cut the number of strips needed from each fabric using a rotary cutter. Cut all strips across the fabric width. All measurements include ¼-inch seam allowances. If you are using scraps that are less than 42 inches wide, you will need to increase the number of strips you cut accordingly. You will need to make a template for the A pattern on page 83.

PIECING THE BLOCKS

STEP 1. Referring to the **Block Diagram,** join six A pieces along the long sides to form a gentle arc. At the narrow ends of the wedge pieces, stop stitching ¼ inch from the bottom raw edge of the inner curve of the arc and backstitch two or three stitches. This will make it easier to turn under seam allowances along the inner edge of

the arc. Press seam allowances in one direction.

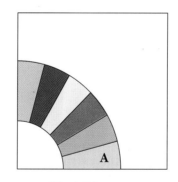

Block Diagram

STEP 2. Baste under a ¼-inch seam allowance along the top and bottom curves of the arc.

STEP 3. Position the arc on top of a background square and pin it in place. Appliqué the top and bottom curves. Remove the basting. Baste the sides of the arc to the background square.

STEP 4. Repeat to make a total of 120 blocks.

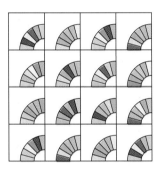

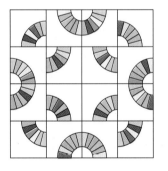

Try out other arrangements of the blocks to decide which setting you like best. The illustrations suggest some alternatives.

Quilt Diagram

ASSEMBLING THE QUILT TOP

STEP 1. Referring to the **Quilt Diagram,** lay out the blocks in 12 horizontal rows with ten blocks in each row. Arrange them in concentric rings as in the quilt shown.

STEP 2. Join the blocks into rows. Press the seam allowances in alternate directions from row to row. Join the rows.

QUILTING AND FINISHING

STEP 1. Mark quilting designs as desired, or see "Quilting Ideas" for suggestions.

STEP 2. To piece the quilt back, cut the backing fabric into two 2-yard pieces. Cut one piece in half lengthwise. Trim the selvages, and sew a half panel to each long side of the full panel. Press the seam allowances toward the narrow panels. The seams on the quilt

Quilting Ideas

Make a quilting template using the Feather Quilting Design. Quilt the feather in the background area of the blocks, and quilt the remainder of the block, as shown.

back will run parallel to the top and bottom edges of the quilt.

STEP 3. Layer the quilt back, batting, and quilt top. Baste the layers together. Trim the quilt back and batting so they are approximately 3 inches larger than the quilt top on all sides.

STEP 4. Hand or machine quilt as desired.

STEP 5. Make approximately 300 inches of French-fold binding. See "Finishing" on page 223 for details on finishing the edges of your quilt.

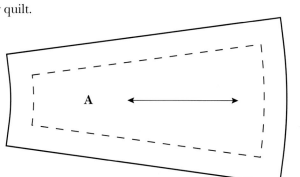

Feather Quilting Design

A

Six-Pointed String Star

SKILL LEVEL: Challenging

SIZE: Finished quilt is
74 × 111 inches

Finished star is approximately 18
inches from point to point

Number of pieced stars: 28

FABRICS AND SUPPLIES

- 4³/4 yards of medium green solid
  fabric for background

- Approximately 3¹/2 yards
  total of assorted print
  scraps in the fol-
  lowing pastel
  colors: yellow,
  blue, pink, green,
  peach, lavender,
  white, and cream
  for patchwork

- Freezer, butcher, or
  photocopy paper for
  patchwork foundation

- 6¹/2 yards of fabric for quilt back

- ³/4 yard of fabric for binding

- Quilt batting, at least 80 × 117
  inches

- Rotary cutter, ruler, and mat

- Template plastic

AMERICAN COUNTRY
SCRAP QUILTS

Tennessee quilter Nancy Granner chose many

medium-value pastel print fabrics for her pieced dia-

monds. Each diamond features some blue,

yellow, and green fabrics to unify the

patchwork. The distinctive gray-green

solid setting and border fabric, sometimes

called Nile green, kitchen green, or institutional

green, adds to the impression that this is an antique

rather than a new quilt. String quilts such as this

first became popular around 1890.

74 × 111 inches

SCRAP RECIPE

To achieve the scrappy look of the quilt shown, use a large variety of different prints. This project is a great way to use up small pieces of fabric. If green isn't your color, imagine these stars on a background of another hue, such as medium or navy blue, deep pink, or a muted shade of plum. Just be sure to use a large selection of scraps to make them blend well with whatever background color you choose.

QUICK CUTTING			
Fabric	**Cut**		
BLOCKS	No.	Shape	**Note:** *String star points are pieced from scraps. If you are using yardage, you may want to cut it into random-width strips ahead of time for quicker and easier piecing.*
Green	81	A diamond	
	14	B	
Foundation paper	184	A diamond	
BORDERS	No. of Strips	Strip Width	
Green	4	6½"	

CUTTING

Referring to the "Quick Cutting" chart, cut the number of strips needed using a rotary cutter. Cut all strips across the fabric width. For A and B pieces, refer to "Making and Using Templates" on page 215, and make templates from the patterns on pages 92–93. Follow the grain arrows on the pattern pieces when cutting your fabric. All measurements include ¼-inch seam allowances.

If you plan to hand piece this quilt, make finished-size templates for patterns A and B. If you plan to machine piece, make both a finished-size template (to mark the paper pieces) and a template that includes seam allowances (to mark the green fabric pieces) for the A diamond. Use a large needle, such as a sewing machine needle, to pierce holes in your template at the points marked with dots on the pattern. As you mark your fabrics, mark dots through the holes in the templates. You can use the dots to match points for pinning and sewing.

CRUMB-PIECING THE DIAMONDS

During the hard times of the Great Depression, quilters utilized even the smallest fabric scraps (crumbs) to piece their patchwork. In a true quilting tradition, quilts made in this manner satisfied a desire for frugality, creativity, and beauty at the same time. While similar to crazy quilts, crumb-pieced quilts are made of cotton fabrics, are generally quilted, and are not usually embellished with embroidery.

STEP 1. Referring to **Diagram 1,** pin the wrong side of an irregular shaped fabric piece that has straight, not curved sides, on top of the approximate center of a paper foundation diamond. The beginning piece can be virtually any shape with straight edges, such as a square, rectangle, triangle, or other polygon.

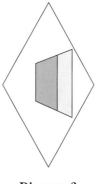

Diagram 1

STEP 2. Place a fabric scrap on top of the previous fabric piece with right sides facing and one raw edge aligned. Join the pieces, stitching through the fabric and the paper foundation. Make the seam the length of the underneath fabric piece as shown in **Diagram 2.** Place a pin at the start and end of your underneath piece so you can easily tell where to start and stop stitching.

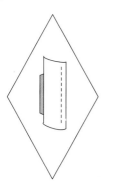

Diagram 2

STEP 3. Open out the top fabric piece and press. Trim the edges of the new piece so they are in a

straight line with the edges of the beginning piece as shown in **Diagram 3.**

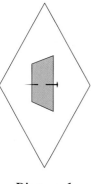

Diagram 3

STEP 4. To add the next piece, place a new fabric scrap along an edge created by the first and second pieces. Stitch and trim to create a straight line. In foundation piecing, it's important to plan your trimming carefully to avoid creating L-shaped openings between fabric pieces, as shown in **Diagram 4.** These spaces are difficult to fill in.

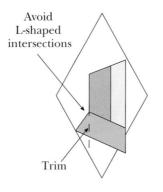

Avoid L-shaped intersections

Trim

Diagram 4

STEP 5. Working around the center piece, add additional pieces in the same manner until the paper diamond is covered with

When using paper foundation pieces, set your sewing machine stitch length at approximately 15 stitches per inch. Using a shorter stitch length will make it easier to remove the paper when piecing is completed. Don't worry about having to tear out mistakes. Since you are piecing randomly, if you have to remove a piece for any reason, simply cut away the piece as close to the stitching as possible on both sides of the seam. Then pull out any remaining threads. Now you're ready to choose another scrap and stitch it on without removing any tiny machine stitches!

fabric. Since the paper diamonds are finished size, plan your piecing and trimming to allow at least ¼ inch of fabric to extend over the paper diamond. Turn the diamond over so the paper side is facing up. Using a rotary cutter and ruler, trim the excess fabric to create an even ¼-inch seam allowance on all sides of the diamond.

STEP 6. Repeat to cover all of the paper diamonds with crumb piecing.

PIECING THE STARS

STEP 1. You will need six crumb-pieced diamonds for each star. Make two half stars by joining diamonds into groups of three, as shown in **Diagram 5.** As you assemble the diamonds and other pieces for this quilt, use the tips of the paper diamonds and dots on the points to align the pieces. To

create smooth star centers and to make setting in pieces easier, sew seams only from dot to dot without stitching into the seam allowances, as shown in **Diagram 6.** If you are machine stitching, secure the beginning and end of each seam by backstitching.

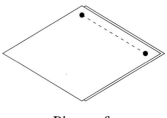

Diagram 6

STEP 2. Join the half stars. Press all seam allowances clockwise so they radiate around the star.

STEP 3. Repeat to make 28 stars.

STEP 4. Referring to **Diagram 7,** join groups of four crumb diamonds to make a total of four partial stars.

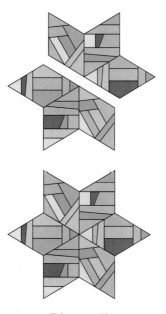

Diagram 5

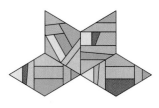

Diagram 7

ASSEMBLING THE QUILT TOP

STEP 1. Referring to the **Quilt Assembly Diagram,** join the stars, partial stars, green A diamonds, and B pieces to make the quilt top. Work in vertical rows and then add the diamonds between the rows. Add the B pieces last. (See "Setting In Pieces" on page 217.) Use the matching dots as guidelines to align and join pieces as you set in the many pieces for this quilt. Tear away the paper from the wrong side of the crumb-pieced diamonds as you work. The paper can be removed when a diamond has been sewn on all four sides. Press all seams toward the green diamonds.

STEP 2. Trim the bottom and top edges of the quilt as indicated on

the **Quilt Assembly Diagram.** IMPORTANT: Be sure to leave ¼ inch beyond the points of the diamonds for seam allowance.

STEP 3. Make two long borders by joining pairs of green border strips. Measure the width of the quilt top through the center, and trim the borders to this size. Sew the borders to the top and bottom edges of the quilt. See the **Quilt Diagram** on page 90. Press the seam allowances toward the borders.

When adding the top and bottom borders, it may be easier to sew them on before trimming the diamonds. Use your ruler and mark a line ¼ inch above the points of the diamonds all the way across the top and bottom of the quilt. Align the edge of the border with the marked line and sew. Then remove the paper from the crumb-pieced diamonds and trim even with the border using a rotary cutter and ruler. This method helps to ensure that the seams do not come apart after trimming.

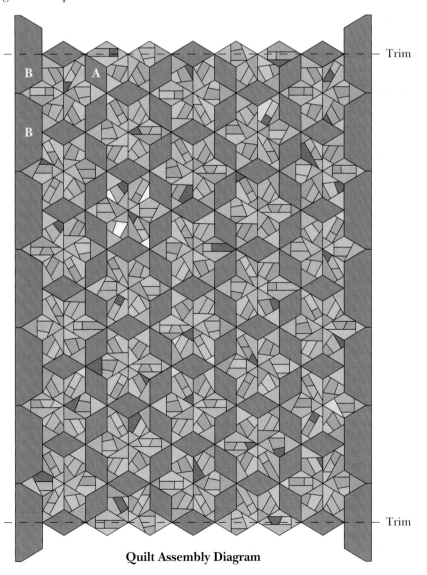

Quilt Assembly Diagram

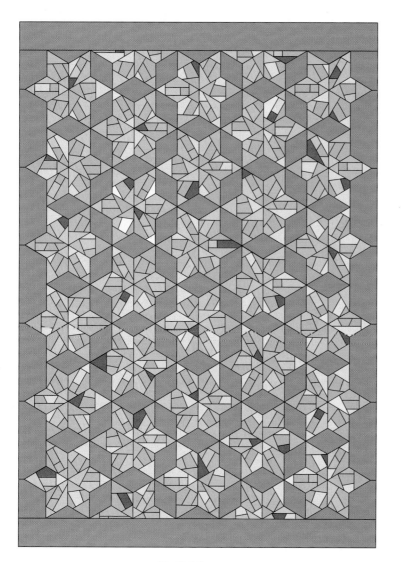

Quilt Diagram

QUILTING AND FINISHING

STEP 1. Mark quilting designs as desired, or see "Quilting Ideas" for suggestions.

STEP 2. To piece the quilt back, cut the backing fabric into two 3¼-yard pieces. Cut one piece in half lengthwise. Trim the selvages, and sew a half panel to each long side of the full panel. Press the seam allowances toward the narrow panels.

STEP 3. Layer the quilt back, batting, and quilt top. Baste the layers together. Trim the quilt back and batting so they are approximately 3 inches larger than the quilt top on all sides.

STEP 4. Hand or machine quilt as desired.

STEP 5. From the binding fabric, make approximately 390 inches of French-fold binding by joining the binding strips with diagonal seams. See "Finishing" on page 223 for details on finishing the edges of your quilt.

Quilting Ideas

This quilt was quilted in the ditch within the crumb-pieced areas. The green diamonds are quilted with the curved motif given on page 92, and the borders are quilted diagonally to form Vs, as shown.

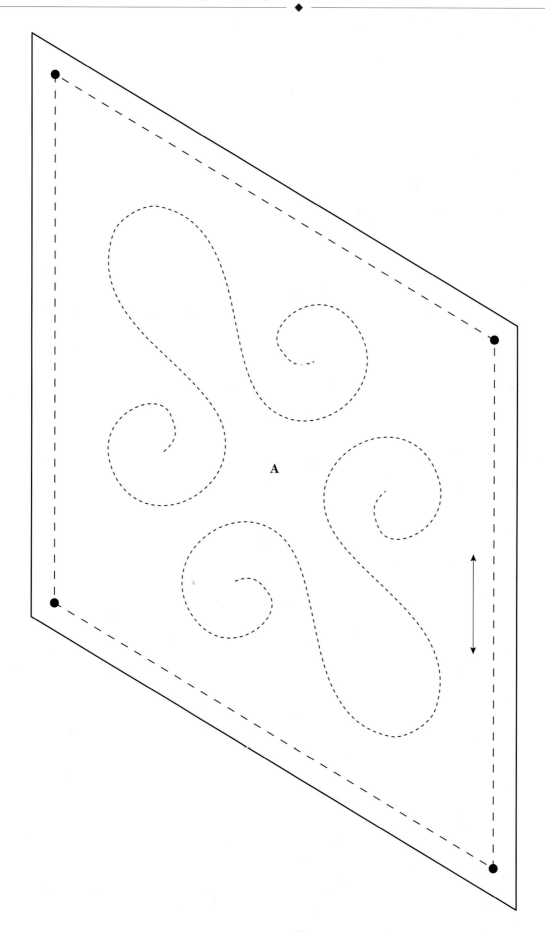

A

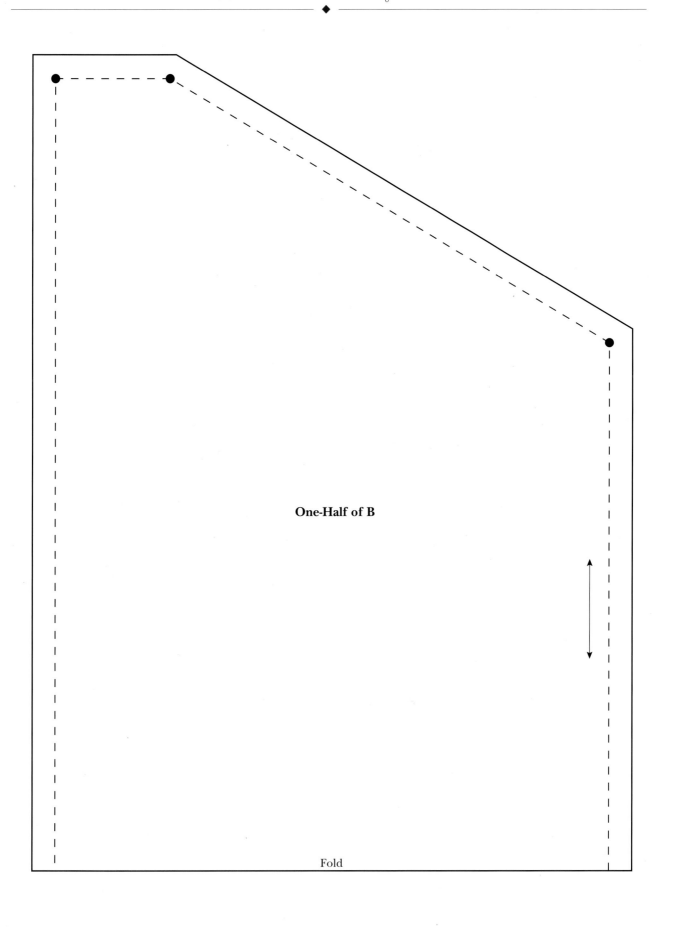

One-Half of B

Fold

Sunbonnet Sue

SKILL LEVEL: Easy

SIZE: Finished quilt is
15$\frac{1}{2}$ × 22$\frac{1}{2}$ inches

Finished block is 5$\frac{1}{2}$
inches square

Number of blocks: 6

FABRICS AND SUPPLIES

- $\frac{1}{4}$ yard of muslin or off-white solid fabric for block background

- $\frac{1}{4}$ yard of blue solid fabric for sashing

- $\frac{1}{4}$ yard of pink solid fabric for sashing

- Scraps of six different floral print fabrics for dresses

- Scraps of six different solid fabrics for bonnets, sleeves, and shoes (The solid blue and pink fabrics for sashing can be used for two of the blocks.)

- $\frac{1}{4}$ yard of medium green solid fabric for binding

- $\frac{2}{3}$ yard of fabric for quilt back

- Quilt batting, at least 22 × 29 inches

- Rotary cutter, ruler, and mat

- Black embroidery floss and embroidery needle

- Paper-backed fusible web (optional)

Sunbonnet Sue was a favorite pattern during Depression Era times. Inspired by illustrations in earlier children's storybooks, Sue and her beau, Overall Bill, often appear on quilts fashioned from flour and feed sacks. This cute miniquilt by Mary Radke of Illinois probably would not be mistaken for an authentic 1930s piece, since miniaturizing blocks like Sue is a modern-day practice. However, Mary's choice of feed-sack reproduction fabrics and her use of black blanket stitching for the appliqué are certainly reminiscent of the mid-1930s time period.

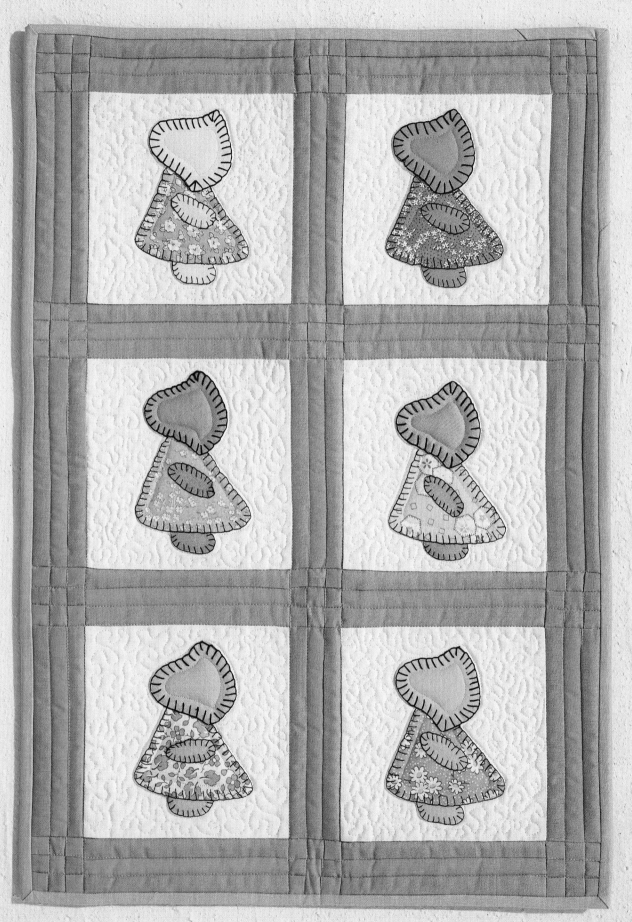

15½ × 22½ inches

SCRAP RECIPE

If you want Sunbonnet Sue to look just as she did in the 1930s, then reproduction fabrics are probably your best bet. But if you're flexible about what Sue wears, just about any scraps will work. For a homespun Sue, use plaids for her dresses and deeper colors for the bonnets, shoes, and lattice. It's best to stay with small- or medium-scale prints, and if you have a lot of calico scraps, these would work well, too.

QUICK CUTTING				
Fabric	**First Cut**		**Second Cut**	
BACKGROUND SQUARES	No. of Strips	Strip Width	No.	Shape
Muslin or off-white	1	6"	6	▢
SASHING	No. of Strips	Strip Width	No.	Shape
Blue solid	7	1"	—	—
Pink solid	5	1"	—	—
APPLIQUÉ	No.	Shape		
Floral prints	6	Dress pieces		
Solid colors	6	Matching sets of the bonnet and shoe pieces		

CUTTING

Referring to the "Quick Cutting" chart, cut the number of strips and background squares needed from each fabric using a rotary cutter. Cut all strips across the fabric width. All measurements include ¼-inch seam allowances.

Make plastic templates for the Sunbonnet Sue appliqués using the patterns on page 99. Mary used easy fusible appliqué for the quilt shown, securing the pieces to the background fabric with fusible web and then adding decorative blanket stitching. For the fused method, pieces are cut finished size. See "Fusible Appliqué" for further instructions.

If you plan to use traditional appliqué methods, add seam allowances to the fabric pieces when cutting. Turn under the seam allowances, appliqué the pieces in place using a blind stitch and matching thread, and then add decorative blanket stitching as well.

MAKING THE BLOCKS

STEP 1. Prepare the dress, bonnet, sleeve, and shoe pieces for appliqué.

STEP 2. Referring to the photograph of the quilt on page 95, position the appliqués for one block on a background square and either pin or fuse in place. Add stitching as desired. Refer to **Diagram 1** if you are adding decorative blanket stitching.

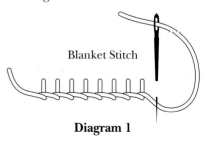

Blanket Stitch

Diagram 1

STEP 3. Make a total of six blocks.

Fusible Appliqué

Make the preparation of appliqués for blanket stitching quick and easy by using fusible web to secure the pieces to your background blocks. Several brands of paper-backed fusible web are available at quilt shops and fabric stores. If you plan to do the decorative hand stitching, make sure you get a lightweight, sewable fusible web.

STEP 1. Trace appliqué patterns onto the paper side of the fusible web. Make a separate tracing for each appliqué piece. If you want your Sue to face right, as shown in the quilt in the photograph, you will need to do your tracing in two steps. (If you trace directly from the book, Sue will be facing left.) First trace the patterns onto paper, then reverse them and trace onto the paper side of the fusible web.

STEP 2. Cut out each appliqué shape, cutting slightly larger than the traced outline.

STEP 3. Follow the manufacturer's instructions to fuse the web side of each appliqué to the wrong side of the appliqué fabric.

STEP 4. Carefully cut out the appliqué pieces along the traced lines.

STEP 5. Peel off the paper backing and position the appliqué pieces on the background block, overlapping them as needed.

STEP 6. Following the manufacturer's instructions, fuse the appliqué shapes to the background block.

SEW WISE

Many sewing machines will do a beautiful blanket stitch in half the time it takes you to do it by hand. Consult your machine manual and experiment with stitch length and width settings before you do your blocks.

PIECING THE SASHING AND NINE-PATCH SASHING SQUARES

STEP 1. Referring to **Diagram 2**, make Strip Set 1 with two blue fabric strips and one pink fabric strip. Press seam allowances toward the blue strips. Repeat to make three strip sets.

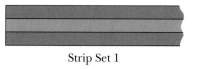

Strip Set 1

Diagram 2

STEP 2. From Strip Set 1, cut seventeen 6-inch-long sashing strip segments. Also cut twelve 1-inch segments for the sashing squares. See **Diagram 3.**

STEP 3. Referring to **Diagram 4,** make one Strip Set 2 with two pink fabric strips and one blue fabric strip. Press seam allowances toward the blue strip. From Strip Set 2, cut 24 segments, each 1 inch wide, for the sashing squares.

STEP 4. Lay out three segments as shown in **Diagram 5.** Join the segments to make a nine-patch sashing square. Use the remaining segments to make a total of 12 sashing squares.

ASSEMBLING THE QUILT TOP

STEP 1. Referring to the **Quilt Diagram,** lay out the pieced sashing, sashing squares, and blocks in seven horizontal rows. Four of the rows will be made of sashing and sashing squares. Three of the rows will be made of sashing and blocks.

STEP 2. Join the units to make the rows. Press seam allowances toward sashing. Join the rows.

QUILTING AND FINISHING

STEP 1. Mark quilting designs as desired, or see "Quilting Ideas" for suggestions.

STEP 2. For the quilt back, cut a piece of backing fabric 22 × 30 inches.

STEP 3. Layer the quilt back, batting, and quilt top. Baste the layers together.

STEP 4. Hand or machine quilt as desired.

STEP 5. From the binding fabric, make approximately 85 inches of French-fold binding. See "Finishing" on page 223 for details on finishing the edges of your quilt.

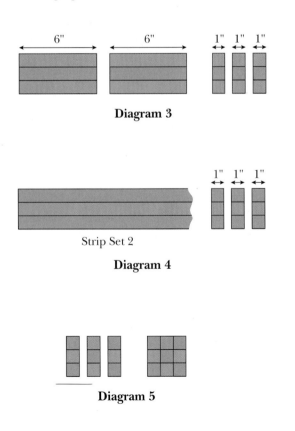

Diagram 3

Strip Set 2

Diagram 4

Diagram 5

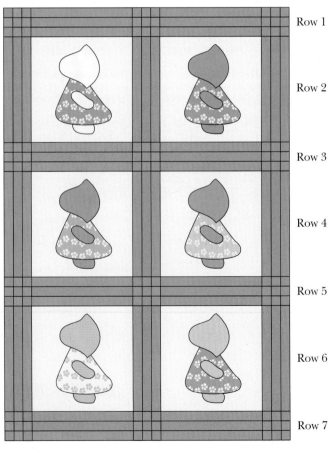

Row 1

Row 2

Row 3

Row 4

Row 5

Row 6

Row 7

Quilt Diagram

Quilting Ideas

This quilt has machine-quilted stippling in the background area around the appliqués on each block. The dress and bonnet are machine quilted ¼ inch inside the appliqué shapes. The sashing pieces are quilted in the ditch. Another approach would be echo quilting to enhance the appliqués.

Appliqué Patterns

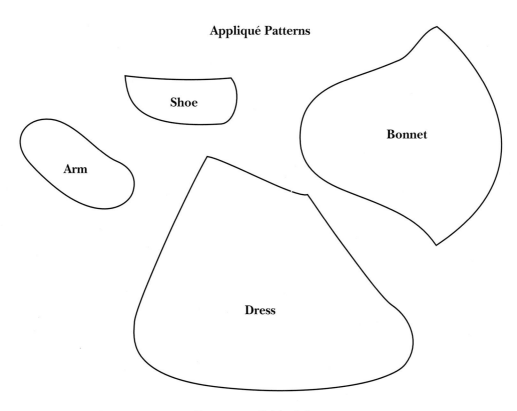

Patterns are finished size.
(Trace and reverse for fusible appliqué.)

SKILL LEVEL: Easy

SIZE: Finished quilt is approximately 86 × 96 inches

Finished block is 10 inches square

Number of blocks: 72

Quilt owner: LaNelle Bentz

FABRIC AND SUPPLIES

In the quilt shown, fan blocks are arranged so that they produce diagonal rows of color. Each single fan block contains only two fabrics, one solid and one coordinating print. The fabric amounts given list total yardage of one particular color; it can be the same fabric or assorted shades of the same basic color.

- 7½ yards of white solid fabric for block background

- 1 yard of lavender solid fabrics for fans

- 1 yard of orange solid fabrics for fans

- 1¼ yards of pink solid fabrics for fans

- 1¼ yards of green solid fabrics for fans

- 1½ yards of yellow solid fabrics for fans

- 1½ yards of blue solid fabrics for fans

- Assorted print scraps, at least 6 × 12 inches *each*, to coordinate with the solid fabrics for fans: 5 orange prints, 7 lavender prints, 12 pink prints, 13 green prints, 17 yellow prints, and 18 blue prints

- ¾ yard of fabric for binding

- 7½ yards of fabric for quilt back

- Quilt batting, at least 92 × 102 inches

- Rotary cutter, ruler, and mat

- Template plastic

Grandmother's Fan

Although this colorful fan quilt was made during

the Depression years, it seems to evoke images of

idyllic days gone by when ladies

cooled themselves with hand-held

fans and coyly hid behind them

while flirting with prospective beaux.

Graceful feather quilting above each fan and a

quilted tulip at each fan center add to the simple

beauty of this charming quilt. Whether made for a

master bedroom or a guest room, this quilt would

add a romantic touch.

86 × 96 inches

SCRAP RECIPE

The quilt shown uses pastels that were very popular in the 1930s. Imagine how strikingly different this quilt would look if you chose an Amish color scheme—black in the background and rich solids in deep pink, purple, blue, and green. Or use bold black and white geometric prints with bright solids in gradated colors as we did in this block.

You could also put your scrap basket to the test and try a multicolored scrap theme!

QUICK CUTTING				
Fabric	**First Cut**		**Second Cut**	
FANS	No.	Shape	No.	Shape
Blue solid	54	A fan blade	18	B fan base
Yellow solid	51	A fan blade	17	B fan base
Green solid	39	A fan blade	13	B fan base
Pink solid	36	A fan blade	12	B fan base
Lavender solid	21	A fan blade	7	B fan base
Orange solid	15	A fan blade	5	B fan base
Blue prints*	72	A fan blade	*From the blue, yellow, green, pink, lavender, and orange prints,* cut the print fabric A pieces in sets of four from each print.	
Yellow prints*	68	A fan blade		
Green prints*	52	A fan blade		
Pink prints*	48	A fan blade	†*From the white,* first cut the four 3½"-wide border strips lengthwise from a 100" length of fabric.	
Lavender prints*	28	A fan blade		
Orange prints*	20	A fan blade	‡ *From the white,* cut six 10½" strips crosswise from the remainder of the 100"-long piece.	
BORDERS & BACKGROUND	No. of Strips	Strip Width	No.	Shape
White	4†	3½" × 100"	—	—
	6‡	10½"	12	☐
	15	10½"	60	☐

CUTTING

Referring to the "Quick Cutting" chart, cut the white background squares and borders using a rotary cutter. Measurements for these pieces include ¼-inch seam allowances.

If you plan to hand piece the fan blades, make finished-size templates by tracing the *dashed* outlines for pattern pieces A and B on page 106. Remember to leave enough space around the templates on all sides when tracing them onto fabric to allow for seam allowances when the pieces are cut.

For machine piecing the fan blades, trace the *solid* outlines around pattern pieces A and B to make templates that include the seam allowances.

Cut fan blades (A pieces) in sets of three solid color pieces and four coordinating print pieces for each block.

MAKING THE FAN BLOCKS

Follow the instructions below for either hand piecing or machine piecing to make a total of 72 Fan blocks. Make 18 blocks with blue fabrics, 17 with yellow fabrics, 13 with green fabrics, 12 with pink fabrics, 7 with lavender fabrics, and 5 with orange fabrics.

To make one Fan block as shown in the **Block Diagram,** you will need the following pieces: one background square, one solid color fan center piece B, three fan blades A that match the center piece, and four matching print fan blades A that coordinate with the solid fabric pieces.

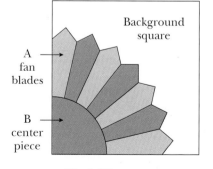

Block Diagram

Hand-Piecing Method

STEP 1. Beginning with a print fan blade, alternate print and solid blades as you join seven blades along the long sides to form a quarter circle.

STEP 2. To appliqué the fan, turn under and hand baste the pointed edges at the top of the fan. Baste under the curved edge of the fan center piece B.

STEP 3. Pin the fan center piece B to one corner of a white background square.

STEP 4. Pin the fan blade unit to the background square, slipping the curved inner edge of the fan approximately ¼ inch under the curved edge of the fan center piece and aligning the raw side edges with those of the white background block.

STEP 5. Using matching thread, appliqué the curved edge of the fan center piece and the pointed edges of the blades to the background square. Then, stitching within the seam allowance, baste the sides of the fan and center piece to the background square to stabilize the edges of the block.

STEP 6. Repeat to make 72 fan blocks.

Machine-Piecing Method

STEP 1. Referring to **Diagram 1,** fold a fan blade in half lengthwise

with wrong sides facing. Taking a ¼-inch seam, stitch across the top edge of the blade.

Diagram 1

STEP 2. Unfold the fan blade and center the seam. Press the seam open and trim the seam allowances to ⅛ inch to reduce bulk.

STEP 3. Turn the stitched section right side out and center the seam along the wrong side of the blade as shown in **Diagram 2,** and press.

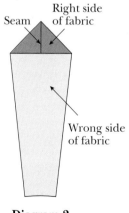

Diagram 2

STEP 4. Prepare each fan blade in this manner.

SEW WISE

If you want to round off the corners of your quilt as in the one shown, use a saucer or teacup from your cupboard. Choose a piece of china that will give you the size curve you want, and use it as a guide for tracing a curve on each corner of the borders. Sew the binding to the quilt top using the marked line as a guide at the corners. Trim off excess batting and backing, trimming along your traced line at the corners, and you'll have gently curved corners that coordinate nicely with the fan shapes on your quilt top.

STEP 5. Beginning with a print fan blade, alternate print and solid fabric blades as you stitch the seven blades for one fan together along the long sides to make a quarter circle. Press the seams to one side.

STEP 6. Baste under the seam allowance along the curved edge of the fan center piece B.

STEP 7. Follow the instructions in Steps 3 through 6 under "Hand-Piecing Method" on page 103 to complete 72 Fan blocks.

ASSEMBLING THE QUILT TOP

STEP 1. Referring to the **Quilt Diagram** for color placement, lay out the blocks in nine horizontal rows with eight blocks in each row.

STEP 2. Sew the blocks together in horizontal rows. Press the seams in alternate directions from row to row. Join the rows and press the quilt top.

STEP 3. Measure the width of the quilt through the center and trim two borders to this length. Sew the borders to the top and bottom

Quilt Diagram

Quilting Ideas

This quilt was outline quilted ¼ inch from the inner edges of the fan blades. A tulip is quilted in each fan center piece, and this design is printed on pattern piece B on page 106. The feathered arc quilted in each block is provided on page 107; the interwoven diamond design used for the borders of the quilt is shown on this page.

edges of the quilt top. Press the seams toward the borders.

STEP 4. Measure the length of the quilt through the center, including the top and bottom borders, and trim two borders to this length. Sew the borders to the sides of the quilt top. Press the seams toward the borders.

QUILTING AND FINISHING

STEP 1. Mark quilting designs as desired, or see "Quilting Ideas" for suggestions.

STEP 2. To piece the quilt back, cut the backing fabric into two 3¾-yard lengths. Cut one piece in half lengthwise. Trim the selvages, and sew a half panel to each side of the

full panel. Press the seams toward the narrow panels.

STEP 3. Layer the quilt back, batting, and quilt top. Baste the layers together. Trim the quilt back and batting so they are approximately 3 inches larger than the quilt top on all sides.

STEP 4. Hand or machine quilt all marked designs. Outline quilt ¼ inch from the edges of the fan blades.

STEP 5. From the binding fabric, make approximately 380 inches of French-fold binding. See "Finishing" on page 223 for details on finishing the edges of your quilt.

Border Quilting Design

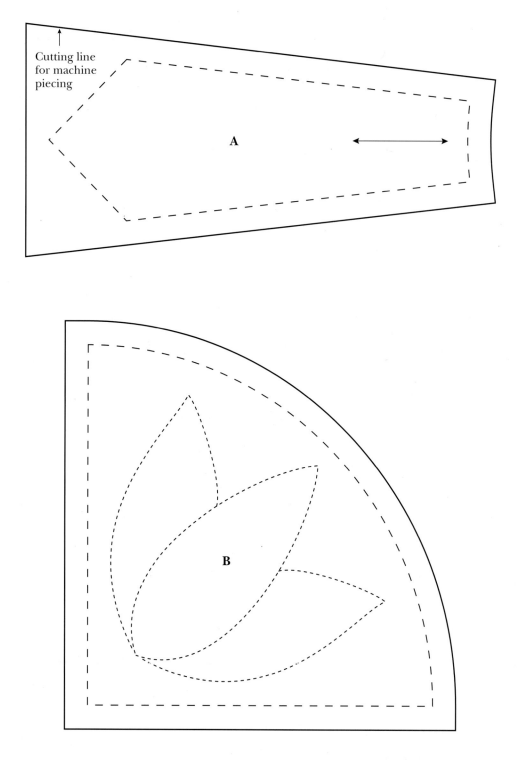

Cutting line
for machine
piecing

A

B

Block Quilting Design

Kansas Twister

SKILL LEVEL: Intermediate

SIZE: Finished quilt is 54 × 68 inches

Finished block is 3½ inches on each hexagonal side

Number of blocks: 71

Number of half blocks: 12

FABRICS AND SUPPLIES

- 2 yards of bright pink solid fabric for borders and binding

- ⅛ yard *each* of 40 assorted pastel print fabrics for blocks and middle borders (yellows, blues, pinks, greens, and lavenders)

- 3½ yards of fabric for quilt back

- Quilt batting, at least 62 × 74 inches

- Rotary cutter, mat, and ruler

- Master Piece 60 ruler (optional; see "Sew Wise" on page 111 for information on where to find this tool)

- Master Piece Static Stickers (optional; see "Sew Wise" on page 111)

- Template plastic (optional)

- Tracing paper (optional)

Kansas Twister, Whirligig, Texas Trellis, and Whirling Triangles in a Hexagon—all of these action-packed names have been used to describe this whirling, twirling quilt design. Although this Depression-era pattern was traditionally made using white fabric for the small background triangles, Iowa quiltmaker Jill Reber chose to make her 1990s blocks entirely from print fabrics. She's added more color without detracting from the spinning star effect.

We've included two methods for making the triangle units for this quilt: the traditional template method and a quick-cutting and quick-piecing method that requires a special rotary ruler called Master Piece 60.

54 × 68 inches

SCRAP RECIPE

The key word here is *contrast.*
Whether you use an all-American red, white, and blue theme or a kaleidoscope of colors, contrast is important between the two colors or prints used in each individual Kansas Twister block. You need 39 pairs of strips, so you can use up to about 80 different fabrics, or create a more subdued effect with just a few prints and colors.

QUICK CUTTING					
Fabric	**First Cut**		**Second Cut**		**From the pink solid, if you are using the Master Piece 60 ruler, cut only the 4¼" strip. Directions for cutting the A and A reverse pieces from the strip are given in the step-by-step instructions.*
BLOCKS	No. of Strips	Strip Width	No.	Shape	
Prints	78	2"	—	—	
Pink solid*	1	4¼"	14	A	
			14	A reverse	
BORDERS	No. of Strips	Strip Width	†*From the pink solid, reserve the remaining fabric for binding.*		
Pink solid†	2	2"			
	9	3½"			

CUTTING

Referring to the "Quick Cutting" chart, cut the number of strips needed from each fabric using a rotary cutter and ruler. Cut all strips across the fabric width. All measurements include ¼-inch seam allowances. If you are using scraps that are less than 42 inches wide, you will need to increase the number of strips you cut accordingly.

If you are not using the Master Piece 60 ruler, make a plastic template for pattern piece A and the Quick-Cutting Guide on page 115. See "Making and Using Templates" on page 215.

PIECING THE TRIANGLE UNITS

Each Kansas Twister block is made of six pieced triangles. You will be sewing strip sets and cutting the triangles from these using the Quick-Cutting Guide on page 115 and a rotary cutter with either a regular see-through ruler or the Master Piece 60 ruler.

Making the Strip Sets

Choose two print strips that have good contrast in color. Sew the strips together to make a strip set, as shown in **Diagram 1.** Press the seam allowances toward the darker fabric. Repeat to make a total of 39 strip sets, each with lots of contrast. Choose one of the following methods to make these blocks.

Diagram 1

Option 1: Using a Ruler and Rotary Cutter

STEP 1. Place the Quick-Cutting Guide template over the wrong side of the strip sets, having the center line directly over the seam line. Mark around the template with a pencil. Mark 12 triangles on each strip set as shown in **Diagram 2.** The remainder of the strip sets will be used in the pieced border.

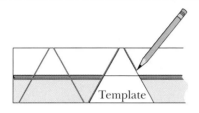

Diagram 2

STEP 2. Use your ruler and rotary cutter to cut the triangles from the strip sets. You will have 78 sets of six matching triangles, but only 77 sets are needed. To speed cutting, you can stack several strip sets under the marked set to cut.

Option 2: Using the Master Piece 60 Ruler

STEP 1. Make two paper tracings of the Quick-Cutting Guide on page 115 and cut them out. Tape the tracings to the Master Piece 60 ruler as shown in **Diagram 3.** Or, if you are using Master Piece Static Stickers, glue the tracings to the paper side of the Static Sticker sheet. Cut out the Static Stickers, remove the paper backing, and adhere the Static Sticker triangles to the ruler.

STEP 2. Position the Master Piece 60 ruler on a strip set with the length of the ruler parallel to the long edges of the strip set. Use the seam alignment line on the Quick-Cutting Guide for proper placement. Begin cutting at the right end of the strip set and make a cut through the slot in the ruler that angles from the upper left to lower right, as shown in **Diagram 4.** Slide the ruler over so the edge of your Quick-Cutting Guide that is pasted to the right-angled slot is aligned with the first cut. Cut through the right-angled slot to make a triangle.

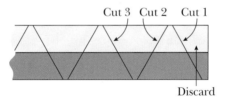

Diagram 4

Then slide the ruler over so the edge of your Quick-Cutting Guide at the left-angled slot is aligned with the cut edge of the fabric, and cut through the left-angled slot. Now you have cut a second triangle. Continue in this manner to cut a total of 12 triangles: 6 of one color arrangement and 6 of an-

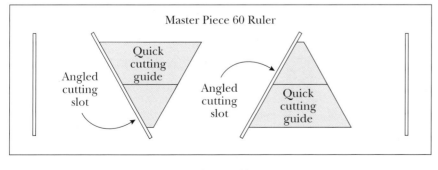

Diagram 3

For the best results in planning color placement in your quilt, lay out all the blocks on a flannel board, design wall, or other flat surface (see "Make an Instant Design Wall" on page 209). It will help you get a better balance of color in your quilt, and it will also help you to determine how the rows match up to form the completed blocks. And for failproof results, number the rows as you make them so you can sew them together in the correct order. Press the seam allowances in even-numbered rows in one direction and in odd-numbered rows in the other direction.

other. Save the remainder of the strip for cutting pieces for the middle border.

STEP 3. Repeat to cut a total of 12 triangles from each of the 39 strip sets. You will have 78 sets of 6 matching triangles, but only 77 sets are needed.

ASSEMBLING THE INNER QUILT TOP

STEP 1. Join each set of six matching triangle units into two half blocks as shown in **Diagram 5.** Press the seam allowances toward the trapezoids. Make sure that all half blocks twist in the same direction.

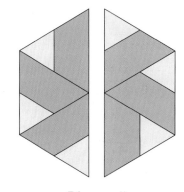

Diagram 5

STEP 2. Arrange the half blocks in 14 vertical rows with 11 half blocks in each row. You will need to make seven rows that start with a right half of a block and seven rows that start with a left half of a block, as shown in **Diagram 6.** Arrange the half blocks so that matching half blocks will meet to form Kansas Twister blocks when the rows are joined.

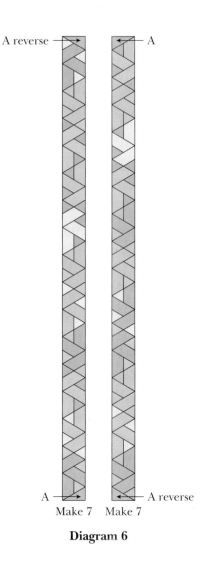

A reverse ⟶   A

Make 7   Make 7

Diagram 6

STEP 3. To cut the A and A reverse triangles with the Master Piece 60 ruler, refer to **Diagram 7.** Position the Master Piece 60 ruler on top of the 4¼-inch-wide pink strip with the long edges of the ruler parallel to the long edges of the strip. Beginning at the right end of the strip, cut through the vertical slot on the right end of the ruler to trim the selvage from the fabric strip. To cut a triangle, slide the ruler over so the left-angled slot meets the bottom of the first cut; cut through the angled slot. Slide the ruler over so a vertical slot meets the top edge of the angled cut; cut through the vertical slot. Continue cutting in this manner until you have 28 triangles; 14 will be A triangles, and 14 will be A reverse triangles.

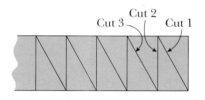

Diagram 7

STEP 4. Add an A or A reverse triangle to the top and bottom of each row, as indicated in **Diagram 6.**

STEP 5. Join the rows, pinning at the seam intersections. Place the pins at 60 degree angles to the edge when matching seams, as shown in **Diagram 8,** so you can more accurately match the six seams where they join. Begin by joining the two different types of rows to make seven pairs. Press seam allowances to one side. The pairs of joined rows should look like the one in **Diagram 9.** Join the pairs of rows to complete the quilt top.

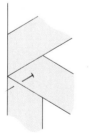

Diagram 8

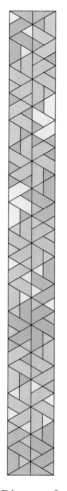

Diagram 9

ADDING THE BORDERS

STEP 1. Measure the quilt width through the center of the quilt top and trim the two 2-inch-wide pink border strips to this length. Sew the borders to the top and bottom edges of quilt top. Press the seam allowances toward the borders.

STEP 2. Measure the quilt length through the center, including the top and bottom borders. Piece three 3½-inch-wide border strips together, and then cut two borders to the length needed. Sew the borders to the sides of the quilt.

Press the seam allowances toward the borders.

STEP 3. The middle border is pieced from scraps from the remaining strip sets. Cut 78 segments, each 1½ inches wide, as shown in **Diagram 10,** from the strip set leftovers.

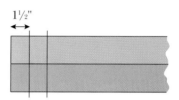

Diagram 10

STEP 4. Make two borders with 17 segments in each for the top and bottom quilt edges, randomly mixing the colors. Make two borders with 22 segments each for the quilt sides.

STEP 5. Sew the pieced borders to the top and bottom quilt edges. Matching the corner seams, as shown in **Diagram 11,** sew the side borders to the quilt top. Press the seam allowances toward the pink borders. Trim off the excess side borders at the corners, forming a square at each corner.

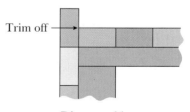

Diagram 11

STEP 6. Measure the quilt width through the center, including all borders. Piece two borders to this length from the 3½-inch-wide pink strips. Sew the borders to the top and bottom quilt edges. Press the seam allowances toward the pink borders.

STEP 7. Measure the quilt length through the center, including all borders. Piece two borders to this length from 3½-inch-wide pink

strips. Sew the borders to the quilt sides, as shown in the **Quilt Diagram.** Press the seam allowances toward the pink borders.

QUILTING AND FINISHING

STEP 1. Mark quilting designs as desired, or see "Quilting Ideas" for suggestions.

STEP 2. To piece the quilt back, cut the backing fabric into two 1¾-

yard lengths. Cut one piece in half lengthwise. Trim the selvages, and sew a half panel to each side of the full panel. Press the seams toward the narrow panels. The seams on the quilt back will run parallel to the top and bottom quilt edges.

STEP 3. Layer the quilt back, batting, and quilt top. Baste the layers together. Trim the quilt back and batting so they are approximately 3 inches larger than the quilt top on all sides.

STEP 4. Hand or machine quilt as desired.

STEP 5. From the binding fabric, make approximately 260 inches of French-fold binding. See "Finishing" on page 223 for instructions on finishing the edges of your quilt.

Quilt Diagram

Quilting Ideas

The patchwork was hand quilted
¼ inch from each seam in the
Kansas Twister blocks. The borders
were quilted with three-tier fans
that span all three borders.

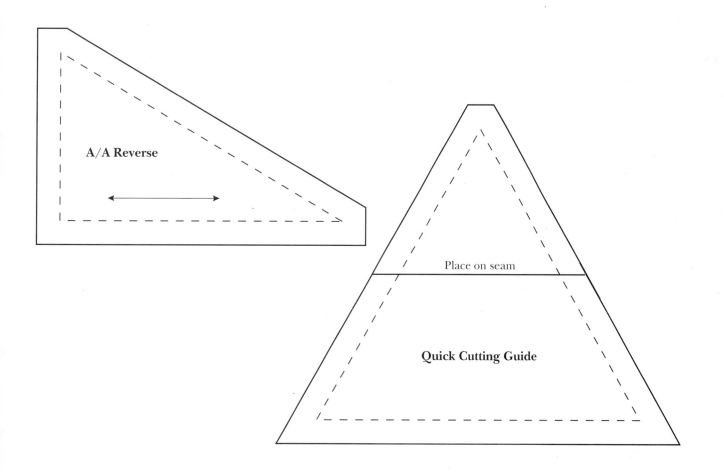

A/A Reverse

Place on seam

Quick Cutting Guide

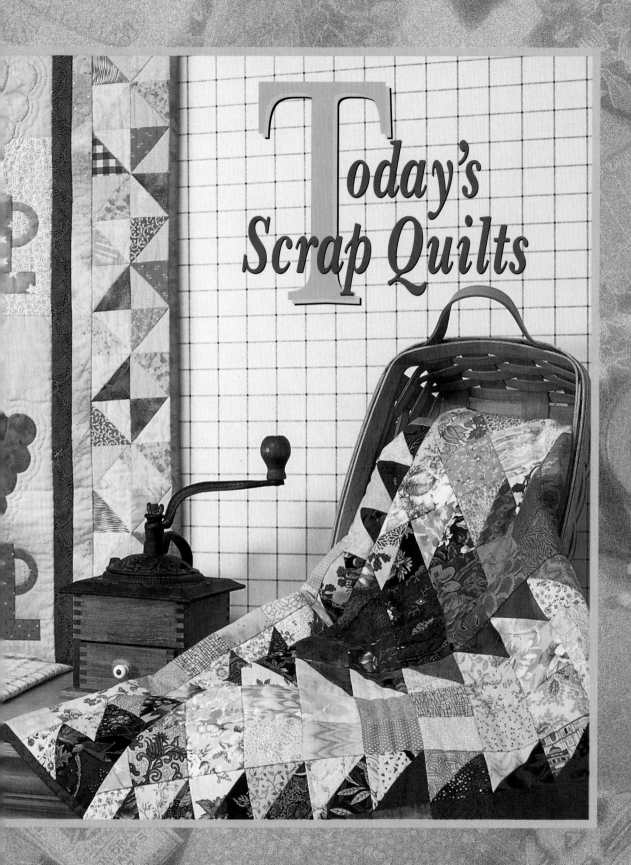

Today's Scrap Quilts

THE LOOK OF TODAY'S QUILTS

A resurgence of interest in quilts and quiltmaking took place in the mid-1970s. At that time, had any quilter been interested in making scrap quilts, she would have been frustrated in her search for enough cotton scraps to create a multifabric quilt. The quiltmaking revival that began with the 1976 American bicentennial thrived for several years on quilts made from only a few fabrics. Not until the mid-1980s, when the fabric industry began to catch up with quilters' voracious desire for 100 percent cotton printed cloth, did the scrap quilt come again into vogue.

Today's lovers of multifabric quilts often begin their projects inspired by tradition, but the design process and the fabrics they choose result in quilts that could never be mistaken for quilts from an earlier time.

Among the fabric styles that distinguish contemporary quilts are bright, strong jewel tone colors, large-scale exotic prints, and light printed background fabrics. Metallic fabrics such as lamé or prints with metallic ink find their way into many of today's quilts. A global trade environment makes batiks, Madras plaids, and ethnic fabrics from all over the world available for use in American quilts. Some quilters make a personal science out of dying their own cloth, carefully achieving subtle color gradations. Others shop for funky, whimsical fabrics.

When working up a pattern, quiltmakers today may use a computer to create a new patchwork block, superimposing one tradi-

Fabrics that incorporate silver or gold metallic ink in their designs are used by many contemporary quiltmakers.

Subtle low-contrast prints are typical background fabrics for today's quilters. Muslin, plain and simple, was the common "light" in quilts of the past. Modern quilters prefer the energy and texture of background prints.

tional design atop another or starting from scratch to invent a completely new one. Some quiltmakers have gone on to experiment with asymmetrical overall designs; quilts become design areas with little or no relation to the block-style quilt.

In the 1990s, quilters are making quilts to keep their families warm in bed, but they are also designing art pieces for the walls of their homes or even for commercial installations, exhibitions, and galleries.

Here are some hints for achieving a contemporary look for your own scrap quilts.

- Use exotic jewel tone prints, sophisticated large-scale decorator fabrics, and neutral printed backgrounds (see Tulips in the Spring and Feathered World without End).

- Create new patterns or settings by combining others (see Tulips in the Spring).

- Choose ethnic fabrics from around the world (see October and African Lattice).

- Work with whimsical fabrics or themes (see Shooting Star and Expresso Yourself).

- Approach the design of your quilt as a whole rather than a collection of blocks (see October, Crazy Cabins, Tulips in the Spring, and Galaxy Star).

- Create visual gradation and shading by careful placement of light-, medium-, and dark-value fabrics (see October and Galaxy Star).

Many of today's quilters become amateur chemists, creating fabric-dying labs in their basements and garages. They use fiber-reactive dyes to create beautiful gradations of color.

Funky, whimsical prints are often just modern versions of the object prints of the last century. These fabrics lend themselves to informal-style quilts.

Quilters in the 1990s love imported fabrics, such as batiks and pseudo-batiks. An appreciation of cultural diversity has put many exotic and ethnic prints on the market for quilters to collect and use.

Expresso Yourself

What coffee lover wouldn't adore this whimsical

wall quilt to display at home or in the office?

Marianne Fons combined her enjoyment

of espresso, cappuccino, and café latté

with her love of feather motifs to create

this contemporary scrap quilt. She used in-

visible machine appliqué for the cup handles and the

feather steam puffs. A friend suggested the perfect

border—Broken Dishes blocks made of

many scrap fabrics.

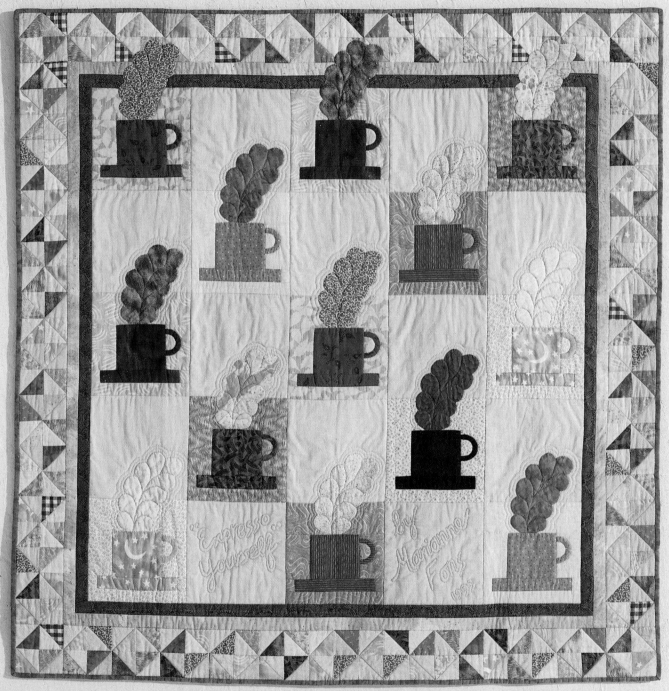

52 X 52 inches

SCRAP RECIPE

Cool shades of blues, pinks, and purples are warmed by rich tones of beige, tan, and brown in this contemporary charmer. It's fun to choose fabrics for a whimsical quilt like this. Marianne rounded up "ethereal" textured prints for the steam coming out of the cups, and more solid geometric prints for the cups. She made a subtle reference to coffeehouse tablecloths by including a large-scale blue-and-white check in the border triangles. Try incorporating your own favorite shades. Or try an avant-garde look with lots of black and white prints set off by a shade or two of hot pink, vivid red, or brilliant yellow. In this quilt, as with coffee, choose the "flavor" that warms your heart.

QUICK CUTTING						
Fabric	First Cut		Second Cut		Third Cut	
BLOCKS	No. of Strips	Strip Width	No.	Shape	No.	Shape
Beige print	3	8½"	12	▢	—	—
	No.	Shape	*From the Coffee Cup background fabrics, for each block, cut two A rectangles, two C rectangles, one E rectangle, and one F rectangle that match.*			
Coffee Cup background prints*	26	A 2½"×4"				
	26	C 1¼"×1½"				
	13	E 1½"×8½"				
	13	F 3"×8½"				
Coffee Cups†	13	B 4"×4½"	*†From the Coffee Cup fabrics and scraps, for each block, cut one B rectangle, one D rectangle, and one handle that match; cut one coordinating steam puff piece.*			
	13	D 1½"×7"				
	13	Handles				
Scraps†	13	Steam puff pieces				
BORDERS	No. of Strips	Strip Width	No.	Shape	No.	Shape
Light beige prints and leftovers	6	2⅞"	96	▢	192	◨
Medium/ dark prints & leftovers	6	2⅞"	96	▢	192	◨
Medium brown print	4	1½"	—	—	—	—
Medium beige print	5	1½"	—	—	—	—

CUTTING

Referring to the "Quick Cutting" chart, cut the number of strips needed from each fabric for the patchwork pieces using a rotary cutter. Cut all strips across the fabric width. All measurements include ¼-inch seam allowances. If you are using scraps that are less than 42 inches wide, you may need to increase the number of strips you cut accordingly.

To cut the cup handles and steam puffs, make plastic templates from the patterns on page 126. The templates can be used to mark the fabric or to make freezer paper templates, if desired.

MAKING THE BLOCKS

You will need to make 13 Coffee Cup blocks, as shown in the **Block Diagram.** These blocks combine piecing and appliqué techniques and are alternated with plain setting squares.

Block Diagram

STEP 1. Prepare the cup handles and steam puffs for your favorite method of appliqué. See "Tips on Appliqué" on page 219 or "Invisible Machine Appliqué" on page 127 for pointers.

STEP 2. Referring to **Diagram 1,** lay out the patchwork pieces and the handle for one block. Use matching A, C, E, and F background pieces. The B, D, and handle pieces should also match.

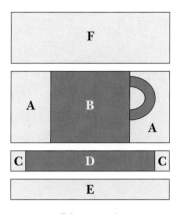

Diagram 1

STEP 3. Appliqué the handle to the A rectangle, as shown in the diagram. Make sure your handle is about ½ inch away from the top of the rectangle so it will not be too close to the seam allowance.

STEP 4. Sew the A pieces to the B coffee cup. In the same manner, sew the C pieces to the ends of the D saucer. Press seam allowances toward the darker fabric.

STEP 5. Sew the coffee cup units together, adding an E background piece to the bottom of the block, as shown. Press the seam allowances toward the coffee cup.

STEP 6. Referring to **Diagram 2,** position a steam puff on top of the cup unit, right sides together, with raw edges aligned. Lay the F background rectangle on top of both pieces, right side down, and raw edges aligned. Stitch the seam to join the pieces. Open out and press the seam allowance toward the cup. The appliqué steam puff will remain loose except at the rim of the cup.

Diagram 2

STEP 7. Repeat to make a total of 13 Coffee Cup blocks.

ASSEMBLING THE INNER QUILT TOP

STEP 1. Referring to the **Quilt Diagram** on page 124, lay out the 13 Coffee Cup blocks and the 12 beige setting squares in five vertical rows. Rows 1, 3, and 5 will have three Coffee Cup blocks and two plain blocks. Rows 2 and 4 will have two Coffee Cup blocks and three plain blocks.

STEP 2. Join the blocks in each row, folding back the steam puff appliqués to keep them out of the way of stitching. Press the seam allowances in opposite directions from row to row.

STEP 3. Stitch the appliqués to the plain blocks above the cups. The puffs at the tops of rows 1, 3, and 5 will remain loose until the borders are added.

STEP 4. Join the rows, keeping puffs free from the seams.

To make certain that your pieced borders will fit your quilt top, be extra careful in piecing the Broken Dishes blocks accurately. They should measure 4$\frac{1}{2}$ inches square after piecing (including seam allowances). Also, make sure your quilt top measures 40$\frac{1}{2}$ × 42$\frac{1}{2}$ inches before adding the narrow borders. If you need to make adjustments in the pieced border, take in or let out several seam allowances by $\frac{1}{16}$ inch.

Quilt Diagram

ADDING THE BORDERS

STEP 1. Join the light and dark border triangles as shown in **Diagram 3** to make a total of 192 triangle squares. Press the seam allowances toward the darker triangles.

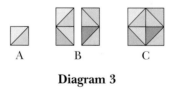

A   B   C

Diagram 3

STEP 2. Join four triangle squares together as shown to make a Broken Dishes block. Repeat to make a total of 48 blocks.

STEP 3. Join 11 blocks to make the top border. Repeat to make a

bottom border in the same manner. Construct the side borders by joining 13 blocks for each border.

STEP 4. Measure the width of the quilt top through the center. Trim two of the medium brown border strips to this length. Sew the borders to the top and bottom of the quilt top. Fold and pin down the appliqués before stitching to avoid catching the steam puffs in the seam at the top edge of the quilt top. Press the seam allowances toward the borders. Measure the length of the quilt top, and trim the two remaining medium brown border strips to this length. Sew the borders to the sides of the quilt. Press the seam allowances toward the borders.

STEP 5. In the same manner, measure and trim medium beige border strips and add them to the quilt top. If necessary, piece strips to achieve the needed length, sewing together with diagonal seams as shown in **Diagram 4.**

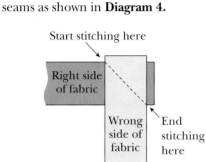

Diagram 4

STEP 6. Sew the two shorter strips of Broken Dishes blocks to the top and bottom of the quilt top. Press the seam allowances toward the narrow borders. Sew the two longer strips of Broken Dishes to the quilt top sides. Press.

STEP 7. Appliqué the edges of the steam puffs along the top to the borders.

QUILTING AND FINISHING

STEP 1. Mark quilting designs as desired, or see "Quilting Ideas" for suggestions.

STEP 2. To piece the quilt back, cut the backing fabric crosswise into two equal lengths. Cut one piece in half lengthwise. Trim the selvages, and sew a half panel to one side of the full panel. Press the seams toward the narrow panel.

STEP 3. Layer the quilt back, batting, and quilt top. Baste the layers together. Trim the quilt back and batting so they are approximately 3 inches larger than the quilt top on all sides.

STEP 4. Machine or hand quilt as desired.

STEP 5. From the binding fabric, make approximately 220 inches of French-fold binding. See "Finishing" on page 223 for details on finishing the edges of your quilt.

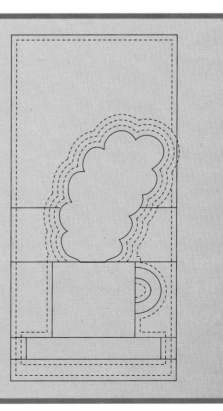

Quilting Ideas

Marrianne's quilt was machine quilted in the ditch around the coffee cups and along the seams that join the blocks, rows, and borders. The steam puffs were outline quilted by hand, with two additional rows of echo quilting around each puff, as shown. Feather quilting was done inside each steam puff, as indicated on the pattern piece on page 126. Don't be shy about quilting your name in one of the blocks as Marianne did!

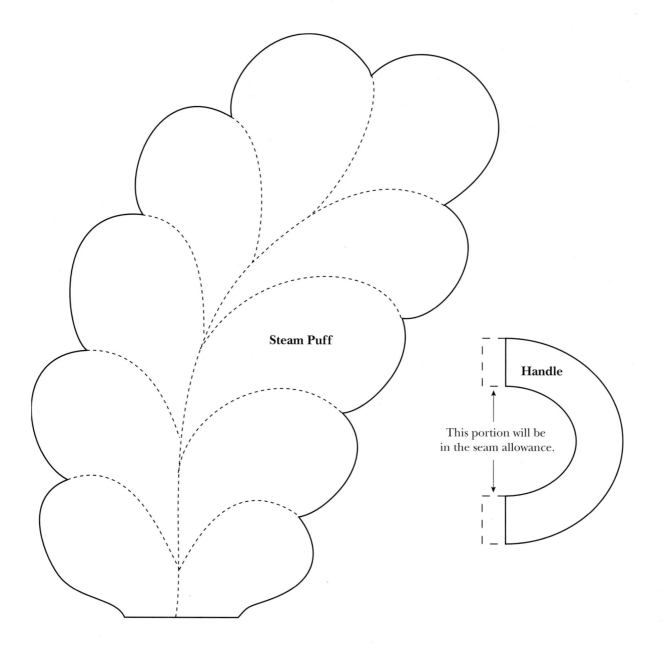

Steam Puff

Handle

This portion will be
in the seam allowance.

Patterns are finished size. Add seam
allowances when cutting the pieces from fabric.

Invisible Machine Appliqué

STEP 1. Following the manufacturer's instructions, press lightweight fusible interfacing to the wrong side of each of your appliqué fabrics.

STEP 2. Make plastic templates that include ¼-inch seam allowances from the Steam Puff and Handle patterns. Trace around the templates onto the interfacing side of your fabric and cut out.

STEP 3. For each steam puff and handle, you will also need a freezer paper template *without* seam allowances. Cut 13 handles and 13 steam puffs from freezer paper. Place the freezer paper template, shiny side up, on the wrong side (the interfacing side) of your appliqué piece. Press the seam allowances to the freezer paper to hold the raw edges in place. Do not press under seam allowances on edges that will be sewn into the seam of the patchwork. Carefully remove the freezer paper after all edges have been pressed.

STEP 4. Position the cup handles on the background fabric, using a glue stick or pins to hold them in place.

STEP 5. Use clear nylon thread on the top of your machine and thread that matches the appliqué fabric in the bobbin. Set your machine for a blind-stitch with a stitch length of 20 stitches per inch. Sew around the edges of the handles. Your stitches should catch the edge of your appliqué piece about every ¼ inch. See the diagram below. Because the thread is invisible, this method is virtually indistinguishable from hand appliqué.

STEP 6. Continue with the block assembly as directed, and appliqué the steam puff in the same manner.

Tree Everlasting

SKILL LEVEL: Easy

SIZE: Finished quilt is 42 × 48 inches

FABRICS AND SUPPLIES

- At least 700 squares, *each* 2¹/2 inches, of assorted multicolored print fabrics
- ¹/2 yard of fabric for binding
- 1¹/2 yards of fabric for quilt back
- Quilt batting, at least 48 × 54 inches
- Rotary cutter, ruler, and mat
- Template plastic

AMERICAN COUNTRY SCRAP QUILTS

The Tree Everlasting quilt pattern is traditionally pieced from just two solid fabrics, often green and white or red and white. For this updated scrappy version, Marianne Fons used almost 700 different fabric pieces. She created the design by careful placement of light and dark value fabrics. By concentrating colors such as reds and teals in the dark areas and yellows and blues in the light areas, she added some extra interest to the design.

42 × 48 inches

SCRAP RECIPE

Fabrics that are printed in a medium-scale design with at least three colors are easiest to use in designs of this type. You will need about half of your fabrics to be light and half medium and dark values. Including medium-value fabrics will help soften your design and make it less contrasting.

SORTING THE FABRIC SQUARES

Sort the fabrics into a light group and a dark group. Keep the groups approximately equal in size by placing the lightest medium fabrics with the light fabrics and the darkest medium fabrics with the dark fabrics.

Medium value fabrics are sometimes difficult to categorize as light or dark. Start by placing them arbitrarily into one group or the other. Later you can force these medium fabrics to work as lights or darks by adjusting the value of fabrics near them in your design. To make a medium fabric appear lighter, surround it with very dark fabrics. To make a medium fabric appear darker, surround it with very light fabrics.

CUTTING SQUARES INTO TRIANGLES

STEP 1. Make a special rotary cutting guide template from the Trimming Pattern on page 132. (You will use this template for cutting the triangles in the quilt. Trimming the tips of the triangle pattern as we have done enables you to easily cut your triangles from the 2½-inch squares.) See "Making and Using Templates" on page 215.

STEP 2. Randomly choose 168 of the light squares and 168 of the dark squares to cut into triangles.

STEP 3. On the wrong side of one square, use the template to draw a diagonal cutting line. See **Diagram 1.** Stack five additional squares (or a suitable number to cut with your rotary cutter) under the marked square. Cut through all layers along the diagonal line. Keep the pieces that are the size of the template; discard the small triangles or save them for another scrap project.

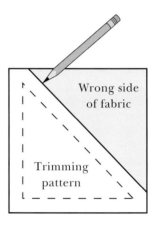

Diagram 1

STEP 4. Repeat to cut a total of 168 light and 168 dark triangles.

ASSEMBLING THE QUILT TOP

STEP 1. Referring to the **Quilt Diagram,** the "Sew Wise" tip, and the photograph on page 129, lay out the pieces for the quilt on a design wall, sheet, or similar surface. See "Make an Instant Design Wall" on page 209 for hints on making a portable design surface.

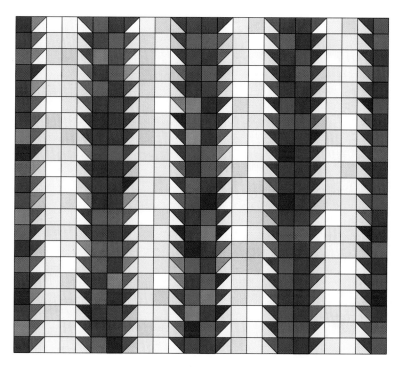

Quilt Diagram

egin by simply arranging pieces of light and dark value to create the design. Then, rearrange pieces to cluster fabrics of similar color such as red, purple, gold, or teal together to create concentrations of color as in the quilt in the photograph. Color concentrations created with dark fabrics will naturally be more intense than those created with light fabrics.

When you are pleased with the layout, you may want to pin the pieces in place to keep them in position until you finish piecing the top. A breeze from an open door or window can quickly toss your "perfect" arrangement on the floor!

STEP 2. Join each light triangle to a dark triangle along the long sides to form a square. Press seam allowances toward the dark fabric.

STEP 3. Join the squares in vertical rows. Press the seam allowances in alternate directions from row to row. Join the rows. Press the seam allowances to one side.

QUILTING AND FINISHING

STEP 1. Mark quilting designs as desired, or see "Quilting Ideas" on page 132 for suggestions.

STEP 2. Layer the quilt back, batting, and quilt top. Baste the layers together. Trim the quilt back and batting so they are approximately

3 inches larger than the quilt top on all sides.

STEP 3. Hand or machine quilt as desired.

STEP 4. From the binding fabric, make approximately 200 inches of French-fold binding by joining the binding strips with diagonal seams. See "Finishing" on page 223 for details on finishing the edges of your quilt.

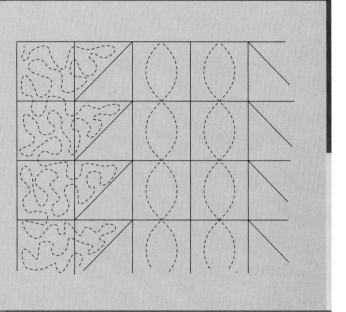

Quilting Ideas

The quilt shown was machine quilted in the ditch along all vertical seams. If you want the quilting to become a more prominent feature, you could also add a simple chain or free-form meander quilting vertically in the dark and light areas using a decorative thread.

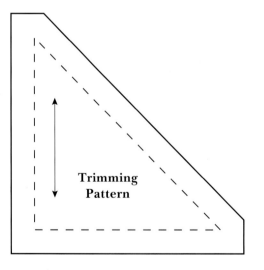

Trimming Pattern

12 Fun Ways to Build Your Scrap Collection

1. When buying for a project, always buy 1/8 yard extra of a couple of fabrics. Set aside these "on-purpose" leftovers and start a scrap library.

2. Connect with your quiltmaking friends and arrange a once-a-month swap. You may want to establish limits on what size scraps you trade (both biggest and smallest sizes).

3. If you belong to a guild, see if the members already have an organized scrap swap. If not, get one going!

4. If there's another guild in a neighboring town, investigate whether this group would be interested in a fabric swap with your guild.

5. Post a note at your local quilt shop asking if anyone would like to participate in a scrap swap with you.

6. If you have a computer, explore the on-line quilting groups and see if there are any current fabric exchanges. If not, post a notice yourself.

7. Mail-order catalogs for quilters often offer collections of miscellaneous fabrics left over after cutting yardage for kits or orders. This way you can add a lot of variety to your collection at one time, often at a very reasonable price.

8. Offer to clean your grandmother's attic or basement (admittedly not the fun part) and keep your eyes open for stashes of unused fabric (*this* is the fun part).

9. Plan a road trip with your quilting friends. Pick a day to drive to all the fabric shops within a 45-mile radius. Make a pact that you will all buy 1/2 yard extra of the fabrics you select, then cut them into smaller pieces to share when you get home.

10. Big cities like New York, Philadelphia, and San Francisco often have a designated garment and fabric district. Visit stores in those areas and stock up on a variety of inexpensive cuts of fabrics (especially the imported or more exotic kinds).

11. Check for bargain boxes of patches at your local quilt or fabric shop. Some stores offer an assortment for a very reasonable amount, like a dime a patch. Or some shops have a designated swap box and ask that for every 6-inch piece you take, you put back in one of your own.

12. If you're taking a quilt class, see if other classmates have some strips or pieces left over from their projects that they would be willing to trade.

SKILL LEVEL: Challenging

SIZE: Finished quilt is
60 × 60 inches

Finished blocks are 7 inches
square

Number of blocks: 16 Tulips
44 Log Cabins

FABRICS AND SUPPLIES

- 3³/4 yards of very light, subtle print for background of Tulip blocks and light side of Log Cabin blocks

- 1¹/2 yards of very dark purple solid for Log Cabin blocks and binding

- ¹/4 yard *each* or scraps of at least 20 different dark jewel tone fabrics for the dark side of the Log Cabin blocks (60 strips, each 1¹/2 × 42 inches)

- ¹/4 yard *each* of eight different rainbow hue fabrics for tulip flower bottoms

- ¹/8 yard *each* of eight different fabrics for tulip flower tops (Choose fabrics in slightly lighter values than the tulip flower bottoms.)

- ¹/2 yard of dark green print fabric for tulip stems and leaves

- 3³/4 yards of fabric for quilt back

- Quilt batting, at least 66 × 66 inches

- Rotary cutter, ruler, and mat (Note: Ruler must have guidelines for making 45 degree angle cuts.)

- Template plastic

Tulips in the Spring

Virginia quilter Linda Fiedler combined high-

contrast Log Cabin blocks with bright pieced tulips

in a unique medallion setting for Tulips

in the Spring. A subtle pastel, almost

white, fabric forms the background for

the rainbow hue tulips and the light side of

the Log Cabin blocks. Tropical and other sophisti-

cated strong prints in deep, dark jewel tones form the

dark side of the Log Cabin blocks.

AMERICAN COUNTRY SCRAP QUILTS

60 X 60 inches

SCRAP RECIPE

Another way to interpret this quilt would be to use a white tone-on-tone background fabric with pastel tulips and medium to dark prints for the dark portion of the Log Cabin blocks. If you have plaids and stripes you want to use, consider them for the darks with a shirting print for the background and deep, rich reds, golds, and blues for the tulips. For an Amish look, use black in place of the light background and Amish solids for the flowers and dark side of the Log Cabin blocks.

QUICK CUTTING				
Fabric	**First Cut**		**Second Cut**	
LOG CABIN BLOCKS	No. of Strips	Strip Width	No.	Shape
Light print	30	1½"	44	1½" B logs
			44	2½" C logs
			44	3½" F logs
			44	4½" G logs
			44	5½" J logs
			44	6½" K logs
Dark jewel tones	30	1½"	44	1½" D logs
			44	2½" E logs
			44	3½" H logs
			44	4½" I logs
			44	5½" L logs
			44	6½" M logs
Dark purple	11	1½"	308	1½" A
LOG CABIN SETTING BLOCKS	No. of Strips	Strip Width	No.	Shape
Dark jewel tones	30	1½"	24	1½" A/B logs
			24	2½" C/D logs
			24	3½" E/F logs
			24	4½" G/H logs
			24	5½" I/J logs
			24	6½" K/L logs
			24	7½" M/N logs
			24	8½" O/P logs
			12	9½" Q logs

Fabric	First Cut		Second Cut		Third Cut	
TULIP BLOCKS	No. of Strips	Strip Width	No.	Shape	No.	Shape
Light print	3	8"	16	▢	32	◩
	10	2½" for Strip Sets 1 and 2	*From each of the eight Tulip bottom and top fabrics, cut the strips as directed in the first column.*			
	8	1¾" for Strip Set 1				
	8	1¼" for Strip Set 1				
	4	1" for Strip Set 3				
Tulip bottom*	1	2⅛" for Strip Set 1				
	1	2⅝" for Strip Set 2				
Tulip top*	2	1⅜" for Strip Sets 1 and 2				
Green print	8	1½" for Strip Set 1				
	2	1¼" for Strip Set 3				

CUTTING

Referring to the "Quick Cutting" chart, cut all the pieces using a rotary cutter. Cut all strips across the fabric width unless directed otherwise. Note that for some of the pieces, the quick-cutting method will result in left-over strips of fabric. All measurements include ¼-inch seam allowances. If you are using scraps that are less than 42 inches wide, you will need to increase the number of strips you cut accordingly. After cutting, label all strips and smaller pieces or "logs" to avoid confusion when piecing.

MAKING TEMPLATES

If you don't have a ruler that is at least 8 inches square, you will need to make a template for squaring up the Tulip blocks. On graph paper, draw a pattern for a 7½-inch square. Make a template for the square. To make a template for the setting triangles, draw a 7⅞-inch square on graph paper. Draw a line diagonally across the square to divide it into two triangles. Make a template for the triangle and label it Setting Triangle.

PIECING THE LOG CABIN BLOCKS

STEP 1. Sew a purple A square to one end of each dark Log Cabin piece (D, E, H, I, L, and M). Press the seam allowances toward the purple squares. Keep the Log Cabin pieces sorted in alphabetical order. Use the remaining purple squares as block centers.

STEP 2. Referring to **Diagram 1,** sew a B square log to a purple center A square. Press seam allowances away from the center square.

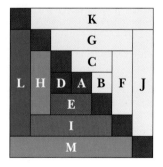

Diagram 1

STEP 3. Sew a C log to the A/B unit. Press all seams away from the center as you add successive logs. Add a D log, then E. Continue adding logs around the center in alphabetical order until the block is complete. Pay close attention as you add the dark logs so that the purple square is positioned correctly.

STEP 4. Repeat to make 44 Log Cabin blocks.

PIECING THE LOG CABIN SETTING TRIANGLES

STEP 1. Referring to **Diagram 2,** add pieces in alphabetical order around the center A square. Press all seam allowances away from the center square. Make 12 blocks, each 9½ inches square, including seam allowances.

Diagram 2

STEP 2. Using the Setting Triangle template, mark and cut two triangles from each block. Position the

triangle template so that the right angle corner of the template is aligned with the corner of the block. You will have a total of 24 setting triangles.

MAKING THE TULIP BLOCKS

STEP 1. Referring to **Diagram 3,** make eight of Strip Set 1, using coordinating tulip top and tulip bottom fabrics for each. Press seam allowances toward the bottom strip.

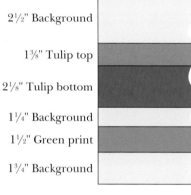

2½" Background
1⅜" Tulip top
2⅛" Tulip bottom
1¼" Background
1½" Green print
1¾" Background

Strip Set 1
Diagram 3

STEP 2. To cut mirror image pieces for the outside of a tulip, fold a strip set in half with wrong sides facing. Cutting through both layers, trim the ends at a 45 degree angle. See **Diagram 4.** Cut parallel to the first cut to make two facing mirror image segments that are 1⅜ inches wide. Cut a second set of segments for a matching Tulip block. In the same manner, cut two pairs of mirror image pieces from each of the remaining seven strip sets. You will make two Tulip blocks from each strip set.

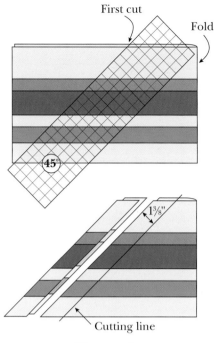

First cut
Fold
45°
1⅜"
Cutting line

Diagram 4

STEP 3. Referring to **Diagram 5,** make eight of Strip Set 2, using coordinating tulip top and tulip bottom fabrics for each. Press seam allowances toward the top strip.

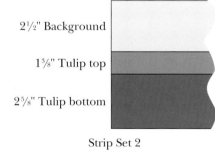

2½" Background
1⅜" Tulip top
2⅝" Tulip bottom

Strip Set 2
Diagram 5

STEP 4. To cut mirror image pieces for the center of a tulip, fold a strip set in half with wrong sides facing. Cutting through both layers, trim the ends at a 45 degree angle as you did in Step 2. Make a cut parallel to the first cut to make two facing mirror image segments that are 1⅜ inches wide. Cut a second set of segments for a matching Tulip block. In this manner, cut two sets of mirror image pieces from each of the seven remaining strip sets.

STEP 5. Referring to **Diagram 6,** make two of Strip Set 3. Press seam allowances toward the center strip.

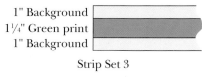

1" Background
1¼" Green print
1" Background

Strip Set 3

Diagram 6

STEP 6. From the strip sets, cut 16 segments, each 5 inches long for the flower stems. See **Diagram 7**

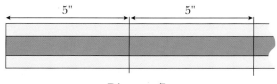

5"   5"

Diagram 7

STEP 7. To make one block, sew mirror image tulip center segments cut from Strip Set 2 together, as shown in **Diagram 8.** Press the seam allowances open. Square off the lower edge of the tulip center, as shown.

STEP 8. Add the stem segment cut from Strip Set 3 to the bottom edge of the tulip center. Refer to **Diagram 9.**

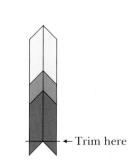

← Trim here

Diagram 8

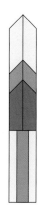

Diagram 9

STEP 9. Sew one side segment cut from Strip Set 1 to each side of the tulip, as shown in **Diagram 10.** Press seam allowances open.

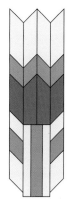

Diagram 10

SEW WISE

As you trim the Tulip blocks in Step 10 on page 140, make certain that you allow ¼ inch for the seam allowance beyond the points of the tulip top so that you will have nice sharp points at the top of the flower. It's easiest to do this with a see-through square ruler. Be extra careful if you are using a square template of opaque material.

Log Cabin Block

Setting Triangle

STEP 10. Sew a background triangle to each side of the tulip to make a square. The tulip should be oriented diagonally in the block. See **Diagram 11.** Press the seam allowances open. Using the Square Template or a square rotary ruler, trim the Tulip block to 7½ inches square.

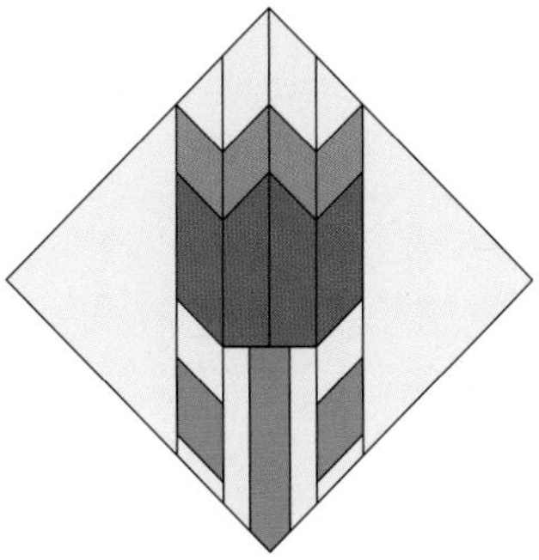

Diagram 11

STEP 11. Repeat Steps 7 through 10 to make a total of 16 Tulip blocks.

Quilt Assembly Diagram

ASSEMBLING THE QUILT TOP

STEP 1. Referring to the **Quilt Assembly Diagram** and the **Quilt Diagram,** lay out the Tulip blocks, Log Cabin blocks, and Log Cabin setting triangles.

STEP 2. Sew the pieces together in diagonal rows, as shown in the **Quilt Assembly Diagram.** Press the seams in alternate directions from row to row. Join the rows.

QUILTING AND FINISHING

STEP 1. Mark quilting designs as desired, or see "Quilting Ideas" for suggestions.

STEP 2. To piece the quilt back, cut the backing fabric into two 1⅞-yard pieces. Cut one piece in half lengthwise. Trim the selvages, and sew a half panel to each long side of the full panel. Press the seam allowances toward the narrow panels.

STEP 3. Layer the quilt back, batting, and quilt top. Baste the layers together. Trim the quilt back and batting so they are approximately 3 inches larger than the quilt top on all sides.

STEP 4. Hand or machine quilt as desired.

STEP 5. Make approximately 260 inches of French-fold binding by joining the binding strips with diagonal seams. See "Finishing" on page 223 for details on finishing the edges of your quilt.

Quilt Diagram

Quilting Ideas

The quilt shown was heavily quilted in the light background areas using the Tulip Quilting Designs on pages 142–143. Place them randomly within the light areas of the quilt. The dark areas were quilted in a 1-inch grid, as shown. The tulips were outline quilted.

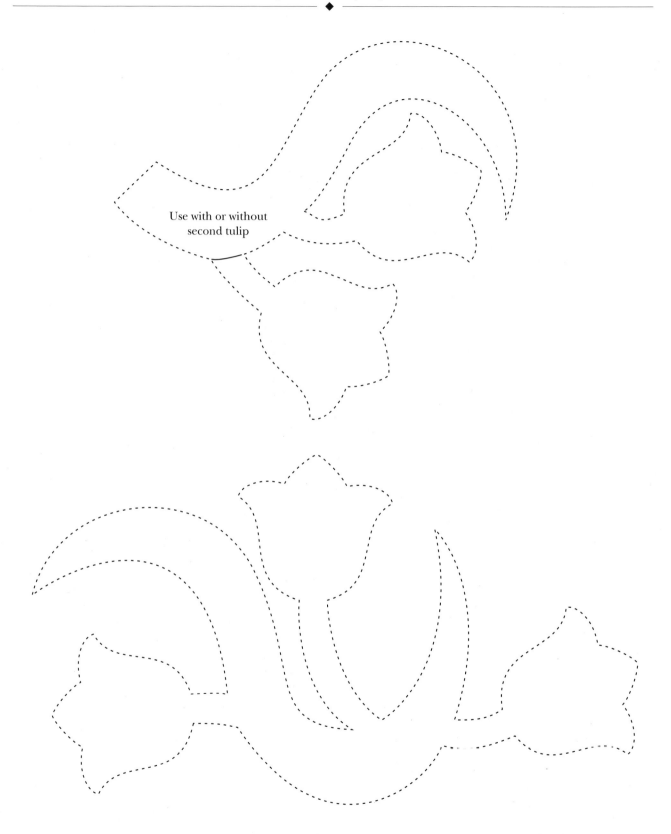

Use with or without
second tulip

Tulip Quilting Designs

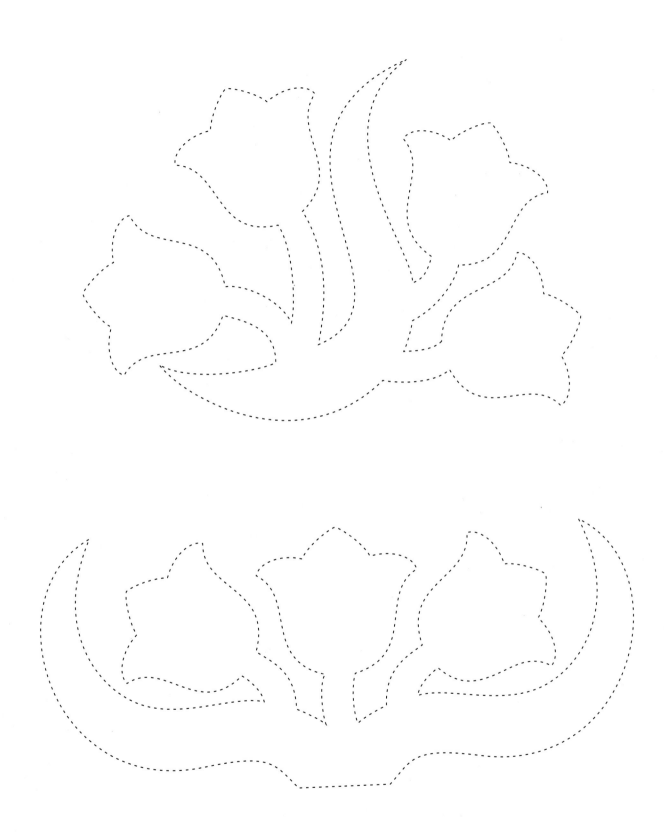

Tulip Quilting Designs

October

Features that will undoubtedly characterize the "art quilts" of the 1990s are manipulation of dark and light values to create asymmetrical design orientations throughout the entire quilt. Iowa quiltmaker Kathy Corones likes to use simple blocks such as the Courthouse Steps Log Cabin to experiment with values and symmetry. She chooses unusual fabrics—such as Indian madras plaids, hand-dyed solids, and batik prints—and sets them together in unique arrangements. This quilt is part of a series of works exploring the use of such fabrics.

30³/₈ × 30³/₈ inches

SCRAP RECIPE

There's no doubt about it. The fabrics in this quilt make a very dramatic presentation. You can make your own statement by choosing entirely different fabrics. Try hot tropical prints instead of cool batiks. Or, for a more subdued look, work in a few homespun plaids instead of the madras ones. Just remember to pay close attention to the placement of light, medium, and dark values.

QUICK CUTTING				
Fabric	**First Cut**		**Second Cut**	
BLOCKS	No. of Strips	Strip Width	No.	Shape
Dark blues	10	$1\frac{5}{8}$"	7	$1\frac{5}{8}$" A logs
			10	$3\frac{7}{8}$" B logs
			10	$6\frac{1}{8}$" C logs
			10	$7\frac{7}{8}$" D logs
			3	$10\frac{5}{8}$" E logs
Light blues	6	$1\frac{5}{8}$"	6	$1\frac{5}{8}$" A logs
			6	$3\frac{7}{8}$" B logs
			6	$6\frac{1}{8}$" C logs
			6	$7\frac{7}{8}$" D logs
			3	$10\frac{5}{8}$" E logs
Dark plaids and prints	11	$1\frac{5}{8}$"	7	$1\frac{5}{8}$" A logs
			11	$3\frac{7}{8}$" B logs
			11	$6\frac{1}{8}$" C logs
			11	$7\frac{7}{8}$" D logs
			7	$10\frac{5}{8}$" E logs
Light plaids and prints	9	$1\frac{5}{8}$"	7	$1\frac{5}{8}$" A logs
			9	$3\frac{7}{8}$" B logs
			9	$6\frac{1}{8}$" C logs
			9	$7\frac{7}{8}$" D logs
			5	$10\frac{5}{8}$" E logs

QUICK CUTTING

Referring to the "Quick Cutting" chart, cut the number of pieces or "logs" needed for each fabric; each letter represents a dimension as specified in the chart. Cut one of each length from each of the fabric strips. You will have some extra pieces; not all are needed for this project. All measurements include ¼-inch seam allowances.

PIECING THE BLOCKS

STEP 1. Referring to the **Fabric Key,** the **Block Diagram,** and the photograph on page 145, lay out the pieces for Block 1. The heavy lines on the block diagrams indicate where two different dark, medium dark, or light prints should be positioned. Use the same print for all pieces within an outlined area.

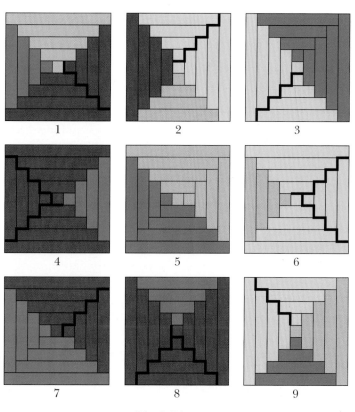

Block Diagram

FABRIC KEY

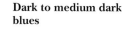

 Dark to medium dark blues

Light to medium light blues

 Dark to medium dark plaids and prints

Light to medium light plaids and prints

STEP 2. Join the three A squares, as shown in **Diagram 1.** Press the seam allowances away from the center square.

Diagram 1

STEP 3. Add a B piece to the long sides of the A squares, as shown in **Diagram 2.** Press the seams toward the B pieces. Then add two B pieces to opposite ends of the center unit, as shown.

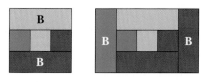

Diagram 2

STEP 4. Continue to add pieces around the center in alphabetical order, as shown in **Diagram 3,** pressing the seam allowances away from the center of the block.

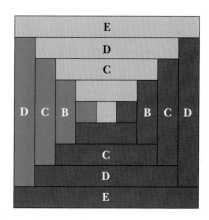

Diagram 3

STEP 5. Repeat Steps 1 through 4 to make one each of Blocks 2 through 9, as shown in the **Block Diagram** on page 147, carefully following the color placement.

ASSEMBLING THE QUILT TOP

STEP 1. Lay the completed blocks out in three rows of three blocks each, following the order given in the **Block Diagram.**

STEP 2. Join the blocks in three horizontal rows. Press the seam allowances in opposite directions from row to row. Join the rows to complete the quilt top.

QUILTING AND FINISHING

STEP 1. Mark quilting designs as desired, or see "Quilting Ideas" for suggestions.

STEP 2. Layer the quilt back, batting, and quilt top. Baste the layers together. Trim the quilt back and batting so they are approximately 3 inches larger than the quilt top on all sides.

STEP 3. Hand or machine quilt as desired.

STEP 4. Finish the top and right side of the of the quilt with light rust binding, and the left side and lower edge with dark rust binding. See "Binding with Overlapped Corners" for tips on how to do this.

STEP 5. To hang your quilt, see "Making a Hanging Sleeve for a Quilt" on page 226.

Quilting Ideas

This quilt was quilted with diagonal lines that form a diamond, as shown in the photograph on page 145. Or you could simply outline quilt ¼ inch from all of the seams of the blocks, as shown.

Binding with Overlapped Corners

STEP 1. Sew binding to two opposite sides of the quilt. Trim away excess binding, batting, and backing. Fold the binding to the back of the quilt and stitch in place by hand.

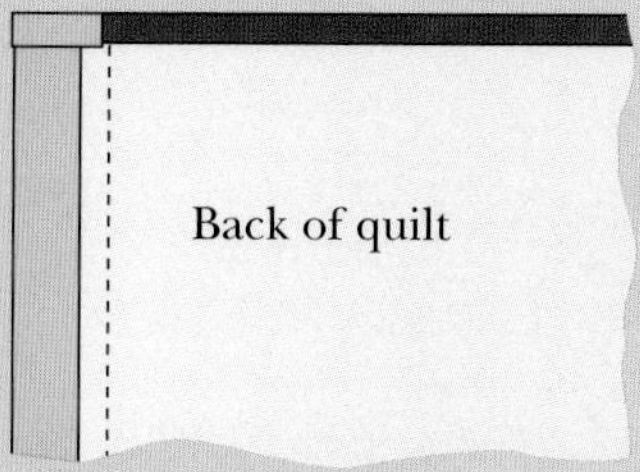

Back of quilt

Diagram 2

STEP 2. Sew binding to the remaining opposite two sides of the quilt, allowing the binding to extend 1 inch past the corner at each end as shown in *Diagram 1.*

STEP 4. Fold the binding over to cover the machine stitching and raw edge of binding corner as shown in *Diagram 3.*

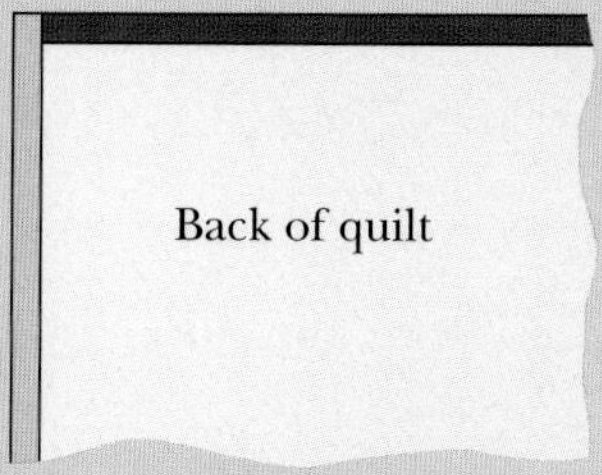

Back of quilt

Diagram 1

Back of quilt

Diagram 3

STEP 3. Trim the ends of the binding so they extend 1/2 inch beyond the adjacent bound edge. With the back of the quilt facing you, fold the end of the binding over, even with the bound edge as shown in *Diagram 2.*

STEP 5. Blindstitch the binding to the quilt backing, adding extra stitches to secure the corners.

Crazy Cabins

SKILL LEVEL: Intermediate

SIZE: Finished quilt is 30 × 33½ inches

Finished block is 6 inches square (approximately 8½ inches on the diagonal)

Number of pieced blocks: 13

FABRICS AND SUPPLIES

- ¾ yard of muslin for block foundations

- ¼ yard of burgundy stripe for bottom outer border

- ¼ yard of dark gray stripe for side border

- ⅛ yard of black-and-white stripe for narrow top and bottom borders

- Scraps or 1½ × 42-inch strips of 30 assorted striped fabrics for blocks

- Scraps, each at least 5¼ inches square, of four medium or dark striped fabrics for corner triangle blocks

- ½ yard of tan stripe for binding

- 1 yard of fabric for quilt back

- 1 yard of polyester fleece

- Embroidery floss or pearl cotton and large needle to tie the quilt

- Rotary cutter, ruler, and mat

The Log Cabin pattern is one of the most classic and beloved of all quilt designs. In a display of its seemingly limitless versatility, quilters continuously invent their own versions of strips organized around a center shape. Crazy Cabins was an experiment in using striped fabrics for North Dakota quilter Kim Baird. She began by cutting a 1½-inch-wide strip from each of the striped fabrics in her collection. She then let go of her inhibitions and pieced a variety of traditional and crazy Log Cabin blocks for her exciting and unconventional wall quilt.

30 × 33¹/₂ inches

SCRAP RECIPE

The large variety of stripes in this quilt certainly makes your eyes dance across the design. However, it's not just the stripes that make this Log Cabin quilt crazy. You could substitute plaids or prints and come up with an equally exciting wall quilt, since the blocks are not all alike. Upon closer examination you'll find Courthouse Steps, Spirals, triangular centers, and more. All these features lead to the high-energy feel of the quilt. By mixing in some geometrics, florals, and woven plaids, you can add to the fun-filled impact of the design.

QUICK CUTTING						
Fabric	**First Cut**		**Second Cut**		**Third Cut**	
BLOCKS	No. of Strips	Strip Width	No.	Shape	No.	Shape
Muslin	1	8"	4	☐	—	—
	2	6½"	13	☐	—	—
Assorted stripes*	30	1½"	—	—	—	—
Dark stripes*	4	5¼"	4	■	4	◩ †
BORDERS	No. of Strips	Strip Width				
Burgundy stripe	1	6"				
Dark gray stripe	1	5"				
Black-and-white stripe	2	1¾"				

From the assorted and dark stripes, cut one strip or piece from each fabric to get the total number required.

†*From the dark stripes, only one-half of each square will be used for the corner triangle blocks.*

QUICK CUTTING

Referring to the "Quick Cutting" chart, cut the number of strips needed from each fabric using a rotary cutter. All measurements include ¼-inch seam allowances. Directions are for cutting all strips across the fabric width. However, if you want to achieve a variety of visual effects with your strips, cut some lengthwise or on the bias, as shown in the photograph on page 151. If you are using scraps that are less than 42 inches wide, you will need to adjust the number of strips you cut accordingly.

Measurements for the borders are longer than needed; trim them to the exact length before adding them to the quilt top.

PIECING THE BLOCKS

The Log Cabin blocks and the triangle half blocks are pieced on muslin foundation squares to ensure stability and a consistent finished size. The half blocks are pieced as squares and then cut into two triangles. As each strip is added around the center, it is pressed to form a ⅛-inch-deep pleat to give the blocks extra texture.

This quilt contains several blocks that are shading variations of the traditional Log Cabin block, including Half Light/Half Dark, Spiral, and Rings. You'll also find Courthouse Steps and Off-Center Log Cabin variations, which are pieced a bit differently. Finally, the Crazy Cabin variation begins with a center piece that is not square. Some fun center shapes to experiment with are rectangles, triangles, trapezoids, and other straight-sided polygons. See the **Block Diagram** to help you plan the type of blocks you want to make. Notice the color placement in the diagrams for light and dark fabrics.

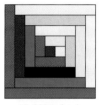

Half Light/
Half Dark

Courthouse
Steps

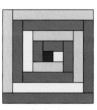

Spiral

Off-Center

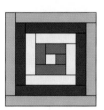

Rings

Crazy Cabin

Block Diagram

STEP 1. Cover the 6½-inch foundation squares with Log Cabin patchwork. In the quilt shown, three of the 6½-inch blocks are Crazy Cabins, one is Half Light/Half Dark, three are Spiral, four are Rings, one is Courthouse Steps, and one is Off-Center. You can follow the same layout for your quilt, or vary the types of blocks to create an original design.

STEP 2. To piece a block with the foundation method, position the center piece on the muslin square, with the right side of the fabric face up.

STEP 3. Place a strip on top of the center patch, with right sides facing and raw edges aligned along one side. Stitch the length of the center piece. Open out the strip and press, forming an approximately ⅛-inch-deep pleat along the seamed edge. Trim the ends of the strip even with the center piece.

STEP 4. In the same manner, continue to add strips, following the numerical order shown in **Diagram 1** on this page and **Diagrams 2, 3,** or **4** on page 154. The block is completed when the foundation square is covered with fabric.

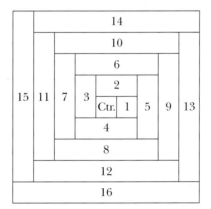

Basic Log Cabin
Use for Half Light/Half Dark,
Spiral, and Rings variations

Diagram 1

STEP 5. To make the eight setting triangles, cover the four 8-inch muslin foundations as you did for the smaller foundations using your choice of block type. Cut

Our "Fabrics and Supplies" list on page 150 recommends using fleece rather than traditional batting since the Crazy Cabins quilt calls for a combination of quilting and tying. Fleece is similar to a thin batting, yet it is a denser polyester filling that will hold up better to occasional laundering in a tied project. If you prefer to quilt your project, you may want to substitute your favorite quilt batting for the fleece. If you use fleece, you'll want to avoid the fusible type, since it will be more difficult to stitch through, whether quilting or tying.

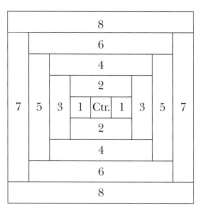

Courthouse Steps

Diagram 2

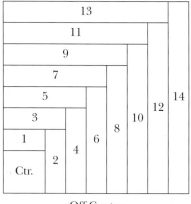

Off-Center

Diagram 3

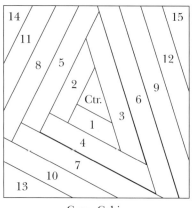

Crazy Cabin

Diagram 4

each of the 8-inch blocks in half diagonally to make two pieced triangles.

ASSEMBLING THE QUILT TOP

STEP 1. Referring to the **Quilt Diagram,** lay out the blocks, half blocks, and corner triangles in a pleasing arrangement.

STEP 2. Sew the blocks and half blocks together in diagonal rows. The heavy lines on the diagram indicate the rows. Press the seam allowances to one side, alternating directions from one row to another. Join the rows and press the seam allowances to one side.

STEP 3. Using a rotary cutter and ruler, trim the triangle half blocks and corner triangles so that the sides are even and the quilt top is square. Be sure to allow ¼ inch beyond the corners of the blocks for the seam allowance.

STEP 4. Measure the width of the quilt top through the center of the quilt. Trim the two black-and-white striped border pieces to this size. Sew a border to the top and

Quilt Diagram

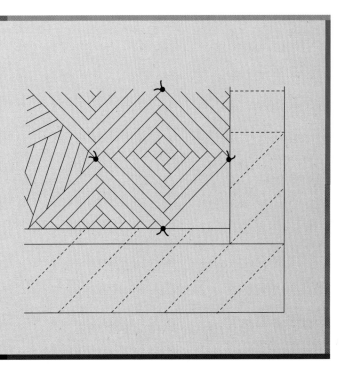

Quilting Ideas

This quilt was tied at the block intersections. The only quilted areas are the borders, which have rows of diagonal and horizontal line quilting spaced 3 inches apart, as shown. Directions for tying your quilt are given in Step 3 of "Quilting and Finishing."

bottom edges of the quilt top. Press the seam allowances toward the borders.

STEP 5. Measure the length of the quilt top through the center, including the two borders. Trim the gray striped border piece to this size. Sew the border to the right side of the quilt. Press the seam allowances toward the border.

STEP 6. Measure the width of the quilt top through the center, including the side border. Trim the burgundy striped border piece to this size. Sew the border to the bottom edge of the quilt. Press the seam allowances toward the outer border.

QUILTING AND FINISHING

STEP 1. Mark quilting designs as desired, or see "Quilting Ideas" for suggestions.

STEP 2. Layer the quilt back, fleece, and quilt top. Baste the layers together. Trim the quilt back and fleece so they are approximately 3 inches larger than the quilt top on all sides.

STEP 3. Using embroidery floss or pearl cotton and a large needle, tie the quilt at the corners of all the blocks. On the quilt shown in the photograph on page 150, the ties were made from the quilt back so the tie ends would not show on the quilt front. As an extra feature, the

quiltmaker attached a different style button on the back at each place where the quilt was tied. You may choose to make the ties on the quilt front as an added design element, and add buttons as embellishment to the front as well.

STEP 4. Hand or machine quilt the border as desired.

STEP 5. From the tan striped fabric, make approximately 140 inches of French-fold bias binding. See "Finishing" on page 223 for details on finishing the edges of your quilt.

Feathered World without End

SKILL LEVEL: Challenging

SIZE: Finished quilt is
60 × 60 inches

Finished block is 12 inches square

Number of blocks: 16

FABRICS AND SUPPLIES

- 2 yards of multicolored, large-scale print for borders and block background

- 2 yards of white print for patchwork

- 1³/₄ yards *total* of assorted prints for feathered triangles

- 1 yard of black solid for diamonds, borders, and binding

- Scraps of 16 large-scale prints for centers of blocks (minimum size 5 × 5 inches each)

- ¹/₈ yard *each* or scraps of 16 solids for patchwork

- 3¹/₂ yards of fabric for quilt back

- Quilt batting, at least 66 inches square

- Rotary cutter, ruler, and mat

- Template plastic

AMERICAN COUNTRY SCRAP QUILTS

Unmistakably from the present, this quilt's distinctive

feature is a large-scale printed fabric. Quiltmaker

Bev Munson let the multicolored leaf

print dictate the choice of the printed

and solid scraps. The solid black dia-

monds at the corners of each block and the

subtle white printed background fabric used

throughout the quilt work effectively to unify the mul-

titude of colors and fabrics.

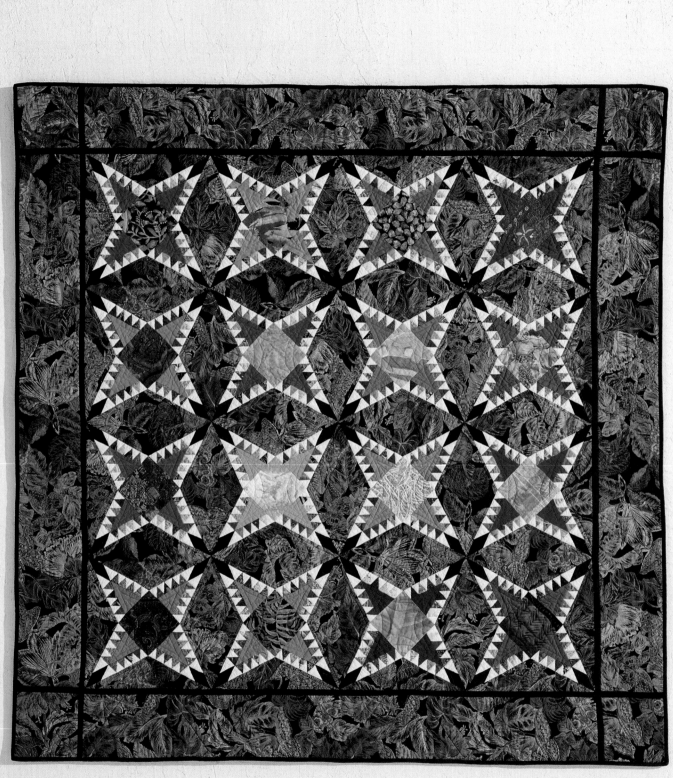

60 × 60 inches

SCRAP RECIPE

Today we are lucky to have so many beautiful, large-scale prints available from which to choose. Whether you prefer florals or geometrics, a trip to your local fabric shop is bound to get your imagination going. Choose a print that appeals to you, whether for the color scheme or for the design. Then mix and match your scraps or fat quarters to build from there. While the quilt in the photograph on page 157 is predominately black, fuchsia, and teal, you could plan a traditional navy and red quilt, or look to nature for deep greens, rusts, and golden hues as your main colors.

QUICK CUTTING				
Fabric	**First Cut**		**Second Cut**	
BLOCKS	No. of Strips	Strip Width	No.	Shape
Black solid	5	1½"	64	A diamonds
White print	3	2⅛"	128	B triangles
	6	2"	256	C triangles
	6	2"	256	C reverse triangles
Assorted prints	6	2"	256	C triangles
	6	2"	256	C reverse triangles
	No.	Shape		
Assorted solids*	64	D triangles	*From each of the assorted solids, cut four D triangles.	
Large-scale prints	16	E squares		
Multicolored print†	64	F triangles	†From the multicolored print, cut the 6" × 49" border strips lengthwise before cutting other pieces from that fabric.	
BORDERS	No.	Shape		
Multi-colored print†	4	6" × 49" strips		
	4	6" squares		
	No. of Strips	Strip Width		
Black solid	6	1"		

CUTTING

Whether you plan to piece this quilt by hand or machine, you will need to make templates for patterns A, B, C, D, and F on pages 162–163. Piece E is a 4¾-inch square. Follow the directions under "Making and Using Templates" on page 215.

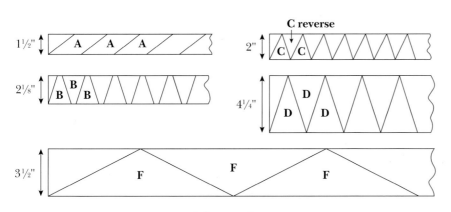

Diagram 1

Referring to the "Quick Cutting" chart, cut the number of strips and pieces needed from each fabric, using a rotary cutter or scissors. To use a rotary cutter, refer to **Diagram 1** for tips on placing the A, B, C, D, and F templates on fabric strips to cut the diamonds and triangles. Mark the outline of the templates and place a ruler over the lines to cut with a rotary cutter. You can also trace the templates and cut them traditionally with scissors. Cut all strips across the fabric width unless otherwise noted. All measurements include ¼-inch seam allowances. If you are using scraps that are less than 42 inches wide, you will need to increase the number of strips you cut accordingly.

PIECING THE BLOCKS

STEP 1. Referring to the **Block Diagram,** lay out the pieces for one block. Pay careful attention when positioning the C and C reverse pieces.

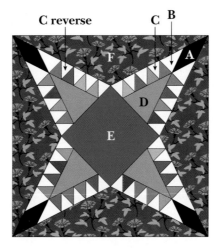

Block Diagram

STEP 2. Referring to **Diagram 2,** sew B triangles to opposite sides of the four A diamonds that are needed for the block. Press the seam allowances toward the B triangles.

Diagram 2

STEP 3. Join four white print and four scrap print C triangles into a

Because the C and C reverse triangles are very similar in shape, but not *exactly* the same, it is easy to confuse them. To avoid a frustrating experience in trying to make a C triangle fit where you should have a C reverse, store the two shapes in different zipper-type plastic bags. Label each bag and then simply slip a triangle out of the appropriate bag when needed.

strip, as shown in **Diagram 3A.** Make four such strips. Referring to **Diagram 3B,** make four similar strips using white print and scrap print C reverse triangles. Press all seams toward the print triangles.

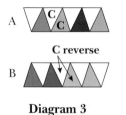

Diagram 3

STEP 4. Sew the C and C reverse strips to opposite sides of four D triangles, as shown in **Diagram 4.** Press the seam allowances away from the D triangles.

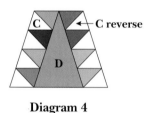

Diagram 4

STEP 5. Sew an A/B triangle unit to the top of each C/D unit, as shown in **Diagram 5** to complete the feathered points.

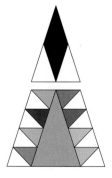

Diagram 5

STEP 6. Referring to the **Block Diagram** on page 159, sew a feathered point to each side of the E center square. Press the seam allowances away from the square.

STEP 7. Set in the F triangles as indicated in the **Block Diagram.** See "Setting In Pieces" on page 217 for more details. Press seam allowances toward the F triangles.

STEP 8. Repeat to make a total of 16 blocks.

ASSEMBLING THE QUILT TOP

STEP 1. Referring to the **Quilt Diagram,** lay out the 16 blocks in four horizontal rows with four blocks per row.

STEP 2. Join the blocks to make the rows. Press the seam allowances in opposite directions from row to row. Join the rows, and press the quilt top.

STEP 3. Measure the width of the quilt top through the center. Trim the four multicolor print border strips to this length, which should be about 48½ inches.

STEP 4. Join the narrow black border strips as needed to make two borders the same length as the wide border. Stitch together using diagonal seams, as shown in **Diagram 6.**

Quilt Diagram

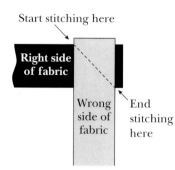

Start stitching here

Right side of fabric

Wrong side of fabric

End stitching here

Diagram 6

STEP 5. Sew a black border strip to the long side of two of the print borders. Press the seam allowances toward the print borders. Sew the borders to the top and bottom edges of the quilt top, with the black borders next to the inner quilt.

STEP 6. From the remaining 1-inch black border strips, cut four

1 × 6-inch pieces. Sew one of these short black strips to each end of the two remaining print border strips. Press the seam allowances toward the print border. Sew a 6-inch print corner square to each end of the two borders. Press the seam allowances toward the corner squares.

STEP 7. Make two black borders the length of the print borders. Sew a black border to one long edge of each print border. Sew the borders to the two sides of the quilt, with the black border toward quilt center. Press the seam allowances toward the black borders.

QUILTING AND FINISHING

STEP 1. Mark quilting designs as desired, or see "Quilting Ideas" for suggestions.

STEP 2. To piece the quilt back, cut the backing fabric into two 63-inch lengths. Cut one piece in half lengthwise. Trim all of the selvages, and sew a half panel to each side of the full panel. Press the seams toward the narrow panels.

STEP 3. Layer the quilt back, batting, and quilt top. Baste the layers together. Trim the quilt back and batting so they are approximately least 3 inches larger than the quilt top on all sides.

STEP 4. Hand or machine quilt as desired.

STEP 5. From the binding fabric, make approximately 252 inches of French-fold binding. See "Finishing" on page 223 for details on finishing the edges of your quilt.

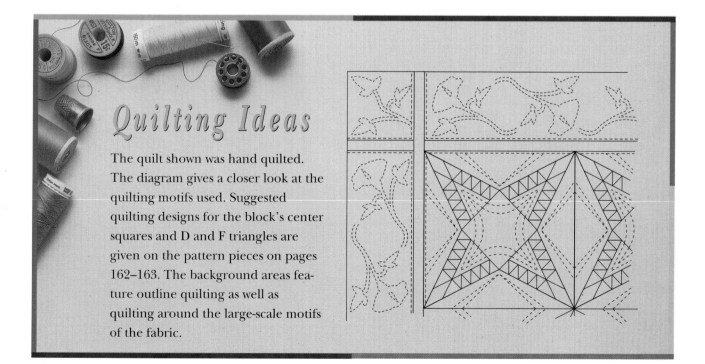

Quilting Ideas

The quilt shown was hand quilted. The diagram gives a closer look at the quilting motifs used. Suggested quilting designs for the block's center squares and D and F triangles are given on the pattern pieces on pages 162–163. The background areas feature outline quilting as well as quilting around the large-scale motifs of the fabric.

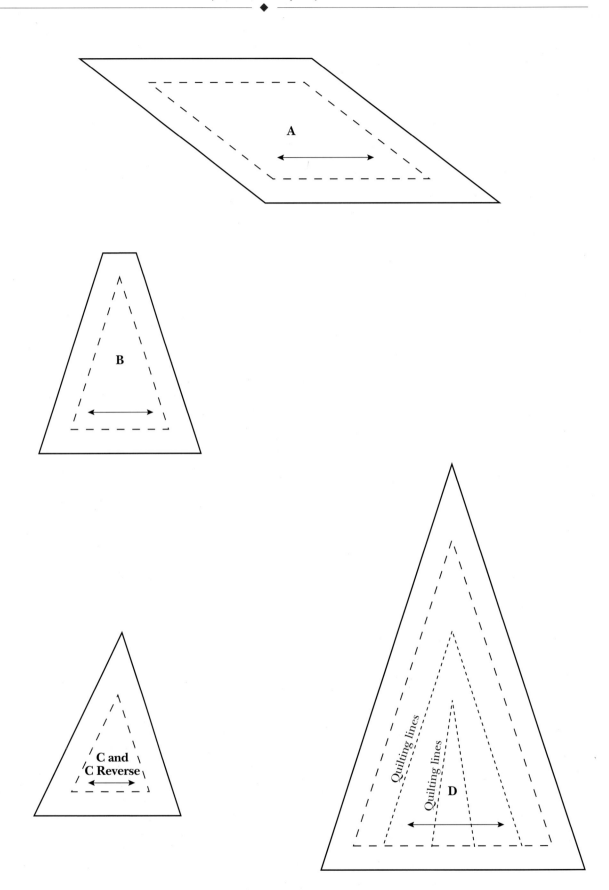

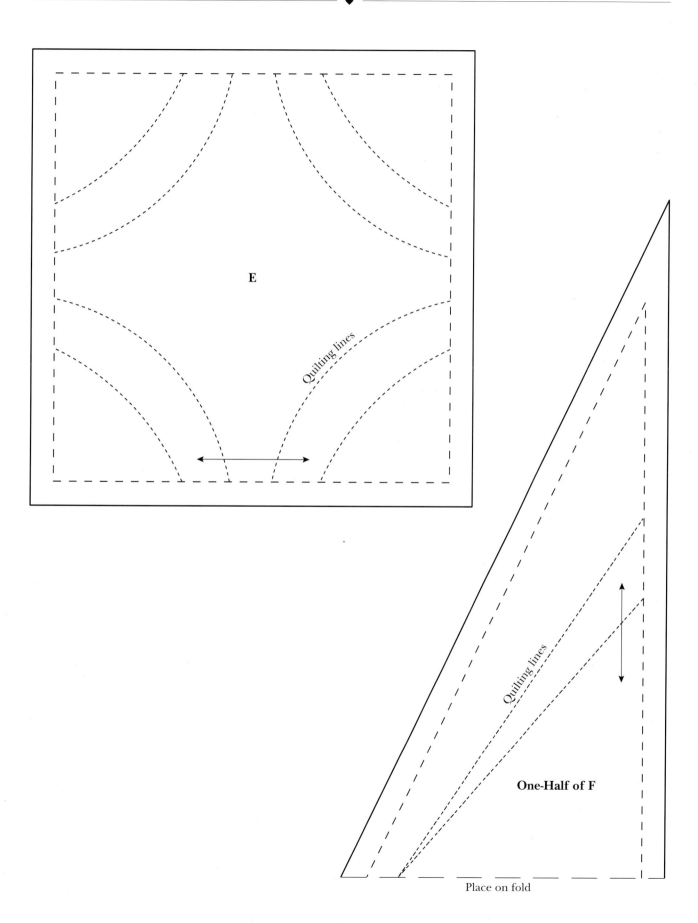

E

Quilting lines

Quilting lines

One-Half of F

Place on fold

African Lattice Wall Quilt

SKILL LEVEL: Easy

SIZE: Finished quilt is 46 × 46 inches

Finished block is 14 inches square

Number of blocks: 9

Made by Fern Stewart

FABRICS AND SUPPLIES

- Approximately 1¼ yards *total* of various black and other dark value print fabrics for rectangles and large squares

- Approximately 1 yard *total* of various gold, black and gold, black and cream, and rust print fabrics for rectangles and large squares

- ¼ yard of red and black print for small squares

- ½ yard of striped fabric for border

- 3 yards of fabric for quilt back

- ½ yard of fabric for binding

- Quilt batting, at least 52 × 52 inches

- Rotary cutter, ruler, and mat

A simple combination of squares

and rectangles is the perfect way to

display interesting fabrics. We used

prints influenced by African motifs to design

a contemporary wall quilt that celebrates ethnicity.

The nine blocks are arranged in an overall nine-

patch configuration.

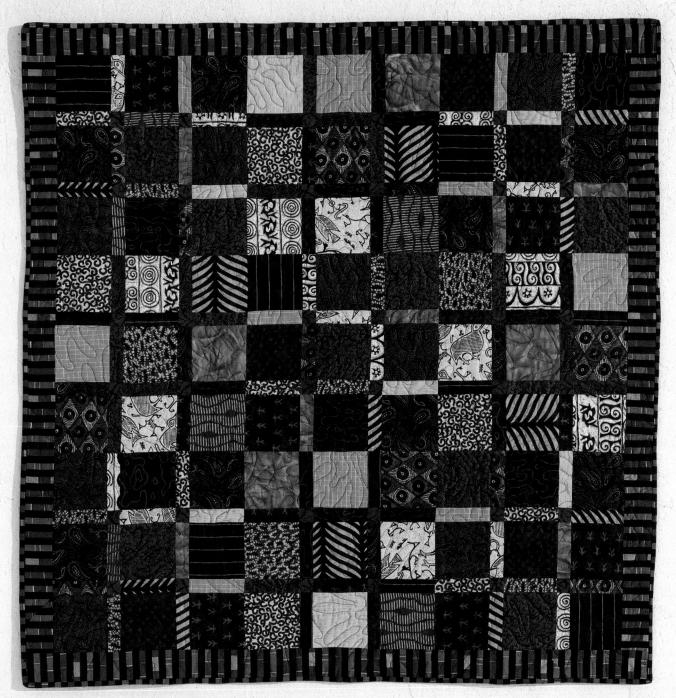

46 X 46 inches

SCRAP RECIPE

This is a quilt that lets your fabrics be the stars. The 4-inch finished squares are large enough and the overall structure of the quilt simple enough to make the fabric itself be the primary feature. It's a wonderful way to highlight any category of fabric, from African prints or bright florals to batiks or Japanese fabrics. Often these are the fabrics we love the most and readily buy but don't quite know how to use in a quilt. Just be sure to stick to one genre, and pick a color scheme. Use 10 to 15 different black print fabrics and 10 to 15 gold print fabrics.

QUICK CUTTING				
Fabric	**First Cut**		**Second Cut**	
BLOCKS	No. of Strips	Strip Width	No.	Shape
Dark prints	5	4½"	45	A ⬛
	3	4½"	48	C 1½"×4½"
Gold prints	4	4½"	36	A ⬛
	3	4½"	60	C 1½"×4½"
Red and black print	2	1½"	36	B ⬛
BORDERS	No. of Strips	Strip Width	No.	Shape
Stripe	5	2½"	—	—

FABRIC KEY

Black prints

Gold prints

Red print

Stripe

QUICK CUTTING

Referring to the "Quick Cutting" chart, cut the number of strips needed from each fabric using a rotary cutter. Cut all strips across the fabric width. All measurements include ¼-inch seam allowances. If you are using scraps that are less than 42 inches wide, you will need to increase the number of strips you cut accordingly.

PIECING THE BLOCKS

STEP 1. Referring to the **Block Diagram,** lay out 9 A squares, 4 B squares, and 12 C rectangles. There are two types of blocks, Type 1 and Type 2.

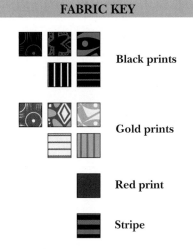

Type 1

Type 2

Block Diagram

STEP 2. For Type 1 blocks, join the pieces into five vertical rows as shown in **Diagram 1.** Press the seam allowances toward the darker fabrics. Join the rows. Repeat to make a total of five Type 1 blocks.

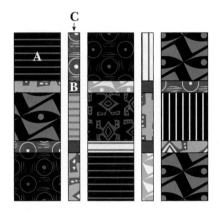

Diagram 1

STEP 3. In the same manner, lay out the pieces for Type 2 blocks. Join the pieces to make the rows as shown in **Diagram 2.** Join the rows to make a block. Make a total of four Type 2 blocks.

Diagram 2

ASSEMBLING THE QUILT TOP

STEP 1. Referring to the **Quilt Diagram** on page 168, lay out the nine blocks in three horizontal

rows, alternating Type 1 and Type 2 blocks. Join the blocks into rows. Press seam allowances toward the Type 1 blocks. Join the rows.

STEP 2. Join the five border strips end to end to make one long strip. Measure the length of the quilt through the center. From the long strip, cut two borders to this length. Sew the border strips to the sides of the quilt top. Press the seams toward the borders.

STEP 3. Measure the width of the quilt top through the center, including the side borders. Cut two border strips to the needed length. Sew the borders to the quilt top. Press seams toward the borders.

QUILTING AND FINISHING

STEP 1. Mark quilting designs as desired, or see "Quilting Ideas" on page 168 for suggestions.

STEP 2. To piece the quilt back, cut the backing fabric crosswise into two 54-inch lengths. Cut a 10-inch-wide lengthwise strip from one panel. Trim the selvages, and sew the narrow strip to one side of the full panel. Press the seams toward the narrow panel.

STEP 3. Layer the quilt back, batting, and quilt top. Baste the layers together. Trim the quilt back and batting so they are approximately 3 inches larger than the quilt top on all sides.

U nusual fabrics, especially large-scale ones, sometimes present a special cutting challenge. If the print is one with strong light/dark or color contrast, you'll find your squares or other shapes for patchwork may not read as they should. If you're unsure how well a particular fabric will work for this or any other quilt, use a piece of posterboard or heavy paper to make a viewing "window" for auditioning specific areas of the print. For this quilt, cut a 4-inch window in the center of an 8-inch square of posterboard. Try the window out on different sections of fabric.

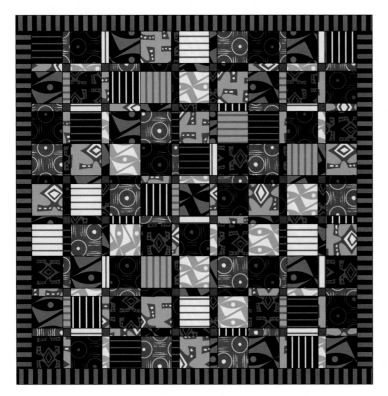

Quilt Diagram

STEP 4. Hand or machine quilt as marked.

STEP 5. From the binding fabric, make approximately 200 inches of French-fold binding. See "Finishing" on page 223 for details on finishing the edges of your quilt.

Quilting Ideas

Our quilt is machine quilted in free-motion meandering fashion, as shown. Leaf motifs predominate, with occasional animal shapes like turtles and fish worked in where space allowed.

Shooting Star

This delightful crib-size quilt will never be mistaken

for one from an earlier time period. Its clear, "hot"

colors, whimsical prints, and tropical plaids

all say "I was made in the 1990s." But

the surprise is that Michigan quilter Bev

Munson used an adaptation of a 1930s news-

paper pattern as the starting point for this spirited

quilt. Our instructions call for partial seaming when

constructing the blocks—an easy technique to avoid

setting in pieces. We've also simplified the border with

instructions for easy straight seam borders. Mitered

border directions are included as an option.

SKILL LEVEL: Easy

SIZE: Finished quilt is 40$\frac{1}{2}$ × 51 inches

Finished block is 9 inches square

Number of blocks: 12

FABRICS AND SUPPLIES

- 1$\frac{1}{2}$ yards of navy and medium blue polka dot fabric for sashing, borders, and binding

- 2 yards *total* of 12 to 15 assorted print and solid scrap fabrics for patchwork blocks

- 1$\frac{1}{2}$ yards of fabric for quilt back

- Quilt batting, at least 47 × 57 inches

- Rotary cutter, ruler, and mat

- Template plastic

40½ × 51 inches

Shooting Star

QUICK CUTTING					*From the prints and solids, for each block, cut one A square, four matching B triangles, four matching C triangles, four matching D pieces, and four matching E triangles.
Fabric	**First Cut**		**Second Cut**		
BLOCKS	No.	Shape	No.	Shape	
Prints and solids*	12	2⅝" A ■	—	—	
	24	2⅜" ■	48	B ◫	
	24	3" ■	48	C ◫	
	48	D pieces	—	—	
	12	7¼" ■	48	E ⊠	
SASHING	No.	Shape	No.	Shape	
Print or solid	20	2" ■	—	—	†From the navy and blue polka dot, reserve remaining fabric for binding.
	No. of Strips	Strip Width	No.	Shape	
Navy and blue polka dot	8	2"	31	2"×9½"	
BORDERS	No. of Strips	Strip Width	No.	Shape	
Navy and blue polka dot†	5	4¼"	—	—	

CUTTING

Referring to the "Quick Cutting" chart, cut the number of strips needed from each fabric using a rotary cutter. Cut all strips across the fabric width. All measurements include ¼-inch seam allowances. If you are using scraps that are less than 42 inches wide, you will need to increase the number of strips you cut accordingly.

You will need to make a template for pattern piece D, shown on page 175. If you prefer to use traditional cutting methods to make all the pieces, see "Making and Using Templates" on page 215.

PIECING THE BLOCKS

STEP 1. Lay out the pieces for one block. You will need one A square, four matching B triangles, four matching C triangles, four matching D pieces, and four matching E triangles, as indicated in the **Block Diagram.**

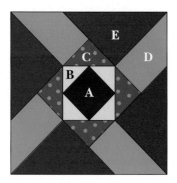

Block Diagram

STEP 2. Referring to **Diagram 1,** sew two B triangles to opposite sides of the A square. Press seam allowances toward the triangles. Add B triangles to the remaining two sides. In the same manner, sew the four C triangles to the center unit. Press seam allowances toward triangles.

Diagram 1

STEP 3. Join the D and E pieces to make four units, as shown in **Diagram 2.** Press the seam allowances toward the E triangles.

Diagram 2

STEP 4. Referring to **Diagram 3,** sew a D/E unit to the center unit, sewing a partial seam, starting at the D edge and stopping at the dot, as indicated. Press the seam allowances toward the D/E unit.

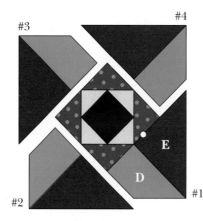

Diagram 3

STEP 5. Follow the numbers in the diagram and work clockwise around the center. Sew another D/E unit to the long side of the partially completed block. Press the seam allowances away from the center unit. Continue adding D/E units around the block. After adding the last unit, complete the partial seam.

STEP 6. Repeat to make a total of 12 blocks.

ASSEMBLING THE QUILT TOP

STEP 1. Referring to the **Quilt Diagram** on page 174, lay out the blocks, sashing strips, and sashing squares in nine horizontal rows.

STEP 2. Join the pieces to make the rows. Press the seam allowances toward the sashing strips. Join the rows.

STEP 3. Measure the length of the quilt top through the center. Piece three 4¼-inch-wide border strips together using diagonal seams, as shown in **Diagram 4.** From this long strip, cut two strips the length of your quilt measurement. Sew the borders to the sides of the quilt top. Press the seam allowances toward the borders.

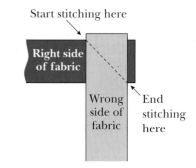

Diagram 4

STEP 4. Measure the width of the quilt top, including the borders you just added. Trim the two remaining border strips to this length. Sew the borders to the top and bottom of the quilt top. Press the seam allowances toward the borders.

Mitered Borders

If you prefer to add mitered borders to your quilt, measure your finished quilt top through the center as described in Steps 3 and 4 of "Assembling the Quilt Top." Add extra length to allow for the miters. A good rule of thumb is to add two times the width of the finished border plus 5 inches. Sew each border as follows:

STEP 1. With a ruler and pencil, mark a 1/4-inch sewing line on the wrong side along one long edge of the border strip. Fold the strip in half crosswise and press it lightly to mark the halfway point.

STEP 2. Measure out from the halfway point along the drawn line, and mark one-half the desired finished border length at each end of the border.

STEP 3. Using a ruler with a 45 degree angle line, mark the sewing line for the miter, as shown in the diagram, measuring

from the end mark made in Step 2 to the outer edge of the border strip. Mark a cutting line 1/4 inch to the outside of the sewing line, but do not trim the excess fabric away until after the border is sewn to the quilt top.

STEP 4. Pin the marked border strip to the quilt top, matching the crease at the halfway point to the midpoint on the side of the quilt. Match the end marks of the sewing lines on the border strips to a point 1/4 inch in from the raw edges of the quilt top.

STEP 5. Stitch the borders to the quilt top, starting and stopping at the end marks, exactly 1/4 inch in from the corner of the quilt top. Backstitch to secure the begin-

ning and end of each seam, without stitching into the seam allowances. Press the seams away from the quilt top.

STEP 6. Fold the quilt diagonally right sides together and align the marked miter lines on adjacent borders. Sew on the angled stitching line from the inner corner mark all the way to the outer raw edge. Backstitch at the beginning and the end of the seam, without stitching into the seam allowance at the inside corner.

STEP 7. Check the accuracy of each mitered corner and then trim away any excess fabric, creating a 1/4-inch seam allowance at each corner.

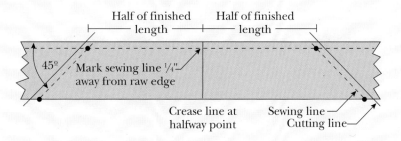

Half of finished length — Half of finished length
45° — Mark sewing line 1/4" away from raw edge
Crease line at halfway point — Sewing line — Cutting line

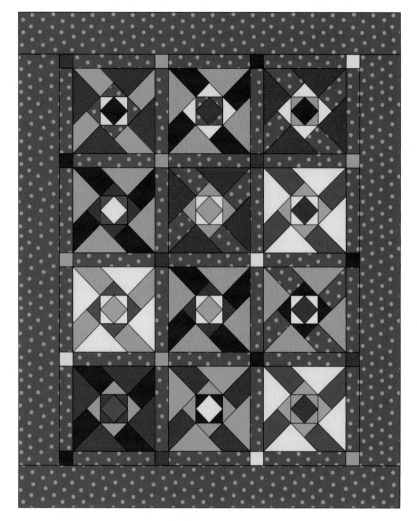

Quilt Diagram

QUILTING AND FINISHING

STEP 1. Mark quilting designs as desired, or see "Quilting Ideas" for suggestions.

STEP 2. Layer the quilt back, batting, and quilt top. Baste the layers together. Trim the quilt back and batting so they are approximately 3 inches larger than the quilt top on all sides.

STEP 3. Hand or machine quilt as desired.

STEP 4. From the binding fabric, make approximately 195 inches of French-fold binding. See "Finishing" on page 223 for instructions on finishing the edges of your quilt.

Quilting Ideas

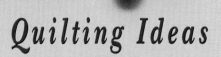

Rather than following the outline of each shape with quilting stitches, this quilt has fan-type quilting over the whole surface of the quilt, as shown. An easy way to create the arcs of a fan without a compass is to trace around a dinner plate, luncheon plate, or soup bowl.

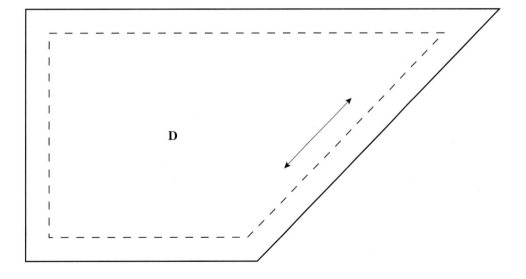

D

Galaxy Star

SKILL LEVEL: Challenging

SIZE: Finished quilt is 48¹/₂ × 48¹/₂ inches

FABRICS AND SUPPLIES

- ¹/₄ yard *each* of four celestial print fabrics for outer borders

- ¹/₄ yard of orange print fabric for inner border

- Four hundred to four hundred fifty 2¹/₂-inch print squares for patchwork. You will need approximately 55 that range from pale yellow to deep yellow-gold, and approximately 350 that are black, dark purple, and pale to dark blue.

- Scraps, approximately 5 inches square, of 16 different yellow and gold print fabrics for large star. Fabrics should range from pale yellow to deep gold.

- 3 yards of fabric for quilt back

- ¹/₂ yard of fabric for binding

- Quilt batting, at least 55 × 55 inches

- Rotary cutter, ruler, and mat

Iowa quiltmaker Mabeth Oxenreider created this dramatic wall quilt by careful shading of dark and light fabrics. Her palette was primarily black, purple, blue, gold, and yellow, with a striking orange narrow border that separates the inner quilt from a wide, pieced outer border. This quilt, with its luminous 1990s colors and celestial theme, is definitely a contemporary scrap quilt.

48½ × 48½ inches

SCRAP RECIPE

Although the basic formula for this quilt is pretty straight-forward, you could alter the color scheme of the interior of the quilt top—making it more blue, for example, depending on the fabrics you have on hand. Just be sure to have plenty of contrast between the stars and the background squares. The star and yellow/gold areas could include some reds, oranges, and pinks in the darker areas, and the sky could handle more greens and teals if you have an abundance of these in your scrap basket.

QUICK CUTTING			
Fabric	**Cut**		
WIDE BORDER	No. of Strips	Strip Width	*From the celestial prints, cut one strip from each of the four border fabrics.
Celestial prints*	4	5"	
NARROW BORDER	No. of Strips	Strip Width	
Orange print	4	1¼"	
LARGE STAR BLOCK	No.	Shape	
Gold and yellow print	32	B diamond	
SMALL STAR BLOCK S	No.	Shape	
Yellow and gold 2½" squares	14	A triangle	
Blue and purple 2½" squares	14	A triangle	

CUTTING

Referring to the "Quick Cutting" chart, cut the number of strips needed from each border fabric using a rotary cutter. Cut all strips across the fabric width. All measurements include ¼-inch seam allowances. If you are using scraps that are less than 42 inches wide, you will need to increase the number of strips you cut accordingly.

Make templates for pattern pieces A and B on page 182. Transfer all markings from the patterns onto the templates. You will use template A to cut triangles for the small Star blocks. The B template is for the diamonds for the large Star block. Make holes at the corners of the B template as described in "Setting In Pieces" on page 217.

PIECING THE SMALL STAR BLOCKS

STEP 1. To make a small star, refer to **Diagram 1** and lay out one gold 2½-inch square, four gold A triangles, four blue or purple A triangles, and four blue or purple 2½-inch squares.

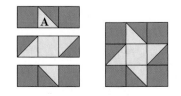

Diagram 1

STEP 2. Join the A triangles to make triangle square units. Press seam allowances toward the darker fabrics.

STEP 3. Join the triangle square units and the squares into rows. Press seam allowances in opposite directions from row to row. Join the rows. Repeat to make a total of two small Star blocks.

STEP 4. In the same manner, refer to **Diagram 2** to make one Half Star block of each type. Pay careful attention to the angles of the seams.

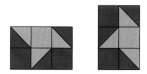

Diagram 2

PIECING THE LARGE STAR BLOCK

STEP 1. To make the large star, refer to the photograph of the quilt on page 177 to lay out 32 B diamonds. Arrange the diamonds so that the star will be light yellow on one side and dark gold on the other.

STEP 2. Join pairs of diamonds, as shown in **Diagram 3**. Press seam allowances in opposite directions. Join paired diamonds to make eight four-diamond units.

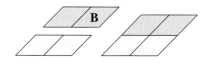

Diagram 3

STEP 3. Lay out the four-diamond units, as shown in **Diagram 4.** Join four four-diamond units to make half the star. When joining units, stop sewing ¼ inch from the raw edge of the fabric at the end of the seam that will be away from the center of the star. Backstitch to secure the seam. Make a second half star. Join the two halves to complete the star.

Diagram 4

STEP 4. Turn under and baste a scant ¼-inch seam allowance around the outside edges of the completed star.

ASSEMBLING THE QUILT TOP

STEP 1. Referring to the **Quilt Assembly Diagram** on page 181 and the photograph of the quilt on page 177, lay out the 2½-inch squares, the small stars, and small half stars, as shown in the diagram. A design wall is very helpful when laying out the squares. See "Make

After you've spent a long time positioning and repositioning your hundreds of squares to create the subtle gradations of color you desire for this quilt, you certainly don't want to "rearrange" your pattern again when transporting the pieces from your design wall to your sewing machine!

We suggest pinning the squares together and joining them in long vertical rows, one row at a time. When you pin the squares together for a row, don't worry about neat pinning—just pin so you know which side to sew. Put two pins at the top of the top square to remind you which end is up.

After you've joined all the squares for one row, press the seam allowances in one direction, toward the top edge of the quilt in the first row, for example. Once you've joined the squares for the second row, press those seams toward the bottom edge of the quilt. Keep alternating pressing directions so that when you join the rows, seam allowances will abut.

an Instant Design Wall" on page 209 for a quick-and-easy version. Position and reposition the colors as needed to achieve the blending and gradation you want.

STEP 2. Sew the squares together in vertical rows. Join the rows to create sections numbered 1 through 6 on the **Quilt Assembly Diagram,** inserting small Star blocks and Half Star blocks, as shown. Sometimes you will need to sew a shorter strip of squares to the side, top, or bottom of a Star block before constructing the larger section.

STEP 3. Join the sections of the quilt top together in numerical order. Join sections 1, 2, and 3 together as vertical rows. Join sections 4 and 5. Sew section 6 to the top of the section 4/5 unit. Sew the resulting unit to the section 1/2/3 unit to complete the inner quilt.

STEP 4. Referring to the photograph of the quilt on page 177, position the prepared large star on top of section 4 of the quilt top. Carefully pin in place and hand appliqué. The straight edges of the star appliqué should line up with the seams of the squares of section 4, as shown in the **Quilt Assembly Diagram.** If desired, turn the work to the wrong side and trim the patchwork from behind the star.

STEP 5. Measure the width of the quilt top through the center. Trim two of the narrow orange print border strips to this length. Sew

borders to the top and bottom edges of the quilt top. Press seam allowances toward borders. Measure the length of the quilt top through the center, including the borders you just added. Trim the two remaining border strips to this length. Sew the borders to the sides of the quilt top. Press seam allowances toward the borders.

STEP 6. Cut each of the four outer border fabric strips in two unequal length pieces. Make a pieced border for each of the four sides of the quilt by joining two different border fabrics. Plan the borders so that the same fabric will be at adjacent corners. Join the strips with diagonal seams, as shown in **Diagram 5.**

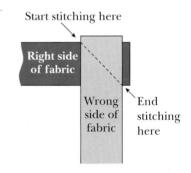

Diagram 5

STEP 7. Measure the width of the quilt through the center. Trim the top and bottom borders to this length. Sew the borders to the quilt top. Press seam allowances toward borders. Measure the length of the quilt top. Measure and trim the side borders to this length. Add the borders to the sides and press.

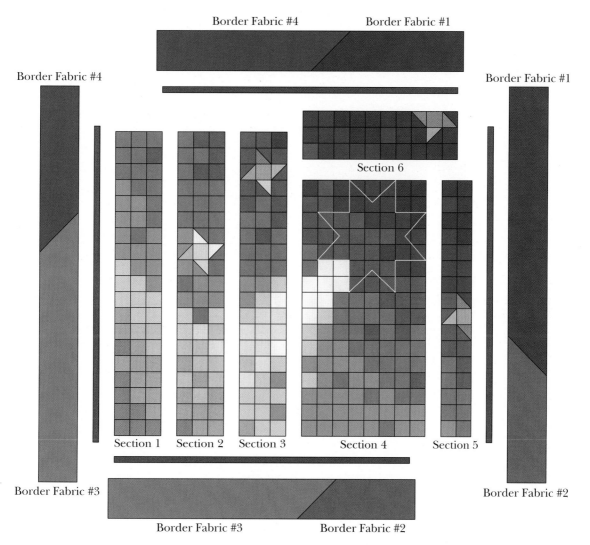

Quilt Assembly Diagram

QUILTING AND FINISHING

STEP 1. Mark quilting designs as desired, or see "Quilting Ideas" on page 182 for suggestions.

STEP 2. To piece the quilt back, cut the backing fabric crosswise into two equal lengths. Cut a 10-inch-wide strip from one piece. Trim the selvages, and sew the narrow strip to the side of the full panel. Press the seams toward the narrow strip.

STEP 3. Layer the quilt back, batting, and quilt top. Baste the layers together. Trim the quilt back and batting so they are approximately 3 inches larger than the quilt top on all sides.

STEP 4. Hand or machine quilt as desired.

STEP 5. From the binding fabric, make approximately 210 inches of French-fold binding. See "Finishing" on page 223 for details on finishing the edges of your quilt.

Quilting Ideas

Quilting on the star patchwork is ¼ inch from the seams. The quilt shown also has free-motion machine quilting in the yellow/gold area to resemble the tail of a comet. The other areas of the quilt are machine quilted with the small Star block design and the Moon and Planet Quilting Designs. The border is quilted in a random meandering design, with some of the stars and planets in the fabric outlined in quilting.

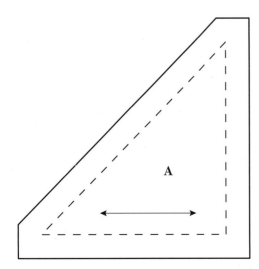

A

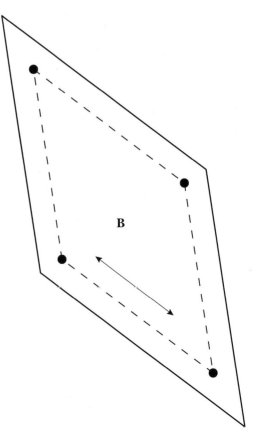

B

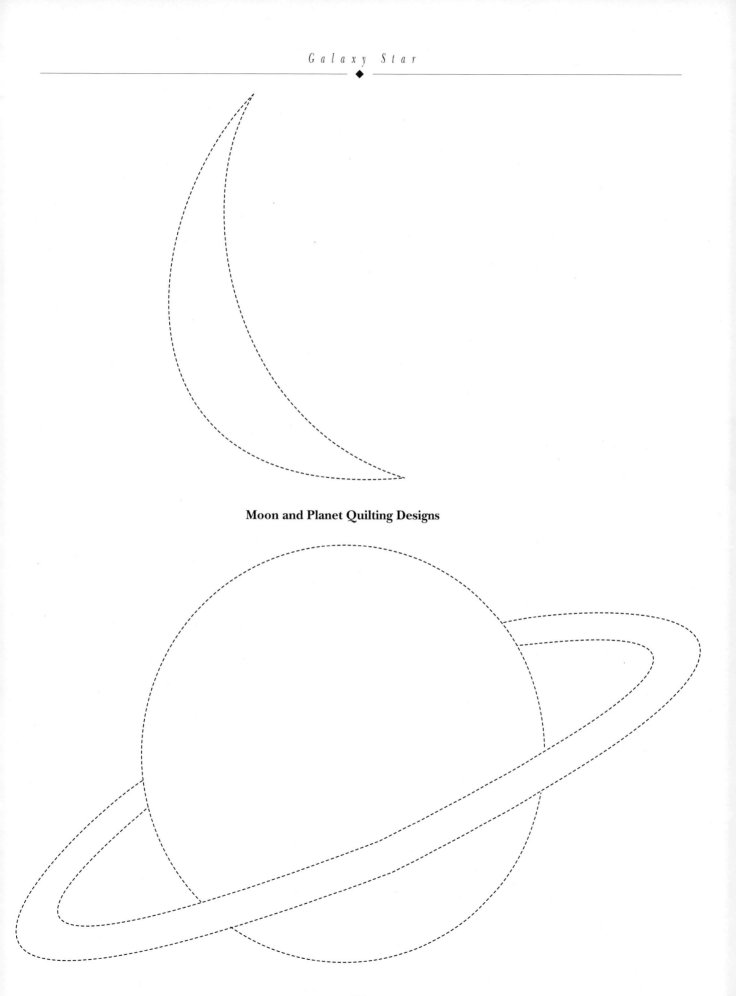

Moon and Planet Quilting Designs

One Patch Wonders

THE MANY LOOKS OF ONE PATCH QUILTS

One patch quilts—quilts made from only one shape repeated in allover fashion—have been popular since pre-Colonial days. Squares, hexagons, and triangles were the patchwork of the day in England during most of the eighteenth century and were probably the shapes used for the earliest American quilts. Charm quilts, one patch quilts with no fabric used more than once, are the rage at least once every century, always when printed cottons are at their most abundant.

It's no surprise that today's quilters still enjoy working with one patch quilts, whether in charm quilt form or otherwise. There is no better way to take pleasure in fabric than by seeing hundreds, even thousands of prints all together in one quilt.

Rectangles lend themselves nicely to a setting of offset rows, like a brick wall, as in Homespun Bricks on page 194. Set lights and darks together as a nine patch or place them in a barn-raising setting. Make miniature quilts by cutting narrow leftover strips into rectangles. Sew them together for doll quilts or wallhangings—a perfect gift for a child.

Use squares as the building blocks for gorgeous watercolor quilts, placing colors to give the illusion of dimension and larger shapes. Colorwash Trio on page 204 is based on 2½-inch squares, a perfect size for making a dent in your scrap collection. Another way to work with squares is simply to alternate lights and darks, 2½ inches or smaller, for a wonderfully simple little quilt.

Forty-five degree diamonds such as those in Hit or Miss Diamonds on page 188 can be sewn together in vertical or horizontal rows in varying color placement schemes for infinite variety.

Triangles of the same size can be set together in myriad ways. In the Hourglass Charm Quilt on page 199, triangles are cut from squares and sewn together randomly without regard to color and value. To get a different effect, sew dark and light triangles together consistently and play with the settings. You could create a pinwheel effect or a zigzag look. Many blocks are composed of half-square triangles, and while they are not technically one patch quilts, each triangle is the same size and shape—a super way to use up leftover bits and pieces of fabric.

Hit or Miss Diamonds

SKILL LEVEL: Intermediate

SIZE: Finished quilt is
$60^1/2 \times 77^1/2$ inches

FABRICS AND SUPPLIES

- 36 strips, *each* 3×44 inches, of assorted red, purple, pink, and turquoise scrap fabrics for the quilt center (Or purchase $1/8$-yard of each fabric and cut strips.)

- $1^1/2$ yards of orange red print fabric for borders and binding

- 1 yard of turquoise print fabric for borders

- $5/8$ yard of fuchsia print fabric for edges of top and bottom borders

- $3^3/4$ yards of fabric for quilt back

- Quilt batting, at least 67×84 inches

- Rotary cutter, ruler with 45 degree angle lines, and mat

Patchwork diamond shapes often appear in star quilts or other designs that call for set-in pieces. This energetic one-patch diamond pattern made by Liz Porter allows you to use diamonds in vertical rows with no setting in. Our instructions are for making strip sets and then rotary cutting strings of prejoined diamonds from the strip sets.

60½ × 77½ inches

SCRAP RECIPE

Liz chose analogous colors of red and purple for most of the diamonds in the center of her quilt. To add interest to the quilt center she used a variety of prints, ranging from multi-colored tropical ones to sub-dued patterns that appear almost solid. A few turquoise diamonds add spice to the quilt center. Vibrant orange red and a clear turquoise work well as the border fabrics.

Some alternate color schemes for this quilt include soft pastels, bright jewel tones, or subdued country colors. Begin by choosing the scrap fabrics for the quilt center; then choose border fabrics that complement the center fabrics.

QUICK CUTTING			
Fabric	**Cut**		**From the red print, reserve the remaining red print fabric for binding.*
BORDER STRIP SETS	No. of Strips	Strip Width	
Red print*	10	3"	
Turquoise print	10	3"	
Fuchsia print	6	3"	

QUICK CUTTING

Referring to the "Quick Cutting" chart, cut the number of strips needed for the borders from each fabric using a rotary cutter. Cut all strips across the fabric width. All measurements include ¼-inch seam allowances. If you are using scraps that are less than 42 inches wide, you will need to increase the number of strips you cut accordingly.

MAKING THE RANDOM SEGMENTS

STEP 1. Referring to **Diagram 1,** make six Type A strip sets and six Type B strip sets by combining the 36 strips for the quilt center. Combine the strips randomly to get different color combinations for each strip set. Offset the strips by 3 inches, as shown. Type A and Type B strip sets are offset in opposite directions. Press seam allowances to one side.

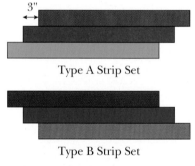

Type A Strip Set

Type B Strip Set

Diagram 1

STEP 2. Cut a total of 45 segments of three joined diamonds from the Type A strip sets, as shown in **Diagram 2.** Begin by trimming the left end of a strip set at a 45 degree angle. Cut three-diamond segments by making cuts parallel to the 45 degree angle cut and 3 inches apart. Label Type A segments and set aside.

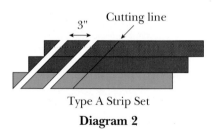

Type A Strip Set

Diagram 2

STEP 3. In a similar manner, cut a total of 45 segments of three joined diamonds from the Type B strip sets. See **Diagram 3.** Be sure to cut at different slants for the Type A and Type B strip sets. Label Type B segments and set aside.

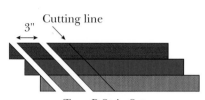

Type B Strip Set

Diagram 3

MAKING THE TOP AND BOTTOM BORDER SEGMENTS

STEP 1. Combine the border strips, offsetting them by 3 inches, in the order shown in **Diagram 4.** Make three Type A border strip sets and three Type B border strip sets. Press seam allowances to one side.

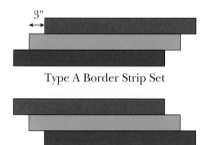

Type A Border Strip Set

Type B Border Strip Set

Diagram 4

STEP 2. Cut 22 Type A and 22 Type B three-diamond border segments as you did in Steps 2 and 3 for "Making the Random Segments." Refer to **Diagrams 2** and **3.** Cut the Type A and Type B segments in opposite directions, as shown in the diagrams.

Quilt Diagram

ASSEMBLING THE QUILT CENTER

STEP 1. Referring to the **Quilt Diagram,** lay out the three-diamond segments in vertical rows, placing border segments along the top and bottom edges. Make nine rows with Type A segments and nine rows with Type B segments. Each row should have five random and two three-diamond border segments.

STEP 2. Join the segments into vertical rows. Press seam allowances toward the top of the quilt in the Type A rows and toward the bottom of the quilt in the Type B rows. Join the rows. You may want to pin at the point where diamond seams meet along the rows. Press the seam allowances to one side. Be very careful when pressing, since you are working with many bias edges.

To make your quilt longer, simply make additional random strip sets and add extra diamonds to each vertical row. Keep an odd number of diamonds in each vertical row so the side border sequence works out correctly. To make the quilt wider, make more vertical rows for the inner quilt before adding the side borders.

MAKING AND ADDING THE SIDE BORDERS

STEP 1. Referring to **Diagram 5,** make one Type A and one Type B strip set. Remember to offset the strips differently in the two types of strip sets. Press seam allowances to one side.

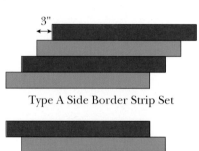

3"

Type A Side Border Strip Set

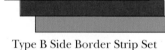

Type B Side Border Strip Set

Diagram 5

STEP 2. Cut eight four-diamond segments from each strip set, referring to **Diagrams 2** and **3** on pages 190–191.

STEP 3. Make two Type A and two Type B vertical rows with four four-diamond border segments in each row. Remove one diamond from each row so the rows have 15 individual diamonds in them, and the color sequence will work correctly with the top and bottom borders. Add a top and bottom border three-diamond segment to the top and bottom of each row. Press seam allowances toward the top of the quilt in the Type A rows and toward the bottom of the quilt in the Type B rows.

STEP 4. Join Type A and Type B rows to opposite sides of the quilt center. Press seam allowances to one side.

QUILTING AND FINISHING

STEP 1. Mark quilting designs as desired, or see "Quilting Ideas" for suggestions.

STEP 2. To piece the quilt back, cut the backing fabric into two $1\frac{7}{8}$-yard pieces. Cut one piece in half lengthwise. Trim the selvages, and sew a half panel to each long side of the full panel. Press the seam allowances toward the narrow panels. The seams on the quilt back will run parallel to the top and bottom quilt edges.

STEP 3. Layer the quilt back, batting, and quilt top. Baste the layers together. Trim the quilt back and batting so they are approximately 3 inches larger than the quilt top on all sides.

STEP 4. Hand or machine quilt as desired.

STEP 5. Using a ruler and tailor's chalk, mark a binding placement line along the top and bottom quilt edges $\frac{1}{4}$ inch beyond the outer points of the turquoise zigzags. Attaching the binding before cutting the points off keeps the edges from stretching and helps the edges stay sewn.

Quilting Ideas

On the quilt shown, the center random section was machine quilted ¼ inch to each side of all vertical seams. The bottom, top, and side borders have quilting that follows the zigzag pattern ¼ inch from the seams, as shown. An even easier way to quilt would be to extend vertical lines of quilting from the top edge to the bottom edge.

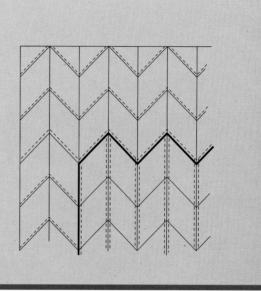

STEP 6. Make approximately 290 inches of French-fold binding. See "Finishing" on page 223 for details on finishing the edges of your quilt.

STEP 7. Sew the binding to the quilt, aligning the raw edges of the binding along the placement line on the top and bottom quilt edges.

Trim excess fabric along the top, bottom, and side quilt edges. Turn the folded edge of the binding to the quilt back and hand finish.

Homespun Bricks

SKILL LEVEL: Easy

SIZE: Finished quilt is
58³/₄ × 69¹/₂ inches

Finished brick is
2¹/₂ × 5¹/₂ inches

FABRICS AND SUPPLIES

- 1³/₈ yards of navy plaid fabric for outer border and binding

- ⁵/₈ yard of red plaid fabric for inner border

- ¹/₈ yard *each* of 20 assorted medium checks, plaids, stripes for bricks

- ¹/₈ yard *each* of 10 assorted light checks, plaids, stripes for bricks

- 3¹/₂ yards fabric for quilt back

- Quilt batting, at least 65 × 76 inches

- Rotary cutter, ruler, and mat

What could be more country than a homespun lap quilt? Mary Jo Kellog of Iowa cut simple rectangles from plaid, checked, and striped fabrics and arranged them in offset rows to create her Homespun Bricks quilt. Don't worry if the plaids are cut off grain or the stripes run in different directions. Break the rules for a casual, homespun-looking quilt that definitely says "curl up with me!"

58¾ × 69½ inches

SCRAP RECIPE

The use of homespun fabrics gives this quilt a distinctive country look. If plaids and stripes are a touch too rustic for your decor, try using scraps in the same color scheme that include florals, geometrics, paisleys, and others. You can even give the quilt a more modern feel by choosing an entirely different color plan. Mellow fall colors would look great, as would a cooler blue-green-purple palette. Just remember that placement of lights and darks is important to the overall design of this quilt.

QUICK CUTTING					
Fabric	First Cut		Second Cut		*From the navy plaid, reserve the remaining fabric for binding.*
BRICKS	No. of Strips	Strip Width	No.	Shape	
Mediums & darks	20	3"	140	3"×6"	
Lights	10	3"	70	3"×6"	
BORDERS	No. of Strips	Strip Width	No.	Shape	
Navy plaid*	7	4½"	—	—	
Red plaid	7	2½"	—	—	

QUICK CUTTING

Referring to the "Quick Cutting" chart, cut the number of strips needed from each fabric using a rotary cutter. Cut all strips across the fabric width. All measurements include ¼-inch seam allowances. If you are using scraps that are less than 42 inches wide, you will need to increase the number of strips you cut accordingly.

PIECING THE QUILT TOP

STEP 1. Referring to the **Row Diagram,** join three light bricks and six medium or dark bricks in the order shown to make one row. Press the seam allowances to one side. Repeat to make a total of 23 rows.

STEP 2. Referring to the **Assembly Diagram,** lay out the rows in a pleasing manner. Join the rows, off-setting the rows as shown. Press the seam allowances to one side.

STEP 3. Trim both sides of the quilt top even with the shorter bricks, as shown in the **Assembly Diagram.**

STEP 4. Cut one red border strip in half. To make the top and bottom borders, join one full-length and one half-length border strip for each border. Join two full-length red border strips to make each side border.

STEP 5. Measure the length of the quilt top through the center, and trim the side borders to this measurement. Sew the borders to the

Row Diagram

Trim   Trim

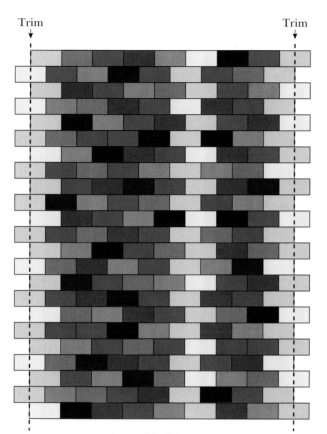

Assembly Diagram

To speed up cutting the many rectangles needed for this quilt, stack strips atop each other before subcutting them. Stack strips so you have six to eight layers if you have a large rotary cutter or four layers if you have a small rotary cutter. Carefully align the raw edges of the strips before cutting.

sides of the quilt top. Press the seam allowances toward the borders. Measure the width of the quilt top through the center, including the side borders, and trim the top and bottom borders to this length. Sew the borders to the top and bottom edges of the quilt top, pressing the seam allowances toward the borders.

STEP 6. In the same manner, make and add the navy plaid borders to the quilt top. See the **Quilt Diagram** on page 198 for the finished quilt top.

QUILTING AND FINISHING

STEP 1. Mark quilting designs as desired, or see "Quilting Ideas" on page 198 for suggestions.

STEP 2. To piece the quilt back, cut the backing fabric into two 1¾-yard pieces. Cut one piece in half lengthwise. Trim the selvages, and sew a half panel to each side of the full panel. Press the seam allowances toward the outer panels. The seams will run parallel to the top and bottom edges of the quilt.

STEP 3. Layer the quilt back, batting, and quilt top. Baste the layers

Quilt Diagram

together. Trim the quilt back and batting so they are approximately 3 inches larger than the quilt top on all sides.

STEP 4. Hand or machine quilt as desired.

STEP 5. From the navy plaid fabric, make approximately 275 inches of French-fold binding by joining the binding strips with diagonal seams. See "Finishing" on page 223 for instructions on finishing the edges of your quilt.

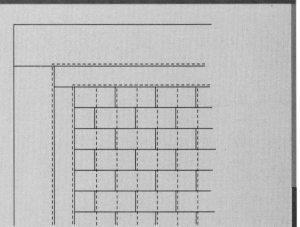

Quilting Ideas

This vesion of Homespun Bricks was quilted in parallel vertical lines that run along the end of some bricks and through the center of the adjacent bricks, as shown. This type of design would not have to be marked, although if you don't trust yourself to eyeball your stitches through the center of the blocks, you could use a strip of masking tape running from the seam allowances in alternate blocks as a guide.

If you want to add more elaborate quilting, try cross-hatching, or perhaps try several different designs in the bricks, such as parallel vertical lines, diagonal lines, cross-hatching, or echo quilting.

Hourglass Charm Quilt

This simple one patch quilt is an exciting scrapbook

for anyone who enjoys fabric history. Each of its 880

different fabrics, or "charms," appears only

once. Charm quilts—quilts with no two

patches alike—were a Victorian fad, pop-

ular in the 1930s and with current renewed in-

terest beginning in the late 1980s. The anonymous

maker of this nineteenth-century quilt surely enjoyed

fabrics just as much as her quilting sisters do today.

SKILL LEVEL: Easy

SIZE: Finished quilt is 94 × 102 inches

Finished block is 8 inches square

Number of blocks: 110

Quilt owner: Judy Roche

FABRICS AND SUPPLIES

- 3 yards of brown print fabric for borders
- Scraps, *each* approximately 5 1/2 inches square, of 880 different fabrics for the patches
- 8 5/8 yards of fabric for quilt back
- 3/4 yard of fabric for binding
- Quilt batting, at least 100 × 108 inches
- Rotary cutter, ruler, and mat

AMERICAN COUNTRY SCRAP QUILTS

94 × 102 inches

Hourglass Charm Quilt

QUICK CUTTING					
Fabric	First Cut		Second Cut		*From the 880 fabrics, you will have an extra triangle of each fabric.
	No.	Shape	No.	Shape	
BLOCKS					
880 fabrics*	880	4⅞" ▢	1,760	◩	
BORDERS	No.	Size	†From the brown print, cut the strips lengthwise.		
Brown print†	4	7½"×108"			

QUICK CUTTING

Referring to the "Quick Cutting" chart, cut the number of pieces needed using a rotary cutter. All measurements include ¼-inch seam allowances. If you prefer to use a template, cut a 4⅞-inch square of paper and cut it once diagonally. Take one of these paper triangles and glue it to your sturdy template material. Seam allowances will be included.

PIECING THE BLOCKS

STEP 1. Referring to the **Block Piecing Diagram,** lay out eight different triangles. Refer to the photograph of the quilt and the **Value Placement Diagram** for ideas on positioning your lights, darks, and mediums.

Block Piecing Diagram

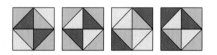

Value Placement Diagram

STEP 2. Join the triangles to make four triangle-square units. Press seam allowances toward the darker fabrics.

STEP 3. Join the triangle squares in two rows of two units per row. Press the seams in opposite directions in the two rows. Join the rows, abutting seam allowances.

STEP 4. Repeat to make a total of 110 Hourglass blocks.

ASSEMBLING THE QUILT TOP

STEP 1. Referring to the **Quilt Diagram** on page 202, lay out the blocks in 11 horizontal rows of ten blocks per row. The heavy lines on the diagram indicate the rows. Join

SCRAP RECIPE

The quilt shown uses lots of brown prints as well as reds, blues, and off-whites, although just about any color is fair game. The quilt is faded, and so the original colors of many of the fabrics have dulled over time. We've pieced a new version of this block using reproduction fabrics to show a totally different look. The Value Placement Diagram will give you some ideas for ways to lay out the Hourglass blocks. Have fun combining fabrics!

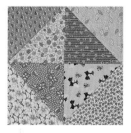

SEW WISE

Y ou can cut two trian-
gles from each fabric

scrap. Keep one and trade the

other with a friend in your

local guild or a "scrap pen

pal" in another state. Several

of the quilting magazines have

classified ad sections in the

back. Each issue includes ads

from quilters who want to

trade fabrics. Or if you sub-

scribe to a computer service,

try one of the online quilting

groups.

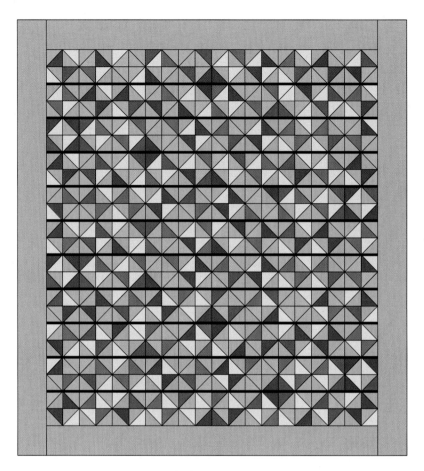

Quilt Diagram

the blocks to make the rows. Press
seam allowances in opposite
directions from row to row. Join
the rows.

STEP 2. Measure the width of the
quilt top through the middle rather
than along an edge. Trim two of
the border strips to this length. Sew
the borders to the top and bottom
edges of the quilt. Press seam allowances toward the borders.

STEP 3. In the same manner, measure the length of the quilt and

trim the remaining two borders to
this length. Sew the borders to the
sides of the quilt top.

QUILTING AND FINISHING
STEP 1. Mark quilting designs as
desired, or see "Quilting Ideas" for
suggestions.

STEP 2. To piece the quilt back,
cut the backing fabric crosswise
into three approximately 103-inch
lengths. Trim the selvages, and sew
the three panels together. Press

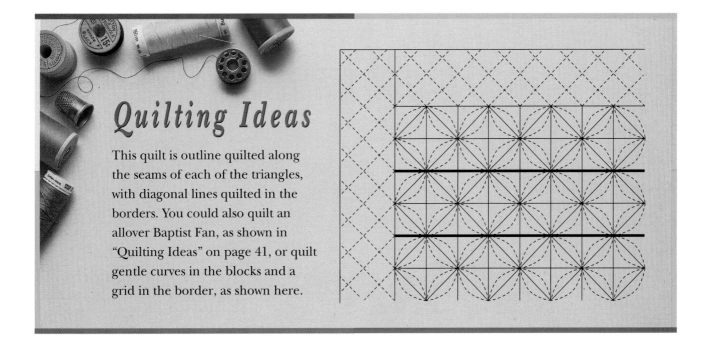

Quilting Ideas

This quilt is outline quilted along the seams of each of the triangles, with diagonal lines quilted in the borders. You could also quilt an allover Baptist Fan, as shown in "Quilting Ideas" on page 41, or quilt gentle curves in the blocks and a grid in the border, as shown here.

the seams toward the outer panels. The seams of the backing will run parallel to the top and bottom edges of the quilt top.

STEP 3. Layer the quilt back, batting, and quilt top. Baste the layers together. Trim the quilt back and batting so they are approximately 3 inches larger than the quilt top on all sides.

STEP 4. Hand or machine quilt as desired.

STEP 5. From the binding fabric, make approximately 405 inches of French-fold binding. See "Finishing" on page 223 for details on finishing the edges of your quilt.

SKILL LEVEL: Easy

SIZE: Color Rotation by JoAnn
Belling is 52 × 52 inches

Square in Square by Julie Hart is
50 × 50 inches

April Showers Bring May Flowers
by Liz Porter is 38 × 38 inches

FABRICS AND SUPPLIES

Color Rotation

- 676 squares, *each* 2½
  inches square, of as-
  sorted multicolored
  print fabrics

- 1⅝ yards of 60-inch-
  wide or 3¼ yards of
  45-inch-wide fabric
  for quilt back

- ⅜ yard of fabric for
  binding

- Quilt batting, at least 58 × 58
  inches square

Square in Square

- 625 squares, *each* 2½ inches
  square, of assorted multicolored
  print fabrics

- 1⅝ yards of 60-inch-wide or 3¼
  yards of 45-inch-wide fabric for
  quilt back

- ⅜ yard of fabric for binding

- Quilt batting, at least 56 × 56
  inches square

April Showers Bring
May Flowers

- 361 squares, *each* 2½ inches
  square, of assorted multicolored
  print fabrics

- 1¼ yards of fabric for quilt back

- ⅓ yard of fabric for binding

- Quilt batting, at least 44 × 44
  inches

Colorwash Trio

Coined by British quiltmaker Dierdre Amsden, the

term colorwash *refers to a style of quilts made with*

many pieces of printed fabric. Amsden spe-

cializes in quilts made from the Liberty

lawn floral prints produced in her

country. Subtle and dramatic shadings are

produced in colorwash quilts by virtually painting

with printed fabrics. Sometimes these quilts are com-

pared with impressionist paintings.

Amsden's methods have interested American

quilters in recent years, and many are experimenting

with her unique approach to creating scrap quilts.

Color Rotation: 52 × 52 inches (top)

Square in Square: 50 × 50 inches (bottom left)

April Showers Bring May Flowers:
38 × 38 inches (bottom right)

SCRAP RECIPE

Fabrics that are printed in a medium-scale design with at least three colors work best in colorwash quilts because they blend more easily with one another. Two-color and tone-on-tone fabrics don't work as well because they don't blend with the other pieces. Floral printed fabrics will help give your project a soft, airy quality, for an impressionist feel. To get this fuzzy, ethereal look, most pieces should be from different fabrics—similar to a charm quilt—but there can be some repetition of fabrics especially in the light areas. You will need light-, medium-, and dark-value fabrics. It's best to cut no more than three or four squares of any one fabric.

THE QUILTS

The Colorwash Trio resulted from get-togethers among our own sewing circle, the May Group. Six of us met at one friend's home on specified days to cut hundreds upon hundreds of fabric squares. Sometimes we cut triangles or diamonds as well.

Before any of the quilts shown were stitched into tops, their makers spent many hours placing and replacing fabrics to achieve just the right value gradations and color shadings. The resulting quilts are quite artistic and, we think, very beautiful.

Choose one of the three designs and use the shaded diagrams that we've included for color placement. Unshaded diagrams are provided if you'd like to create your own shading scheme.

SORTING THE FABRIC SQUARES

Sort the fabrics into five groups by fabric value. When you have completed your sorting, the groups should be approximately equal in size.

The Five Value Groups

- **Group One.** Very light fabrics that are soft pastels or almost white.
- **Group Two.** Medium light fabrics that are pastels and very light backgrounds scantly printed with darker colors.
- **Group Three.** Medium value fabrics—medium blue, mauve, and sage green are typical examples.
- **Group Four.** Medium dark fabrics that have a dark background printed with lighter colors.
- **Group Five.** Very dark fabrics—low contrast print fabrics in black, dark brown, navy, maroon, or dark green.

Choose one square as a representative or model of each of the five values. Use these squares as standards to compare with other squares as you sort. Most people use one of two ways to organize as they sort. Some prefer to make five stacks of squares; others make five long rows of squares.

When you have finished sorting for the first time, your groups may be very unequal in size. Balance the size of the groups by looking back through each group. Move the lightest fabrics in a group down to a lighter group and the darkest fabrics up to a darker group.

Methods for Sorting

- **Method 1.** If you normally wear eyeglasses, try sorting with your glasses off. Fuzzy vision will make the prints less distinct. It is easy to be tricked into thinking that a fabric with a black background and large white flowers is a Group Five rather than a Group Four fabric. Seeing the squares only as light, medium, or dark blobs can make sorting easier. This is one of the few times we have found nearsightedness helpful, so take advantage of it!

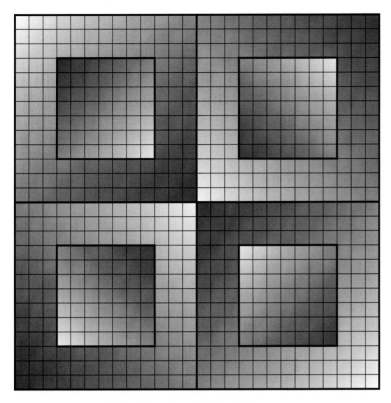

Color Rotation Shaded Diagram

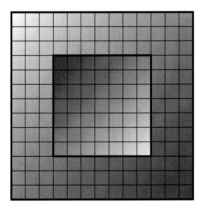

**Color Rotation Basic Unit
(Shaded)**

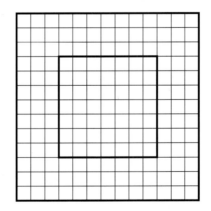

**Color Rotation Basic Unit
(Unshaded)**

S ome medium-value fabrics will be difficult to place so use your best guess to put them into a group. You can always move them to a different group or position in your design later. You can also control the viewer's perception of the value of a fabric square by adjusting the value of fabric squares near it in your design. To make a medium-value fabric square appear lighter, surround it with very dark fabrics. To make a medium-value fabric square appear darker, surround it with very light fabrics.

• **Method 2.** Try looking at the fabric squares through a piece of red plastic. Quilt shops often sell value viewing aids, also called value finders or value filters,

made of red acrylic plastic. You can make a simple, inexpensive value viewing aid by purchasing a red plastic report cover at an office supply store. To intensify the

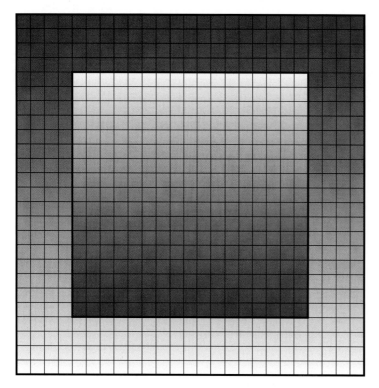

Square in Square Shaded Diagram

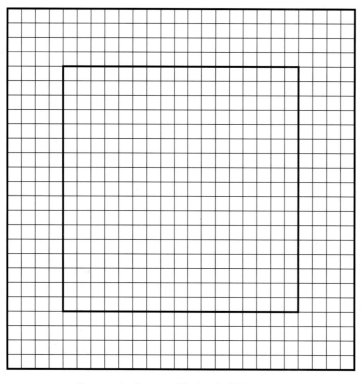

Square in Square Unshaded Diagram

color, cut the folder in half and stack the halves so you look through four layers of plastic.

- **Method 3.** As a way to double-check your value groupings, randomly choose one square from each of the five groups. Tape the squares to a piece of paper and label each square by group. Photocopy the paper with the attached squares. Your photocopy should show five different shades of gray, ranging from almost white to almost black.

PLANNING YOUR DESIGN

A shaded quilt diagram has been given for each of the quilts. If you want to follow these diagrams, use Group One fabrics in the lightest areas and Group Five fabrics in the darkest areas. Use the three medium value groups to shade between the light and dark areas. Build areas of concentrated color by grouping similar color squares together. For example, to make a dark area appear red, include orange red, red, maroon, and squares with dark backgrounds and red printed designs near each other.

If you prefer to try a different shading scheme, use an unshaded layout for each of the wall quilts. The main design areas are indicated with heavy lines. Photocopy these layouts and experiment with shading them in different ways. Use a pencil to shade the diagrams to indicate light, medium, and dark areas.

Make an Instant Design Wall

For an inexpensive and portable design wall that is great to use at home or take to workshops, use flannel-backed plastic. We either purchase this fabric by the yard at a variety or fabric store or purchase a picnic tablecloth at a discount store. As you select your design wall fabric, pay attention to the flannel side of the material. Look for a nice fuzzy flannel on the back side—don't get caught in the trap of being too discriminating about how the printed side looks!

To help you position the squares in straight lines, use a permanent marking pen (such as a Sharpie) and a yardstick to draw a grid on the flannel side. If the plastic side of the material you purchased is printed in a geometric design such as a plaid or checks, you may be able to see the design faintly through the flannel and use those lines as guidelines for the placement of your fabric squares.

Place the plastic side of the material against the wall with the flannel side facing you. Use a gen-erous amount of masking tape to secure the material to the wall. If you do not tape the material adequately, you run the risk of having it fall off the wall as you add fabric squares.

If it becomes necessary to take the design down off the wall, we find we can usually transport it successfully without pinning all the squares in place. Have a friend help you turn up about 6 inches of the material along the bottom edge. Continue to turn up the material so you always have plastic against your fabric squares. The fabric squares will not adhere to the plastic and will tend to stay in place against the flannel. When you have folded all the way to the top edge, loosen the masking tape and remove the folded piece from the wall. Fold the outside edges to the middle and fold again to make a small packet. To rehang your portable design wall, unfold the packet. Have someone help you hold the folded piece against the wall, se-curely tape the top edge in place, and carefully unfold your project.

ASSEMBLING YOUR DESIGN

Referring to your shaded diagram, lay out fabric squares to create the effect you desire. Adjust the position of the squares as needed to improve your design. To get the truest sense of how your design will look when sewn, try to place the squares right next to each other so little or no background from your design wall shows through.

We often like to let our laid-out designs "cure" for a few days before we sew them together. We keep the design on the wall, and as we pass a project each day, we reposition or replace any squares that seem out of place.

Evaluating Your Overall Design

Determining how successful your project is when you are standing just a foot away while placing squares is often difficult. Remember to step back and look. Colorwash quilts are usually most effective when viewed from a bit of a distance. This is why they work so well as wall pieces.

If you are working in a small area, you can try these tricks to get a better overall view of your project.

- View your design through a camera. If you have a Polaroid camera, you may want to take some in-progress photos to study.

- View your design through a re-ducing lens. You can purchase one at many quilt shops or at an art supply store.

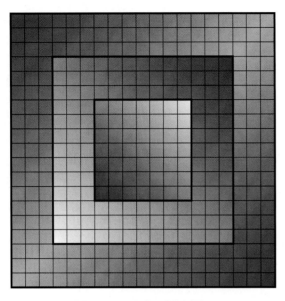

April Showers Bring May Flowers
Shaded Diagram

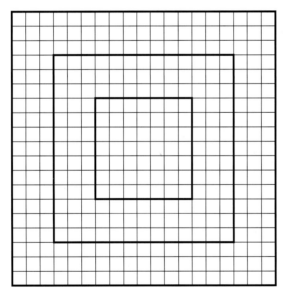

April Showers Bring May Flowers
Unshaded Diagram

- View your design through a peephole like those placed in entryway doors. You can purchase one inexpensively at most hardware stores and lumberyards.

- Try squinting as you view your design. If you are nearsighted, you can get the same effect by looking at your design with your glasses off.

When you are satisfied with your design, join the squares into rows. Press the seam allowances in alternate directions from row to row. Join the rows.

QUILTING AND FINISHING

STEP 1. Mark quilting designs as desired, or see "Quilting Ideas" for suggestions.

STEP 2. If necessary, piece the quilt back so it is approximately 3 inches larger than the quilt top on all sides.

STEP 3. Layer the quilt back, batting, and quilt top. Baste the layers together. Trim the quilt back and batting so they are approximately 3 inches larger than the quilt top on all sides.

STEP 4. Hand or machine quilt as desired.

STEP 5. Measure the perimeter of your quilt. Make enough French-fold binding to go around your quilt plus approximately 15 inches extra for mitering the corners and finishing the end. See "Finishing" on page 223 for details on finishing the edges of your quilt.

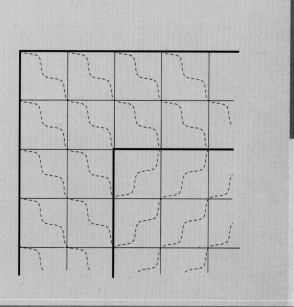

Quilting Ideas

These quilts were all machine quilted in a similar manner with a wavy line going diagonally through the blocks as shown. You may want to change direction wherever darks and lights come together. We were often able to gauge the quilting lines with a quilting guide attached to our machine. Check your sewing machine's accessory box to see if you have one of these curved metal arms.

Quiltmaking Essentials

There were days when templates were made from newspaper or cardboard, piecework was cut out with scissors, and blocks were stitched by hand or treadle sewing machine. Today we cut quickly and accurately with rotary cutters and sew nonstop on computerized machines. But it's still the lure of fabric—the textures, colors, and the tactile quality of cotton—cut into small bits and sewn back together into a wonderful whole that continues to capture the hearts and minds of quiltmakers. Read on to find all the information you need to create a quilt worthy of admiration in any era.

For each quilt in this book, the instructions include a list of all necessary fabrics and supplies, step-by-step directions for making the project, and full-size patterns. In this section, we describe the methods you'll need for many of the projects. You will be referred to these methods as needed throughout the book.

SUPPLIES TO HAVE ON HAND

You'll need some basic sewing supplies such as needles, pins, thread, and scissors. A few of the quilts require specialized supplies, which are listed with those projects. The following list includes other items to have on hand for making most of the quilts.

Rotary cutter: For greater speed and accuracy, cut most of the pieces with a rotary cutter rather than with scissors. See the section on page 214 for tips on rotary cutting. A heavy-duty rotary cutter works better than a small one for cutting fabric strips.

Plastic ruler: High-quality see-through plastic rulers are available in a variety of sizes. The most useful size for rotary cutting is 6 × 24 inches, with increments marked in inches, quarter inches, and eighth inches, as well as marked guidelines for cutting 45 and 60 degree angles. Two other useful tools are a ruled plastic square, 12 × 12 inches or larger, and a 6 × 12-inch ruler handy for cutting strip sets into patchwork segments.

Cutting mat: A self-healing mat won't dull the edge of your cutter blade. A good size for a cutting mat is 18 × 24 inches.

Template plastic or cardboard: Templates are rigid master patterns used to mark patchwork and appliqué shapes on fabric. Thin, semitransparent plastic, available at quilt and craft shops, is ideal, although poster board also works well.

Plastic-coated freezer paper: Quilters have discovered many uses for freezer paper, which is sold in grocery stores. Choose a high-quality brand, such as Reynolds. You'll need this type of paper for several of the methods we've included in our instructions.

ABOUT FABRIC

The instructions for each quilt list the amount of 44/45-inch fabric you will need. When choosing fabrics, most experienced quilters insist on 100 percent cotton broadcloth or dress-weight fabric because it presses well and handles easily, whether you are sewing by hand or machine.

If there is a quilt shop in your area, the sales staff there can help you choose fabrics. You'll find many reproduction fabrics available today that are ideal for achieving the period look of antique quilts. Many other fabric stores also have a section of 100 percent cotton fabrics for quilters.

Keep in mind the amount of time you will be putting into your quilt, and make it a practice to choose high-quality materials. When using scraps left over from other sewing, make certain that they are all-cotton and of similar weight to the other fabrics you're using in your quilt.

Purchasing Fabrics

The amounts listed are based on 44/45-inch fabric, unless stated otherwise. Yardages have been double-checked for accuracy, and they include a bit extra as a margin for error. Be aware, however, that occasionally fabrics are actually narrower than the width listed on the bolt, and that any quilter, no matter how experienced, can make a mistake in cutting. We recommend buying an extra half yard of each of the fabrics for your quilt, just to be safe.

Preparing Fabrics

For best results, prewash, dry, and press your fabrics before using them in your quilts. Use warm water and a mild detergent in your automatic washer. Dry fabric on a medium setting in the dryer or outdoors on a clothesline. Prewashing fabric takes care of shrinkage problems, removes finishes and sizing, and softens the cloth, which makes it easier to handle. It also releases excess dye, making fabrics less likely to bleed after they are combined in a quilt.

Some quilters prefer the crispness of unwashed fabric and feel that they can achieve more accurate machine patchwork by using fabric straight from the bolt. Machine quilters often prefer to use unwashed fabric and wait until the quilt is finished to wash the fabric. This creates a quilt with a crinkled and old-fashioned look, but it also raises the risk of having colors bleed in the finished quilt.

ROTARY CUTTING

We recommend rotary cutting border strips and most of the pieces and have written our instructions accordingly. In addition, for most of the quilts no pattern pieces are given. Instead, the instructions will show you how to measure and rotary cut squares, triangles, rectangles, or diamonds directly from the fabric. For some quilts you will be instructed to cut strips, sew them together into strip sets, and then cut the strip sets into special units to combine with other units.

In addition to being faster than traditional cutting methods, rotary cutting is often more accurate because of the thinness of the cutting blade and the use of precisely calibrated rulers. Here are some helpful tips to keep in mind when rotary cutting.

- Always cover the blade when you're not using it to cut.

- Keep rotary cutters out of children's reach.

- Always cut away from yourself.

- Square off the end of your fabric before measuring and cutting any of the pieces for a quilt, as shown in **Diagram 1.** Align the ruled square exactly with the fabric fold and bring a longer cutting ruler alongside the square. Slide the square away and use your rotary cutter to slice the fabric along the edge of the cutting ruler.

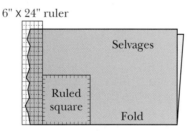

6" X 24" ruler

Selvages

Ruled square

Fold

Diagram 1. Square off the uneven edges of the fabric before cutting the strips.

- Cut strips on the crosswise grain of the fabric, as shown in **Diagram 2,** unless instructed otherwise.

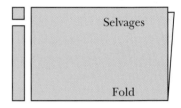

Selvages

Fold

Diagram 2. Cut strips or rectangles on the crosswise grain. Cut the strips into squares.

- Check the fabric periodically to make sure it is square and the strips remain straight.

- To cut squares, begin by cutting one strip. Then cut that strip into squares by cutting across the width of the strip, as shown in **Diagram 2.**

- Cut triangles from squares, as shown in **Diagram 3.** The "Quick Cutting" charts will tell you whether to cut the square into two triangles by making one diagonal cut or into four triangles by making two diagonal cuts.

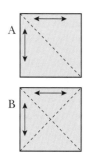

Diagram 3. Cut two triangles from a square by making one diagonal cut (A). Cut four triangles from a square by making two diagonal cuts (B). Dotted lines show cutting. Arrows indicate straight grain.

MAKING AND USING TEMPLATES

The patterns given for patchwork and appliqué pieces are all full size. Whenever possible, instructions are given for using a rotary cutter to quick cut them. If you prefer to make and use templates, use the rotary cutting dimensions to make your templates. For triangles, measure and cut a square out of paper using the "Quick Cutting" chart. Cut the square into triangles and then use the final triangle to make your template.

We favor thin, opaque plastic for templates. Carefully trace the patterns onto the plastic and cut them out with scissors. To make poster-board templates, transfer each pattern to tracing paper, glue the tracing paper to the cardboard, and cut out the templates. Be sure to copy all identification letters and grain line indications onto your templates. Before using them, check your templates against the printed pattern for accuracy.

Most of the patchwork patterns in the book are printed with double lines. If you intend to sew your patchwork by hand, trace the inner line to make finished-size templates. Draw around the template on the wrong side of the fabric, leaving ½ inch between lines for seam allowances, as shown in **Diagram 4.** The lines you draw are the sewing lines. Before you cut out the pieces, add ¼-inch seam allowances around the shapes you have drawn on the fabric.

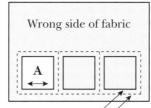

Diagram 4. If piecing by hand, mark around the finished-size template on the wrong side of the fabric. Cut it out, adding ¼-inch seam allowances on all sides.

If you plan to sew your patchwork by machine, use the outer printed line to make templates that have the ¼-inch seam allowances included. Draw around the templates on the wrong side of the fabric, as shown in **Diagram 5.** The line you draw is the cutting line. Sew with an exact ¼-inch seam for perfect patchwork.

Diagram 5. If piecing by machine, use templates with seam allowances included.

Patterns for appliqué pieces are printed with a single line. Make finished-size templates for appliqué pieces. For hand appliqué, draw around templates on the right side of the fabric, leaving ½ inch between pieces, as shown in **Diagram 6.** The lines you draw will be the fold-under lines. Then add scant ¼-inch seam allowances by eye as you cut out each piece.

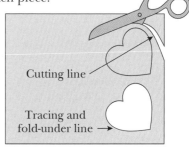

Diagram 6. Draw around the templates on the right side of the fabric for appliqué pieces. Add seam allowances as you cut out the pieces.

TIPS ON PATCHWORK

The standard seam allowance for patchwork is ¼ inch. Accurate seam allowances are a must for accurate patchwork.

When you construct patchwork blocks, keep in mind the basic principles of combining smaller pieces to make larger units, combining larger units into rows or sections, and joining sections into complete blocks. We have included piecing diagrams and step-by-step instructions to help you construct patchwork blocks easily and efficiently.

Whether you sew by hand or machine, lay out the pieces for a block right side up, as shown in the piecing diagrams, before you sew. For quilts with multiple blocks, you may want to cut out the pieces for a sample block first. Piecing this block will allow you to make sure that your fabrics work well together and that you are cutting accurately before you go on to cut out the pieces for the rest of the blocks.

Hand Piecing

For hand patchwork, use finished-size templates to cut your fabric pieces. Join pieces by pin matching marked sewing lines and sewing with a running stitch from seam line to seam line, as shown in **Diagram 7,** rather than from raw edge to raw edge. As you sew,

check to see that your stitching is staying on the lines. Make a backstitch every four or five stitches to reinforce and strengthen the seam. Secure corners with an extra backstitch.

Diagram 7. Join the pieces with a running stitch, backstitching every four or five stitches.

When you cross seam allowances of previously joined smaller units, make a backstitch just before and just after you cross. Leave the seam allowances free, as shown in **Diagram 8,** rather than stitching them down. When your block is finished, press the seam allowances either toward darker fabrics or so they will be out of the way of your planned quilting.

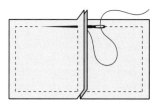

Diagram 8. When hand piecing, leave the seam allowances free by slipping the needle through without stitching them down.

Machine Piecing

For machine patchwork, cut fabric pieces using either templates with ¼-inch seam allowances included or a rotary cutter to quick

cut them as instructed. Before sewing a block, sew a test seam to make sure you are sewing accurate ¼-inch seams. Cut two 3-inch squares and sew them together along one side. Then press the seam, open up the squares, and press the seam again. Measure across the joined squares. If they do not measure exactly 5½ inches, adjust your seam width accordingly.

On many sewing machines, you can use the edge of the presser foot as an accurate seam guide. Another option is to place a piece of masking tape on the throat plate ¼ inch to the right of the needle and use it as a guide.

Adjust the stitch length on your machine to 10 to 12 stitches per inch. Select a neutral-color thread that blends well with the fabrics you are using.

When you join pieces by machine, sew from raw edge to raw edge. Press all seams before crossing them with other seams. When you cross seams, you will be sewing seam allowances down, so before you press, think about the direction in which you want them to lie. When possible, press seam allowances toward darker fabrics to prevent them from showing through lighter ones in the finished quilt. See page 218 for more information on pressing.

When you join rows, press the seams in opposite directions from row to row, as shown in **Diagram 9.** That way, you can abut the seam allowances when you join the rows and produce precisely matched seams.

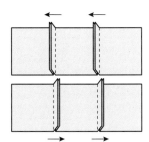

Diagram 9. Press seams in opposite directions from row to row.

When you make multiple blocks, sew pieces together assembly line fashion whenever possible, as shown in **Diagram 10.** Chain piece pairs of pieces or units one after another without cutting the thread between them. Snip units apart, press the seams, and add the next element to growing sections of blocks.

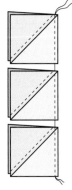

Diagram 10. Feed the units through the machine without cutting the thread.

SETTING IN PIECES

Not all patchwork patterns can be assembled with continuous straight seams. Examples of quilts with set-in pieces are the Feathered World without End on page 156, Rocky Road to Kansas on page 28, and Six-Pointed String Star on page 84.

Setting in pieces by hand is simple. Because you have a marked sewing line, you can easily stop your stitching exactly at the corner, pivot the fabric, adjust and pin the other side of the piece, and complete the seam.

Set-in pieces can be accurately stitched on the sewing machine by adapting hand sewing methods to machine sewing. Follow the instructions below to learn some marking and sewing tricks that can make precision machine stitching easier.

Making Templates

To make the templates, trace both the cutting (outer solid) line and sewing (inner dashed) line onto the template plastic. Carefully cut out the templates along the outer line. Check for accuracy by matching your template to the original pattern.

Use a sewing machine needle or other large needle to make holes in the templates at the corners of the sewing (inner dashed) lines, as shown in **Diagram 11.** The

holes need to be large enough to allow the point of a pencil or other fabric marker to poke through.

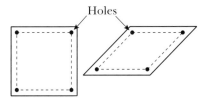

Diagram 11. For setting in pieces by machine, make templates with holes at the setting-in points.

Marking the Fabric

On the wrong side of the fabric, draw around the template. Then, using a pencil, mark dots on the fabric through the holes in the template to create matching points on the fabric piece. Since the templates include seam allowances, you can position pieces next to

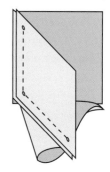

each other so they share cutting lines. Cut out the fabric pieces along the drawn lines. Check to be sure all the pieces have matching points marked on them. If you have forgotten to mark some, reposition the template atop the cutout fabric piece and add the matching points.

Preparing to Sew

Place two fabric pieces right sides together. Put a pin through the matching point on the top piece. Using the same pin, pierce the corresponding matching point on the underneath piece and pin the pieces together. In the same manner, pin the pieces together at the matching point at the end of the seam. **Diagram 12** shows two diamonds pinned at the matching points. Align the raw edges of the pieces between the points, and add additional pins along the seam line as needed.

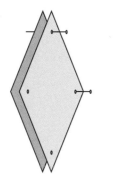

Diagram 12. Place pieces right sides together and pin match at the marked points.

Stitching a Seam

Taking an exact ¼-inch-wide seam, machine stitch from the first matching point to the matching point at the end of the seam, as shown in **Diagram 13**. Stitch only between the points; do not stitch into the seam allowance at the beginning or end of the seam. Secure the beginning and end of your stitching with a few backstitches.

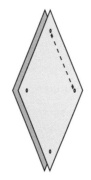

Diagram 13. Stitch from point to point, backstitching at each end of the seam.

To set in a piece, begin by pin matching the piece you want to set in to one side of the opening. Sew the seam from matching point to matching point, as shown in **Diagram 14**. Remove the work from the sewing machine.

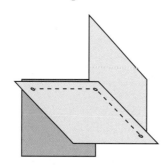

Diagram 14. Pin the piece to one side of the opening, matching dots. Stitch from the edge into the corner.

Align the adjacent edge of the piece you are setting in with the corresponding side of the opening. Pin match and stitch the adjacent seam, sewing from matching point to matching point, as shown in **Diagram 15**. The seam should be smooth, and the corner will lie flat without puckers if you have marked, pinned, and stitched accurately.

Diagram 15. Pin match the adjacent side of the piece and stitch.

Pressing

Because seam allowances at the ends of seams are left unsewn with this method, you are free to wait to make final pressing decisions until the block is assembled. Press the seams in the direction that will make the block lie the flattest, pressing toward the darker fabric whenever possible.

PRESSING BASICS

Proper pressing can make a big difference in the appearance of a finished block or quilt top. Quilters are divided on the issue of whether

steam
or dry pressing
is superior. Experiment
to see which works best for you.
We have included pressing
instructions with each of the quilts,
but here are some general guidelines you can apply to all your
projects:

• Press a seam before crossing it
  with another seam.

• Press seam allowances to one side
  rather than open.

• Whenever possible, press seams
  toward darker fabrics.

• Press seams of adjacent rows of
  patchwork, or rows within blocks,
  in opposite directions so they will
  abut as the rows are joined.

• Press, don't iron. Bring the iron
  down gently and firmly on the
  fabric from above—don't slide it
  across the surface of the patchwork and risk distortion.

• Avoid pressing appliqués after they
  are stitched to the background
  fabric. They are prettiest when
  slightly puffed rather than flat.

TIPS ON APPLIQUÉ

The goal for successful
appliqué is smoothly turned,
crisp edges without unsightly
bumps or gaps. Stitches
should be almost invisible.
Two popular appliqué
methods are:

1. Basting back the seam allowances on appliqué
   pieces before stitching
   them to the background
   fabric;

2. Needle turning the edges
   of appliqué pieces and
   stitching them in place on
   the background fabric as
   you go.

For these methods, use thread
that matches the appliqué pieces,
and stitch the appliqués to the
background fabric with a blind
hem or appliqué stitch, as shown in
Diagram 16. Use long, thin size 11
or size 12 needles marked "sharps."
Make stitches at ⅛-inch intervals
and keep them snug.

Diagram 16. Stitch the appliqués to the
background with a blind hem stitch. The
stitches should be nearly invisible.

When constructing appliqué
blocks, always work from background to foreground. When one
appliqué piece will be covered or
overlapped by another, stitch the
underneath piece to the background fabric first.

Basting Back Method

Mark around finished-size templates on the right side of the
fabric to draw the turning lines.
Cut out pieces, adding a scant ¼-
inch seam allowance to the outside
of the marked line.

For each appliqué piece, turn
the seam allowance under, folding
along the marked line, and thread
baste close to the fold with white or
natural thread. Clip concave curves
and clefts, as shown in **Diagram 17.**

Clip
here

Diagram 17. Clip any clefts and concave
curves, then baste back the seam
allowances.

Do not baste back edges that will
be covered by another appliqué
piece. Pin each appliqué in place

and stitch it to the background fabric, layering pieces where necessary. Remove all basting threads after the pieces are stitched down. Cut away the background fabric from behind pieces when appropriate, as described below.

Needle-Turning Method

For the needle-turning method, cut appliqué pieces a generous ⅛ inch larger than the finished size. Turn under the seam allowances with your needle as you stitch the pieces to the background. Clip concave curves as needed.

Cutting Away Background Fabric behind Appliqués

When appliqué pieces are layered on top of one another, such as the flowers of the Cosmos Garden quilt on page 60, or when quilting is planned on an appliqué piece, such as the pieced blades of fan blocks, then the background fabric should be trimmed away to reduce thickness and make quilting easier. It's also a good idea to trim away the background fabric or underneath layer if they are a darker fabric than the appliqués.

Working from the back, pinch the background or underlying fabric and gently separate it from the appliqué piece. Make a small cut in the background fabric.

Insert scissors in the hole and cut a scant ¼ inch to the inside of the line of appliqué stitches.

ASSEMBLING QUILT TOPS

Most of the quilts we have included have simple settings in which the blocks are sewn together in straight or diagonal rows. On many of our quilt diagrams, we've used heavier lines to indicate rows. For more complicated settings, such as Tulips in the Spring on page 134, or unusual ones, like Expresso Yourself on page 120, pay close attention to the quilt diagram and the detailed assembly instructions.

After all the blocks for a quilt are complete, lay them out right side up, along with any plain blocks and setting pieces, positioned as they will be in the finished quilt. If there are quilting designs for plain setting blocks, it may be helpful to mark them before you sew the top together.

Pin and sew the blocks together in vertical or horizontal rows for straight-set quilts, as shown in **Diagram 18,** and in diagonal rows for diagonal sets, as shown in **Diagram 19.**

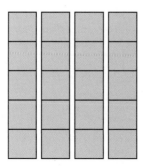

Diagram 18. Join straight-set quilts in vertical rows.

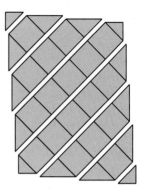

Diagram 19. Join diagonally set quilts in diagonal rows.

Press the seams in opposite directions from row to row. Once all the rows are constructed, join the rows, abutting the pressed seam allowances for accuracy in matching seams. To make the task of assembling a large quilt top manageable, first join rows into pairs and then join those pairs, rather than adding each row to an increasingly unwieldy top.

For medallion-style tops, follow the individual project instructions for constructing the quilt, generally pressing seams toward areas with less patchwork.

When you press a completed quilt top, press the wrong side first, carefully clipping and removing excess threads. Then press the right side, making sure that all of the seams lie flat.

Adding Borders

Directions for adding the appropriate borders are included with the instructions for each quilt. Here are some general tips for successful borders:

• Cut borders the desired finished width plus ½ inch for seam allowances. Always cut border strips several inches longer than needed just to be safe. (Our cutting instructions for borders already include seam allowance and extra length.)

• Before you add borders, measure your completed inner quilt top. Measure through the center of the quilt rather than along the edges, which may have stretched from handling. Use this measurement to determine the exact length to mark and cut borders.

• Measure and mark the sewing dimensions on the borders before sewing them onto the quilt; wait to trim off excess fabric until after the borders are joined to the quilt.

• Fold the border strips in half and press lightly to indicate the halfway mark on each. Align this mark with the center side of your quilt when you pin the border to the quilt.

QUILTING DESIGNS

Along with our quilt instructions, we've included suggestions for quilting in the "Quilting Ideas" boxes and some full-size quilting designs.

Outline quilting is quilting that follows the seams of patchwork, either in the ditch, i.e., right next to the seam, or ¼ inch away from the seams. In-the-ditch quilting does not need to be marked. For ¼-inch outline quilting, you can work by

eye or use ¼-inch masking tape as a stitching guide. You can also mark these and other straight lines lightly with a pencil and ruler.

Motifs such as the feather designs for Aunt Sukey's Choice on page 10 and Grandmother's Fan on page 100 should be marked before the quilt top is layered with batting and backing. The method to use for marking quilting designs depends on whether your fabric is light or dark.

Marking Light Fabrics

If your fabric is a light one that you can see through easily, such as muslin, place the pattern under the quilt top and trace the quilting design onto the fabric. First, trace the design from the book onto good-quality tracing paper or photocopy it. Darken the lines with black permanent marker if necessary. If the pattern will be used many times, glue it to cardboard to make it sturdy. Carefully mark the designs on the fabric, marking a thin, continuous line

that will be covered by the quilting thread. We recommend marking tools such as a silver artist's or quilter's pencil, a mechanical pencil with thin (0.5 mm), medium (B) lead, or a washable graphite pencil sold at quilt shops.

Marking Dark Fabrics

Using a light box, you can trace quilting designs directly onto dark fabrics with the pattern positioned underneath the quilt, as described above. You can also mark quilting designs from the top with a hard-edged template. To make a simple quilting design template, trace the design onto template plastic and cut it out. Draw around the outer edge of the template onto fabric and add any inner lines by eye.

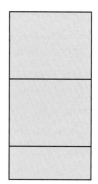

Diagram 21. Divide the yardage crosswise into three equal panels. Sew the three full-width panels together side by side. Layer the backing, batting, and quilt top with the seams running parallel to the short side of the quilt top, as shown. Trim the excess from one panel as needed.

and a center back seam can lead to a more noticeable fold line. For best results, divide one of the fabric backing pieces in half lengthwise, and sew a narrow panel to each side of a full-width central one, as shown in **Diagram 20.** Press all the seams away from the center of the quilt.

QUILT BACKINGS

The materials list that accompanies each quilt includes yardage for the quilt backing. For the small quilts that are narrower than 44 inches wide, simply use a full width of fabric cut several inches longer than the quilt top. For the majority of the quilts, the quilt backing must be pieced, but another option is to purchase 90- or 108-inch-wide fabric sold especially for quilt backings.

Whenever possible, piece quilt backings in vertical panels. Backings for quilts that are 80 inches wide or less can easily be pieced this way from two widths of fabric. You should avoid piecing a back with a seam down the center. The routine folding of a finished quilt can cause creases to form,

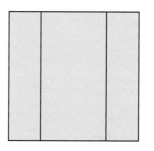

Diagram 20. Divide the yardage in half crosswise; divide one of the pieces in half lengthwise. Sew one of those halves to each side of the full-width piece, as shown.

For quilts that are wider than 80 inches, piecing the back with horizontal seams may make more economical use of your fabric. If this is the case, use three horizontal panels, as shown in **Diagram 21.** Join the full-width panels, layer the backing with the batting and the quilt top, and trim the excess from one of the panels.

TYPES OF QUILT BATTING

Quilters generally spend a lot of time selecting the fabrics for their quilts, but often not enough time choosing the batting they will use. When purchasing a batt, take the time to read the manufacturer's literature and think about the intended use of your quilt. It's also a good idea to talk to experienced quilters about their batting preferences.

One hundred percent polyester battings are very durable and warm. They launder without shrinking and needle easily for hand quilting. All-cotton battings are popular with quilters who like a very flat, old-fashioned appearance, though some cotton battings are more difficult to hand quilt. Another option is cotton/polyester blend batting, which combines the low-loft, sculpted look of cotton with the stability of polyester. Cotton flannel may be substituted for batting for miniature quilts or to give a very thin, flat look.

Before layering the batting with the quilt backing and top, open the package, unroll the batt, and let it relax for several hours to soften the folds, or tumble it in a clothes dryer set on low heat for five to ten minutes.

LAYERING AND BASTING

Once your quilt top is complete and marked for quilting, the batting relaxed, and the backing prepared, you are ready to assemble and baste the layers of the quilt together. Whether you plan to hand or machine quilt, the layers must first be basted evenly, so that the finished quilt will lie flat and smooth. Baste with thread for hand quilting and with safety pins for machine quilting. Follow these steps:

STEP 1. Fold the backing in half lengthwise and press to form a centerline. Place the backing, wrong side up, on a large flat surface, such as two tables pushed together or the floor. To keep the backing taut, secure it with masking tape or clamp it to the table with large binder clips.

STEP 2. Fold the batting in half lengthwise and lay it on top of the quilt backing, aligning the fold with the center crease line of the backing. Open out the batting, and smooth out and pat down any wrinkles.

STEP 3. Fold the quilt top in half lengthwise, right sides together, and lay it on top of the batting, aligning the fold with the center of the batting. Open out the top and remove any loose threads. Check to make sure that the backing and batting are 2 to 3 inches larger than the quilt top on all four sides.

STEP 4. To prepare for hand quilting, use a long darning needle and white sewing thread to baste the layers together, basting lines of stitches approximately 4 inches apart. Baste from the center outward in a radiating pattern, or make horizontal and vertical lines of basting in a grid-work fashion, using seams as guidelines. To prepare for machine quilting, use 1-inch rust-proof brass safety pins to secure the layers together, pinning from the center out approximately every 3 inches.

QUILTING

All of the antique quilts in this book are hand quilted, but most of the new projects are machine quilted. Follow these tips for successful hand or machine quilting:

HAND QUILTING

- Use a hoop or frame to hold the quilt layers taut and smooth while you quilt.
- Use short quilting needles called "betweens" in size 9, 10, or 12.
- Use quilting thread rather than regular sewing thread.
- Pop the knot through the fabric into the batting layer at the begin-

ning and ending of each length of thread so that no knots show on the front or back of the quilt.
- Quilt through all three layers of the quilt with running stitches about ⅛ inch long.

MACHINE QUILTING

- Use a walking or even-feed presser foot for quilting straight lines.
- Use a darning or machine embroidery presser foot for free-motion quilting of curved lines.
- For the top thread, use a color that matches the fabric or clear monofilament nylon thread. Use regular sewing thread in the bobbin.
- To secure the thread at the beginning and end of a design, take extra-short stitches.
- For free-motion quilting, disengage the feed dogs of the sewing machine so you can manipulate the quilt freely. Choose continuous-line quilting designs to reduce the number of times you will need to begin and end a stitching line. Guide the marked design under the needle with both hands, working at an even pace to form even stitches.

FINISHING

The most common edge finish for quilts is binding, cut either on the bias or straight of grain.

We recommend French-fold (double-fold) binding for most quilts. Double-fold binding is easier to apply than single fold binding, and the double thickness adds durability to your quilt. Cut double-fold binding 2 inches wide for quilts with thin batting, such as cotton, and 2¼ inches wide for quilts with thicker batting.

The amount of binding needed for each quilt is included with the finishing instructions. Generally, you will need enough binding to go around the perimeter of the quilt, plus 8 to 10 inches for mitering corners and ending the binding. Three-quarters to 1 yard of fabric will usually make enough binding to finish a full-size quilt.

Joining Straight Strips for Continuous Binding

STEP 1. Refer to the individual project instructions for the amount of binding the quilt requires. Estimate the needed number of strips and cut them across the fabric width.

STEP 2. Join the strips, placing right sides together and sewing diagonal seams, as shown in **Diagram 22.**

STEP 3. For double-fold binding, fold and press the long strip in half lengthwise, wrong sides together.

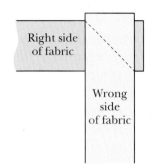

Diagram 22. Place the strips right sides together, positioning each strip ¼ inch in from the end of the other strip. Join with a diagonal seam.

Making Continuous Bias Binding

STEP 1. Measure and cut a square of fabric. A 27-inch square of fabric will yield approximately 350 inches of 2-inch cut binding, which is enough to bind most of the quilts in this book. If you need more than that amount, it's easy to make more binding by cutting another square of fabric in a smaller size. Here's a handy formula for estimating the number of inches of binding you can get from a particular size fabric square: Multiply one side of the square by another side of the square. Divide the result by whatever cut width you desire for the binding strips.

STEP 2. After you've cut the size square of fabric you need for making continuous binding, fold the square in half diagonally and press it lightly. Cut the square into two triangles, cutting on the pressed line.

STEP 3. Place the two triangles right sides together, as shown in **Diagram 23.** Stitch them together with a ¼-inch seam and press the seam open.

Diagram 23. Place the triangles right sides together as shown and stitch.

STEP 4. As shown in **Diagram 24,** mark the cutting lines on the wrong side of the fabric at intervals of the desired strip width, parallel to the bias edges.

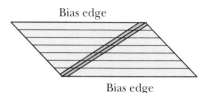

Bias edge

Bias edge

Diagram 24. Open out the two pieces and press the seam open. On the wrong side, mark cutting lines parallel to the bias edges.

STEP 5. Place the marked fabric right side up and fold, as shown in **Diagram 25,** bringing the two non-bias edges together and offsetting the edges by one strip width.

Diagram 25. Bring the nonbias edges together, offsetting them by one strip width. Sew the edges together to create a tube.

STEP 6. Pin the edges together and sew the fabric into a tube,

using a ¼-inch seam. Press the seam open.

STEP 7. Cut on the marked lines, turning the tube as you cut, to make one long bias strip.

STEP 8. To make double-fold binding, fold the long strip in half lengthwise, wrong sides together, and press.

Preparing a Quilt for Binding

Wait to trim excess batting and backing until after you sew the binding strips to the quilt. If the edges of the quilt are uneven after you're finished quilting, use a ruler and pencil to mark a straight line as close as possible to the raw edges of the quilt top. This will help in placing the binding accurately. For best results, use a ruled square to mark placement lines at 90 degree angles at the corners.

Binding a Quilt with Continuous Binding and Mitered Corners

STEP 1. If you have a "walking foot" or even-feed presser foot for your sewing machine, use it to sew on the binding. If you do not have a walking foot, thread baste around the perimeter of the quilt to help avoid puckers.

STEP 2. When you begin to sew on the binding, start at a point that's away from a corner. Place the raw edges of the binding strip even with the raw edge of the quilt top or the placement line.

STEP 3. Turn under the short raw edge approximately 2 inches at the beginning of the binding strip, creating a folded edge. Begin sewing 1 inch away from this fold. With a ¼-inch seam allowance, sew the binding to the quilt, stitching through all three layers.

STEP 4. When you approach a corner, stop stitching exactly ¼ inch away from the corner. Backstitch and remove the quilt from the sewing machine.

STEP 5. Fold the binding up and away from the corner, as shown in **Diagram 26A,** forming a fold at a 45 degree angle.

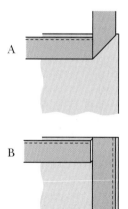

A

B

Diagram 26. Stop stitching ¼ inch from the corner and fold the binding up at a 45 degree angle (A). Fold the binding strip back down, align the raw edges with the side of the quilt top, and stitch the binding in place (B).

STEP 6. Fold the binding strip back down, creating a fold along the top edge of the quilt. Align the raw edges with the adjacent side of the corner.

STEP 7. Begin stitching the next side at the top fold of the binding, as shown in **Diagram 26B** on page 225. Miter all four corners in this manner.

STEP 8. To complete the binding, lay the end of the binding strip over the beginning of the binding. Trim the end of the binding strip so that it extends 1 inch beyond the folded edge at the beginning of the binding and complete the binding seam. The beginning and ending sections overlap approximately 1 inch.

STEP 9. Trim away any excess batting and backing from the edges of the quilt top using scissors or a rotary cutter and ruler. Testing a small section, turn the binding to the back of the quilt to determine the right amount of excess to trim from the quilt. The binding will look better and be more durable if it is filled rather than hollow.

STEP 10. Turn the binding to the back of the quilt and blindstitch the folded edge in place, covering the machine stitches with the folded edge of the binding. Finish the miters at the corners by folding in the adjacent sides on the back of the quilt and placing several blind stitches in the miter, both front and back.

STEP 11. If you plan to add a hanging sleeve to your quilt, follow the instructions below to make and attach the sleeve before turning and finishing the binding.

MAKING A HANGING SLEEVE FOR A QUILT

Many quilters put hanging sleeves on bed quilts as well as on wallhangings so that their work can be exhibited at quilt shows. Use the following procedure to add a 4-inch-wide hanging sleeve.

STEP 1. Cut a strip of muslin or other fabric that is 8½ inches wide and 1 inch shorter than the width of the finished quilt.

STEP 2. Machine hem the short ends by turning under ½ inch on each end of the strip and pressing the fold. Turn under another ½ inch and stitch next to the fold.

STEP 3. Fold the strip in half lengthwise, with wrong sides together, aligning the two long raw edges; press.

STEP 4. After stitching the binding to your quilt and trimming the excess backing and batting, align the raw edges of the sleeve with the top raw edges of the quilt back, centering the sleeve on the quilt. Pin the sleeve in place.

STEP 5. Machine stitch the sleeve to the back of the quilt, stitching from the front by sewing over the stitches used to sew on the binding.

STEP 6. Turn the binding to the back of the quilt and hand stitch in place as described previously. When you turn over the binding along the edge of the quilt with the hanging sleeve, you may need to trim away extra batting and backing in order to turn the binding more easily.

STEP 7. Hand stitch the bottom loose edge of the sleeve in place on the back of the quilt, being careful not to sew through to the front of the quilt.

LABELING YOUR QUILT

The makers of most of the antique quilts in this book are anonymous, since quilters of the nineteenth and early twentieth centuries rarely signed their work.

This is not a tradition we should be continuing. Once you have completed your quilt, be sure to sign and date it. That way, years from now, no one will have to wonder who made that quilt. Be helpful to families, quilt collectors, and historians by including the following information:

• Your complete name

• The month, day, and year the quilt was completed

• The place where the quilt was made

• Any special occasion for making the quilt—new baby, wedding, anniversary, birthday, or holiday, for example

You may also want to include some technical information about the quilt, such as whether it was hand pieced, hand appliquéd, machine pieced, machine appliquéd, or hand quilted. Note any unusual fabrics if you have included any.

If the backing of your quilt is muslin or another light fabric, you can embroider on it, or use a permanent pen to write the information directly on the fabric. If the backing fabric is dark or too busy, make a label and stitch it to the back.

To make a label, choose muslin or other light fabric that has been prewashed. This removes the sizing so that the ink will penetrate the fibers. You will need a permanent pen for writing and freezer paper for stabilizing. A Pigma pen with a point size of 0.01 works well. This pen comes in a variety of colors, with brown and black giving a more "antique" look reminiscent of the ink found on old quilts. Do a test sample on a scrap piece of fabric to get the feel for writing and drawing on fabric.

STEP 1. Cut a piece of your label fabric about ½ inch larger than you want your finished label to be. It can be rectangular, square, circular, heart-shaped, or oval.

STEP 2. Cut a piece of freezer paper the same size, and iron it to the fabric, having the shiny side of the freezer paper facing the wrong side of the fabric. To ensure that your writing will be straight, draw lines using a ruler and a heavy marker on the dull side of the freezer paper. These will be your guidelines for writing.

STEP 3. Sign and embellish your fabric label with the permanent pen. You can add flowers, wreaths, and vines to your heart's content!

STEP 4. Remove the freezer paper, press to set the ink, and press seam allowances under. Blindstitch the label to the back of your quilt.

Glossary

Source: Adapted from *The Quilter's How-To Dictionary*,
published by Leman Publications, Inc. © 1991.

Album quilts. Friendship or sampler quilts that often are made from one-of-a-kind appliqué blocks. One type of album quilt is the Baltimore Album, an elegant style that was popular in the mid-nineteenth century.

All-white quilts. See *White-on-white quilts*.

Amish quilts. A term used to describe quilts made by Amish people; also, an identifiable style of quilt made by the Amish through the early twentieth century. This design style is enjoying popularity among quiltmakers today. These so-called Amish quilts are typically made in bold geometric patterns with solid-color fabrics in vibrant colors and elaborate quilting.

Angled Seam. See *Set-in seam*.

Appliqué. To sew patches onto a background fabric with hand or machine stitching. Appliquéd patches are often curved; curved patches are usually indicative of an appliquéd quilt. Appliqué designs often represent motifs from nature or form a fabric "painting."

Appraisal. A written valuation of a quilt by a certified appraiser to be used for insurance purposes.

Assembly line piecing. An efficient and fast process for joining patches by machine. Patches are cut and stacked in correct sewing order and all necessary supplies are conveniently placed next to the sewing machine. Patches are joined with chain piecing and are pressed in groups to conserve time and effort.

Background fabric. The material (whether print or solid) on which appliqué patches are sewn; the background fabric of an appliqué block is usually cut to the finished block size plus seam allowances. Background fabric also can refer to the fabric chosen for pieced-block patches that appear to recede, thereby allowing other fabrics and patches to form the design.

Background (filler) quilting. An allover design, often horizontal and vertical or diagonal straight lines, that fills in the background around appliquéd or quilting motifs.

Backing. The bottom layer of the quilt. It usually is not pieced or appliquéd, although most bed-size quilts require that panels of fabric be joined to make the backing. Another word for backing is lining.

Backing fabric. Material chosen for the back of the quilt. If the quilt will be hand quilted, select fabric that will be easy to quilt: soft, closely woven, 100 percent cotton. Quilts wider than 40 inches will require one or more seams in the lining unless extra-wide (90 inches) fabric is used. A print fabric will disguise the seam(s) and the quilting stitches, which could be less even on the back of the quilt than on the front.

Bag balm. Ointment used to soothe cow udders and sore quilting fingers. It is available at farm-supply stores and quilt shops.

Baltimore album quilts. One particular group of album quilts made around Baltimore, Maryland, during the mid-nineteenth century. These quilts typically have elaborate appliqué work with a different design in each block. Fabrics used for the appliqué patches are often bright; the background is usually off-white.

Basting. (1) Temporary stitches to hold patches or turn-under allowances in place while the final sewing is done. Basting should be done in thread to match the patch or in light-colored thread so that no marks are left. Basting is removed after the final sewing has been completed.

(2) The fastening of layers of a quilt (backing, batting, and quilt top) with long running stitches in preparation for tying or quilting. The basting stitches can be about 2 inches long in lines that are typically about 4 inches apart and run horizontally and vertically across the quilt.

Batting. The filler or middle layer of the quilt. Batting can be made from polyester, cotton, wool, or silk fibers; a majority of quiltmakers today use batting made of polyester or cotton/polyester blend.

Most batting is white, although black polyester batting and off-white cotton batting are available. Wool batting is naturally off-white. Choosing the most appropriate batting for a quilt is very important. Thick or "fat" batting is best for tied quilts; unbonded cotton batting must be quilted closely (about every 1 to 2 inches) to prevent shifting and bunching.

New cotton battings continue to appear on the market, and many of these need not be quilted any closer than polyester. Quilt-shop personnel can advise about batting selection.

Bearding. Migration of batting fibers through the quilt backing or quilt top. Bearding is particularly

noticeable on dark solid fabric, and the problem may be worse when polyester fabrics are used.

Between. A short needle with a small eye that is used for hand quilting. Betweens are commonly available in sizes 7 to 10 and 12; the higher the number, the smaller the needle.

Bias. The diagonal in relation to the lengthwise and crosswise grain. Bias has considerable stretch. Careful handling in sewing and pressing will prevent problems caused when bias edges stretch out of shape.

Binding. A strip of fabric, either bias or straight grain, used to encase the edges of a quilt. The binding is sewn on after the quilt has been quilted or tied.

Blanket stitch. An embroidery stitch used for embellishing the edges of appliquéd patches and for adding details on Crazy quilts or picture quilts.

Bleeding. The loss of dye when fabric gets wet. This fugitive dye can stain other fabrics, and fabrics that bleed may be noticeably lighter after several washings. It is generally recommended that quiltmakers test each fabric by soaking it (or a scrap of it) in hot water, perhaps with a little soap. If the dye bleeds, continue rinsing until water remains clear. Occasionally you may find a fabric that will not stop bleeding. It may be best to discard

that fabric rather than risk using it in a quilt.

Blind stitch. The most often used method of sewing appliqués in place by hand. A blind stitch leaves only a tiny spot of thread showing on the front of the quilt. Stitches generally should be no farther apart than ⅛ inch.

Block. A design unit, usually a square, that is repeated to make the quilt top. Most quilts are made with blocks although there are other methods for constructing quilt tops (see *Whole-cloth quilts*). The blocks usually are made first and then are sewn together with other parts of the quilt top. The block style of quiltmaking became popular in the United States in the early 1800s.

Border. The outer area of the quilt (inside the binding), much like a frame on a picture. Borders can be made from any number of plain strips of fabric, or they can be pieced or appliquéd. Most quilts have borders, although some do not. Borders can be very wide, very narrow, or any width in between; a quilt can have more than one border.

Broderie perse. A type of appliqué in which motifs are cut from printed fabrics (such as floral designs) and appliquéd to a background.

Butted corner. A corner made when one border strip is sewn past the other at a 90 degree angle. Usually the side borders are added first, the ends are trimmed even with the quilt top, and then the top and bottom borders are added. Bindings may have butted corners.

Cable quilting. Designs that resemble twisted or intertwining cords similar to that of rope.

Calico. Medium-weight fabric of plain weave that is printed in a small, closely repeating design. The name calico comes from Calicut, India, where cotton woodblock prints have been made for hundreds of years.

Chain piecing. A technique of machine sewing where pairs of patches or units are sewn one after the other without lifting the presser foot or clipping threads between patches. Threads connecting the patches are cut later to separate the units.

Challenge quilts. Quilts made from a selected group of fabrics (often with other fabrics added at the individual maker's choosing) to explore the variety of possible combinations. The making of challenge quilts is an activity popular with quilt groups.

Charm quilts. Those made from a single template (such as a triangle,

hexagon, or tumbler shape) and scraps of fabric with no two patches cut from the same fabric. Many quiltmakers enjoy trading small pieces of fabric to collect as many different ones as possible with which to make a charm quilt.

Cheater cloth. A slang term referring to fabric that has been printed with patchwork designs.

Chintz. A cotton fabric with a glaze finish. Chintz is more dense than unglazed fabric and, therefore, more difficult to hand quilt. Its shine gives added highlights to quilting, especially when the fabric is a solid color. The glazing may wash or wear off in time.

Color wheel. Hues arranged in a circle in such a way that the colors blend in sequence like a rainbow. A basic 12-step color wheel arrangement is blue, blue/green, green, yellow/green, yellow, yellow/orange, orange, red/orange, red, red/purple, purple, and blue/purple. Many quiltmakers enjoy using a color wheel to explore color theory and fabric selection.

Comforter. A thick, puffy quilt that is usually tied or machine quilted rather than hand quilted. The term also can apply to quilts, smaller than bed size, to be used for naps and as lap warmers.

Contemporary quilts. A term used to mean quilts that are made in the present, as opposed to those made

in a past era. The term also is used in reference to quilts of new, original design, as contrasted to "traditional" quilts made from an existing pattern. Often a "contemporary" design is nonrepeating, whereas a "traditional" quilt makes use of repeating blocks. There is no universal agreement on this term.

Continuous-line quilting. A technique using unbroken design lines that can be stitched with minimal stopping and starting.

Contrast. Variance in light and dark fabric colors or size/type of prints to allow patches to be distinct.

Corner triangles. Patches (which usually are large) that are sewn on to square up a quilt top made from blocks that are joined in diagonal rows. Outer edges usually should be straight grain.

Cotton fabric. The most suitable fabric to use for appliqué and piecing because of its stability and its ability to retain a crisp crease. Cotton fabric is available in nearly any solid color and a wide variety of prints. Most quiltmakers collect fabric to build an extensive palette of material.

Coverlet. A quilt made to cover the top of a bed and the sides of the mattress but not made large enough to drop to the floor. Coverlets often are used with dust ruffles.

Crazy quilt. Fancy patchwork incorporating silk, velvet, and embroidery popular in the late-nineteenth century and among some quilt-makers today. Crazy quilts are constructed on a muslin foundation fabric and usually do not include batting, although they may have a lining.

Crocking. The rubbing off of fabric dye. If you discover that your fingers take on the color of fabric as you are piecing or quilting, the dye is crocking. Washing or rinsing fabric before cutting and sewing will often remove excess dye so that it does not crock. See also *Bleeding.*

Crosshatching. Parallel lines of quilting that run in two directions, forming either a grid of squares or a grid of diamonds. Crosshatching is sometimes used in the background of appliqué quilts or to set off quilting motifs.

Crosswise grain. The fabric threads that are woven from selvage to selvage, called weft or filling threads. Crosswise grain has some stretch, but not as much as bias.

Curved seams. Lines of stitching joining patches with rounded edges. Curved seams require clips in the seam allowances of the concave curve to allow easier sewing. Careful pinning and sewing are needed for accuracy; marked notches will help in matching seam lines.

Cutter quilts. A term given to old quilts that are cut up to make

stuffed animals, garments, and household accessories. Many quilt-makers strongly oppose cutting up old quilts because they are irreplaceable antiques.

Cutting mat. A special protective surface on which a rotary cutter can be used safely.

Design wall. A handy work surface for mounting patches to see how they look before sewing them together. Cardboard or wood can be covered with fuzzy flannel, or a piece of flannel fabric can be stapled to a wall in your sewing room.

Diagonal row. A row of blocks, with or without sashing, that crosses the quilt at a 45 degree angle. If setting squares are not used, sashing for diagonal rows will be cut in several different lengths to accommodate the varying number of blocks in the rows. If setting squares are used, all sashes will be identical.

Drafting. The drawing of an accurate pattern to be used for marking and cutting patches.

Easing. A technique to make unequal parts of the quilt match at

seams by evenly distributing the fullness of one segment across the edge of the other segment. Easing is used to control unevenness and make the finished quilt lie (or hang) flat and smooth. When pinning two sections with one of them to be eased, use a lot of pins to evenly space the extra fullness. Often the edges of the quilt will be a bit too long and will require easing onto the border. Placing the fuller edge next to the feed dogs and stretching the shorter edge on top as it is sewn helps avoid any tucks.

Echo quilting. Lines of quilting that outline appliqué shapes (often on Hawaiian quilts) in concentric rings or shapes. Lines of echo quilting usually are about $\frac{1}{2}$ inch apart and often are judged by eye without marking.

Edge finishing. Any of several techniques that encase or embellish the perimeter of the quilt. Binding is the most common edge finish; other techniques include adding prairie points, ruffles, or corded edging. As the edges are being finished, the batting should be secured with sewing so that it does not shift. The edges usually are finished after the quilting or tying is complete.

English paper piecing. A technique for piecing in which medium-weight paper is cut to the exact size of a finished patch and fabric is basted over the paper. After patches are basted, they are placed right sides together and joined with tiny overcast stitches. The basting is taken out and the papers are removed. This technique is often used for pieced patterns that would otherwise require set-in patches, such as six- and eight-pointed star designs made from diamonds. Many quilts made with English paper piecing have hexagon-shaped patches that form a design called Grandmother's Flower Garden.

Even-feed foot. See *Walking foot.*

Fabric. For quiltmaking, the material that is favored is usually 100 percent cotton of medium weight. The threads should be woven closely enough so that small quilting stitches will not fall between the threads. Dyes should be colorfast, and the fabric should not have a heavy or stiff finish if it will be hand quilted. Quiltmakers certainly are not limited to cotton fabrics; every imaginable kind of textile has been used to make quilts. However, quilts to be washed should be made of washable fabric.

Fat batting. Extra-thick batting used for tied comforters and, occasionally, for machine-quilted quilts. Fat batting does not allow hand quilters to achieve stitches as small as those possible with thinner batting of light or medium weight.

Fat eighth. A piece of fabric cut half width (approximately 22 inches) by 9 inches. The total number of square inches is the same as that of ⅛ yard of fabric.

Fat quarter. A piece of fabric cut half width (approximately 22 inches) by 18 inches. The total number of square inches is the same as that of ¼ yard of fabric. The advantage of "fat" pieces of fabric is that larger patches can sometimes be cut from them than from the corresponding amount of fabric that is cut full width.

Feather quilting. A favorite design motif, with many variations, that is used in blocks, background, and borders. Individual rounded feathers extend from a center spine that is usually curved but also can be straight.

Feed dogs. The metal teeth that guide and move fabric under the needle of the sewing machine. Feed dogs are lowered (disengaged) for free-motion quilting and free-form appliqué.

Feed sacks. Cloth bags made of cotton, in which grain and flour were (and still are) packaged. They were used to make quilts in the 1930s and 1940s during a time of economic hardship.

Fiber migration. See *Bearding.*

Finger press(ing). To use your fingers to flatten seam allowances or fold guidelines in fabric (for ap-

pliqué, for instance). Cotton fabric is more easily and effectively finger pressed than are other fibers. Finger pressing has two advantages: It can be done anywhere without the need for an iron, and it will press out with no permanent creases.

Flannel board. See *Design wall.*

Foundation fabric. A piece of material used as a base on which patches are sewn for some types of Log Cabin and Crazy quilt blocks. Because foundation fabrics do not show in the finished quilt, many quiltmakers use muslin or their "ugly" fabric as the foundation.

Foundation piecing. A block-construction technique worked on a foundation fabric. One patch is placed face up on the foundation, the next patch is placed face down on the first patch, and the patches are stitched through all three layers. The second patch is folded out to be face up, then the next patch is positioned face down, and it is sewn. A variation of pressed piecing uses pattern lines marked on the underneath side of the foundation fabric, and the stitching is done from this back side. Pressed piecing is one method used for making Log Cabin, Pineapple, and Crazy quilt blocks.

Frame. A wood (or plastic) piece of furniture that stretches and holds the quilt so it can be quilted. Many quilting frames are large enough for six or more people to quilt at one time, making them ideal for group quilts or "quilting bees." These frames have two long rails on which the quilt is rolled, two side stretchers, and legs to position the quilt at a comfortable height for quilting. Many different styles and sizes of quilting frames are available.

Free-motion quilting. Machine quilting for which the feed dogs are lowered and the quilt is maneuvered in any direction (without turning it) under a darning foot, which replaces the regular presser foot.

Freezer-paper appliqué. A popular technique where freezer paper (available at the grocery store for packaging food to be frozen) is cut to the exact size of the finished appliqué patch.

French-fold binding. Binding that finishes with a double layer of fabric. French-fold binding is cut four times the finished width plus two seam allowances (often about 2¼ inches total). Fold binding in half lengthwise (wrong sides together), press, and sew it to the front side of the quilt with both raw edges of binding matching the edge of the quilt. When turning binding to the back, there is no need to turn under the edge. Simply blind stitch the fold so it just covers the stitching.

French knot. A decorative embroidery stitch that makes tiny ball-shape knots that can dot an *i* or embellish appliqué.

Friendship quilts. Group quilts, often made from scraps and varying patterns, that usually have signed blocks. Friendship quilts may commemorate a birthday, wedding anniversary, retirement, or some other special occasion.

Grain lines. Lengthwise and crosswise threads that are woven to make fabric. Grain line placement is indicated on patterns with grain line arrows; arrows should be placed parallel to fabric threads. Crosswise grain provides some stretch but offers only a maximum dimension of about 42 inches without seaming. Lengthwise grain does not stretch, and borders cut this way can be any dimension required without the necessity of seaming short pieces. Border strips can be cut on crosswise grain or lengthwise grain.

Graph paper. Gridded paper that is used in planning quilts by drawing blocks with other components such as, setting squares, and sashing in miniature to experiment with ideas and check proportions.

Greige goods. (Pronounced "gray goods.") Unfinished fabric that is not yet dyed, printed, or finished with sizing. It is the raw material from which fabrics are processed.

Hand (of fabric). The qualities of fabric as perceived by the way it feels. Soft fabric that is neither stiff nor flimsy is the best choice for most quilts.

Hand appliqué. To apply patches with hand sewing, most often using the blind stitch, to a background fabric. Other methods of sewing include slip-stitch, running stitch, and blanket or buttonhole stitch. Patches for hand appliqué should include turn under allowance and usually have marked sewing lines.

Hand piecing. To sew patches together with a hand-held needle and a single strand of thread. Hand piecing is usually done with a running stitch and backstitches to begin and end the seam. Many quiltmakers consider hand piecing to be relaxing and precise because of its slow pace.

Hand quilting. Fastening together the layers of the quilt with running stitches. When a frame or hoop is used, one hand controls the needle on top of the quilt; the other hand guides the needle under the quilt. Beginning quilters might take one stitch at a time; more often quilters use a rocking motion to put several stitches on the needle before pulling it through. Because the needle is pushed with the middle finger of the sewing hand, it is important to wear a thimble on that finger to protect it. Hand quilting a quilt can (but doesn't always) take as long as or longer than making the quilt top. For faster results, the quilt can be machine quilted or tied.

Hawaiian quilting. A style of quilt design, originating in Hawaii and now enjoyed by quilters everywhere, with one large appliqué cut from folded fabric in the same way paper snowflakes are cut. The appliqué is basted to the background fabric, then the allowance is turned under by eye without a marked line. Hawaiian quilts customarily have only two colors of fabric, both of which are solid. They are usually quilted in parallel lines of echo quilting.

Heritage quilt projects. Programs and activities to document historic quilts in a state or region. Quilt guilds are often involved with these events.

Hoop. An alternate kind of frame, much like a large embroidery hoop, for stretching a quilt during quilting. When tightening the hoop screw, allow some slack in the quilt and be certain all the layers are pulled evenly. Hoops are available in round or oval shapes in sizes from 8 to 29 inches (round) and up to 18 x 27 inches (oval).

Horizontal row. A row of blocks, with or without sashing, that crosses the quilt at a 90 degree angle to the lengthwise edge. Many quilts made from blocks are constructed by

joining blocks in horizontal rows and then joining the rows.

In-the-ditch quilting. A line of quilting stitches that is right next to a seam or around an appliqué patch on the side without seam allowances. In-the-ditch quilting is especially good for appliqué quilts because it makes the patches seem to puff up a bit.

Invisible thread. Nylon thread, available in clear or smoke color, that is sometimes used for machine appliqué and machine quilting. Select fine thread (size 0.004 is recommended); heavier thread is too stiff for use on quilts.

Ironing. Moving an iron across fabric (wet or dry) to smooth and flatten it. Ironing is different from pressing, which is a lifting-and-lowering motion. Yardage is ironed before being marked and cut into patches or cut for backing. See also *Press(ing)*.

Join. To sew one patch, unit, or block to another.

Juried shows. Competitions or exhibitions that have a screening

process to select the quilts to be on display. Jurying usually is done from slides, but it can be done with the actual quilts. If the selection process will be done with slides, it is very important to provide the jurors with sharp, well-lit slides that show all of the quilt. Label slides as instructed in the show rules.

Knot. A tie in the end of thread for hand sewing; the knot begins the line of sewing and stops the thread from pulling out. Knots are optional; two or three backstitches also can be used to secure the beginning of thread.

Lattice. See *Sash(ing)*.

Layering. Assembling the quilt "sandwich." Working on a large, flat surface such as the floor or a table, spread out the backing (wrong side up), batting (smoothed over lining), and quilt top (placed over batting right side up). The layers are secured with basting stitches or rustproof safety pins. (Straight pins can be used to temporarily secure the layers while the basting is done.) After quilting or tying, the basting or pins are removed.

Lengthwise grain. The fabric threads that are parallel to the selvages, also called warp threads. Lengthwise grain has very little stretch, if any. Many quiltmakers prefer to cut borders and sashing on the lengthwise grain to avoid any stretch, even if the dimension needed is short enough to allow them to be cut on crosswise grain. Straight grain binding usually is cut on lengthwise grain.

Light box (or table). A work surface that has translucent glass (or plastic) that is illuminated from underneath. A light box or its equivalent makes tracing designs onto fabric much easier.

Light fading. The loss of color density in fabric due to exposure to light. Sunlight is especially detrimental to the dyes in fabrics used to make quilts, but fluorescent lighting also is harmful. The ultraviolet rays that cause light fading can be filtered with special shields for windows and light fixtures, but most quiltmakers either avoid using a quilt in places exposed to excessive light or accept the inevitable fading that occurs with some colors and fabrics.

Lining. See *Backing*.

Loft. The thickness and springiness of quilt batting. High-loft batting is thick and bouncy; low-loft batting is thin and compact. Each batting manufacturer's product has a slightly different loft.

Machine appliqué. To apply patches with machine sewing. One technique uses satin stitches (close zigzag stitches) to define the patches with bold outlines. Patches for this method of machine appliqué usually do not include turn-under allowances. Another machine technique is similar to hand appliqué in its finished appearance; it uses invisible thread and a blind hem stitch. Many newer sewing machines have a blanket stitch that works well for appliqué.

Machine piecing. To sew patches together with a sewing machine. Machine piecing yields seams that are strong, and the work progresses quickly compared with hand piecing.

Machine quilting. Stitching with a sewing machine through all three layers of the quilt to fasten them and add decorative relief and texture to the quilt. Machine quilting is usually done with a walking foot that evenly feeds the quilt under the needle or with a darning foot (with feed dogs lowered) that allows freedom to move the quilt in any direction.

Magnetic pincushion. A magnetized surface for holding steel pins and needles. (Brass does not adhere to a magnet.) Manufacturers of computerized sewing machines recommend caution when using a magnetic pincushion because the magnetic field can make the machine perform erratically.

Masking tape. Sticky tape is available in hardware stores (in many widths and in quilt shops (in ¼-inch width). It is excellent for "marking" lines to be quilted, especially long straight lines and outline quilting ¼ inch from seams. Just quilt next to the masking tape (on one or both sides), then peel it away. Sometimes tape can be used more than once; other times it won't be sticky enough to use again. It is better not to leave tape on a quilt for an extended period of time because it might leave a residue.

Meander quilting. See *Stipple quilting*.

Measuring across the quilt top. Using a tape measure to record the length and width of the quilt top to determine the actual border lengths, which will possibly be different from what is expected because of inaccuracies in sewing. Measure through the center (not the edges) in both directions and record the measurements. Use pins to mark border strips to be these dimensions, allowing the excess length (needed for mitering) to be divided equally at the ends.

Medallion quilts. Those with a central block or design that is surrounded by multiple borders. Borders for medallion quilts are often pieced, but they can be plain, appliquéd, or a combination of techniques.

Memory quilts. Those which are made to remember people, places, events, or anything else.

Methodist knotting (or tying). A quick technique for tying a quilt. Thread a needle with a long piece of floss, yarn, or narrow ribbon. Mark a placement for ties with pins. At the first pin, take a small stitch through all layers and tie a square knot. Proceed to the next pin and make the next knot. Continue across the quilt and clip the thread to leave tails.

Miniature quilts. Those made in reduced size, often one-twelfth, to match the scale of dollhouses.

Mitered corner. A corner formed when two strips (block frame, border, or binding) are joined at a 45 degree angle.

Mock-up. A full-size (or nearly full size) drawing of a block with fabric fastened in position. Many quiltmakers enjoy auditioning fabrics this way to find their favorite combinations.

Muslin. Cotton fabric of medium weight with a slightly coarser weave than that of broadcloth. Unbleached muslin is naturally off-white and has small brown flecks. Bleached muslin is white; muslin also can be dyed. Good-quality muslin is a favorite among quiltmakers; poor-quality muslin will

wrinkle, allow the batting to "beard" and will not hold up well.

Needlepunch batting. Made commercially by pounding batting with needles to make a dense batting with low loft but firm body.

Needles. Those for piecing and appliqué are called sharps; those for hand quilting are called betweens. For hand or machine sewing, change needles as soon as you suspect the old needle is dull).

Needle turning. The use of the needle to gently turn under the allowance on hand-appliquéd patches. After turning under the allowance so that the marked line is barely out of sight, the thumb is used to "finger press" the crease.

Needling. The action of working the needle through the layers when hand quilting. The term often is used to express the ease or difficulty of this action. Some fabrics and battings needle easily; others may be stiff or dense and needle with greater difficulty.

On point. A term used to express the orientation of a quilt block (or

any square) when its corners are placed up, down, and to the sides.

Outline quilting. Quilting that outlines patches in lines that are usually ¼-inch from the patch seams, which places the quilting just beyond the area where the fabric layers in the seam allowance would add extra thickness. Many quilters use ¼-inch-wide masking tape as a guide in outline quilting.

Palette. A quiltmaker's collection of fabric.

Paper basting. See *English paper piecing*.

Partial piecing. A technique (suitable for only some block patterns) used to avoid setting in an angled patch. With this method, the first two patches are sewn only partway. More patches are added and, after joining the last patch of a unit or the block, the partial seam is completed.

Patch. A fabric piece to be sewn into a quilt. Typically, patches are joined to make units, units are joined to make blocks, and blocks are sewn with other components such as sashes and borders to complete the quilt top.

Patchwork. A term that can apply

to appliqué, but more often indicates pieced work.

Patchwork binding. Pieced binding made from square or rectangular patches sewn side by side to make long strips. Remember to allow for seam allowances when figuring the cut size of patches. Patchwork binding works best when applied as single binding because it is too bulky to be applied as French-fold binding.

Pattern. The printed shapes and directions for making a project. Pattern pieces are the actual paper shapes used to make templates for marking and cutting patches.

Pearl cotton. A shiny cotton thread used for embroidery and tying comforters. Pearl cotton comes in many colors and four common sizes: 3 (thick), 5 (medium), 8 (thin), and 12 (very thin).

Pieced borders. Those made from patches, which are assembled with the same methods as for pieced blocks. Graph paper will be very helpful in planning pieced borders.

Pieced sashing. Sashing that is divided into smaller patches to create additional design interest. Pieced sashing can offer endless possibilities for changing the look of traditional quilt blocks or new designs, whether they are pieced or appliquéd. Patches for pieced sashing are marked, cut, and sewn just as those for quilt blocks.

Pieced setting squares. Miniature quilt blocks sewn between sashes at block intersections. Pieced setting squares usually have a simple design because of their small size.

Piecing. Joining with seams the patches, units, blocks, or other elements of a quilt top. Piecing can be done with hand sewing or with machine stitching. Patches to be pieced usually have straight edges, but they also can be curved.

Pin basting. Using straight pins (long "quilting" pins) or rustproof safety pins to secure the three layers of the quilt instead of basting with running stitches. Pin basting is an especially good choice for quilts to be tied or machine quilted because the pins need not stay in the quilt for a long time.

Polyester batting. The top-selling filler for quilts today, made from generic polyester fiber or trade names such as Dacron. Polyester batting, when bonded or glazed (as most are), is lightweight, easy to quilt, and does not readily shift or bunch as cotton batting will. It is available in several weights from "light" to "fat" and various sizes from crib to king. Many quilt shops also sell polyester batting by the yard.

Polyester fleece. Flat, compact batting that is needlepunched. It is sold by the yard and can be used for a variety of craft projects and quilted wallhangings.

Prairie points. Folded squares of fabric that form triangles, which are placed side by side or sewn together to make a zigzag edging on quilts. Quilts with a Prairie-point edge do not need binding because they are sewn between the turned-under edges of the quilt top and quilt lining. Prairie points are also called Portuguese hem.

Press(ing). Lifting and placing the iron to flatten seam allowances and fabric. Pressing can be done with or without steam. Do not move the iron back and forth on a patch or quilt block, as this may stretch and distort the fabric.

Presser foot. The part of a sewing machine that touches the fabric and holds it flat against the throat plate.

Prewashing fabric. The rinsing of fabric in hot water (with or without a little detergent) to shrink it and check for color bleeding. Fabrics should be rinsed one piece at a time to check for colorfastness. If the dye runs, continue rinsing until it stops bleeding. Fabric can be dried by machine or may be hung on a clothesline to dry. Large pieces of fabric can be washed and dried by machine after checking colorfastness. Iron fabric (using steam) to smooth it.

Progressive quilts. Those made as group projects where one person begins a quilt and passes it along to the next person, who adds something (often appliqué or embroidery) and passes it along to the next person. The work continues until everyone involved has had a turn and the quilt is finished. Some quilt groups establish rules or guidelines before beginning a progressive quilt.

Quilting. The stitching that holds the quilt's three layers together. Quilting adds texture and design motifs to the quilt. Quilting can be done by hand with a running stitch or by machine sewing. Long, straight lines of quilting are particularly susceptible to breaking. For this reason, it is a good idea to change directions every few inches so that one-directional stress will not weaken the lines of quilting.

Quilting bee. A social, group effort to work on one or more quilts, usually at the hand-quilting stage. Good conversation and shared food frequently are important elements of a quilting bee.

Quilting thread. Special thread that is extra strong for hand quilting. The thread color can be any that enhances the quilt top and may, in fact, change within the quilt. Some quiltmakers select a color that will blend in; others choose one that will contrast with the fabric(s) and show off the quilting.

Quilt top. The upper layer of the quilt that is usually pieced, appliquéd, embroidered, or any combination of techniques. It is often made from blocks and may incorporate sashes, setting squares, and borders. Quilting usually is planned to accent the design of the quilt top, although the quilting itself can be the primary design feature.

Reverse appliqué. The cutting, turning under, and blindstitching of a top layer of fabric to reveal a shape created by the exposed underlayer of fabric. Reverse appliqué is especially useful when shapes are very small and when an illusion of depth is desired.

Reversed patch. A patch that is a mirror image of another patch. Often such patches are indicated by an *r* following the patch letter. Turn the template over (reverse it) when marking a reversed patch.

Rocking motion. A technique for hand quilting where the needle is pushed with the middle finger of the sewing hand and is guided with the hand underneath the quilt. The needle should be aligned with the finger almost as if it were an extension of the finger. When the alignment is not straight, the needle will slip off the thimble. The sewing hand rocks 90 degrees, from pointing the needle straight

down into the quilt to positioning the needle horizontally.

Rotary cutting. A method recommended for cutting long strips because the rotary cutter allows fast, accurate cutting through several layers of fabric. Always use a cutting mat underneath a rotary cutter.

Rows. Horizontal or vertical units of a quilt. Blocks are usually sewn to make rows, then rows are joined to construct the quilt top.

Ruler. A useful tool for measuring. Many quiltmakers prefer a see-through ruler. Some plastic cutting templates also serve as rulers.

Running stitch. (1) Passing the needle in and out of the fabric along the seam line for hand piecing. The thread color usually matches one or both patches. Running stitches are often about $\frac{1}{16}$ inch.

(2) Passing the needle in and out of the quilt to make even quilting stitches with equal spaces in between.

Safety pins. Items used in a quick method for basting a quilt. Be sure that the safety pins are rust-proof and that they will not leave marks in the quilt after they are removed.

Sampler quilts. Quilts made with a different pattern for each block. Sashing (with or without setting squares) is often used in sampler quilts because the sashes unify the varying blocks and also let each block "shine" alone. Sampler blocks can be set diagonally or they can be set in horizontal rows. Sampler quilts are popular with beginners.

Sandwich. A word used to describe the layers (or layering) of a quilt.

Sash(ing). Strips of fabric sewn between blocks. Sashing separates the blocks, but the visual impact will vary depending on the sash fabric and width. Another name for sashing is lattice.

Sashiko. A Japanese style of decorative stitching that is both embroidery and quilting. It is often done with white thread on a dark, solid background such as indigo.

Satin stitch. A decorative embroidery stitch worked by hand to form solid design areas, often on appliquéd picture quilts. Machine appliqué is done with a close zigzag stitch that resembles a satin stitch.

Sawtooth edging. See *Prairie points.*

Scissors. A necessary tool for quiltmaking. It is important to have special scissors used only for sewing so they will be as sharp as possible. (Cutting paper will dull scissors quickly.) Most quiltmakers enjoy using a pair of dressmaker's shears for cutting patches and a smaller pair of embroidery scissors for clipping threads. Quilters who use a frame often leave their embroidery scissors and thread on the quilt while they work, so they prefer scissors with blunt points that won't accidentally pierce the quilt top.

Seam. The line of stitching that joins patches or other parts of a quilt.

Seam allowance. The fabric between the seam line and the cut edge. Seam allowances are usually ¼ inch wide; both allowances are most often pressed to one side of the seam, often toward the darker fabric.

Seam line. The line, whether marked for hand piecing or unmarked for machine piecing, on which the seam is sewn.

Self-binding. An easy edge finish in which the excess lining fabric is rolled around to the front of the quilt, turned under, and blind stitched in place. When making self-binding, be sure to stitch through to the back of the quilt to prevent the batting from shifting.

Selvages. The lengthwise woven edges of the fabric. Selvages are more densely woven than the rest of the fabric, causing them to shrink considerably and to be difficult to sew through. Selvages are removed by cutting away about ½ inch; they should never be included in border strips.

Set-in seam. A juncture that cannot be sewn in one straight seam. Set-in (or angled) seams are sewn in two steps: First one side of the angled patch or unit is sewn, then the other side. Beginning quiltmakers may want to avoid set-in seams until they are comfortable sewing straight seams with accuracy.

Set(ting). The arrangement of blocks and other components. Sets are usually either horizontal or diagonal, depending on the block orientation.

Setting squares. Squares of fabric sewn at the block intersections and used with sashing. Setting squares can help the blocks lose their individuality to create designs within the overall repeat pattern of the quilt.

Sewing machine. An optional tool for quiltmaking. Quilts were made entirely by hand for hundreds of years, but the invention of the sewing machine in the mid-1800s changed that. Today many quiltmakers work by machine for some or all of the steps in quiltmaking.

Shade. A variation of a color that has had black added to it; a darker version of a hue.

Sharp. A needle, longer than a between, with a small eye. Sharps are excellent needles for hand appliqué. Their length allows a comfortable grip; the narrow shaft slides easily through the appliqué patch and background.

Shrinkage. The reduction in the size of fabric when it is washed and dried; also, the change in size of a quilt when it is quilted. Fabric will shrink up to 8 percent when it is washed and dried, and it can be several inches (or more) smaller after the top is quilted. Finished quilt sizes listed for patterns in books and magazines do not take this after-quilting shrinkage into consideration.

Side triangles. Companion patches to corner triangles, these are used to fill in the triangular gaps at the edges of a quilt that has diagonally set blocks.

Signing quilts. An important final step in quiltmaking. The signature can be done on the quilt's front or back, in embroidery or with a permanent fabric marker or India ink. Add a date and other information such as the name of the recipient or the city and state. Future owners of the quilt will be very grateful for these efforts.

Simple sashing. Plain sashing strips that do not have setting squares to break them up. Simple sashing has short lengths between blocks for the horizontal or diagonal rows and long lengths between rows.

Sleeve. A tube of fabric sewn to the top back side (and sometimes the bottom) of a quilt to accommodate a pole for hanging the quilt. Sleeves can be made of fabric that matches the lining or of contrasting fabric.

Spoon basting. Catching the point of the needle with a spoon when basting. The needle is held in one hand while basting, and the spoon is held in the other. (Both hands are above the quilt.) Catching the needle with a spoon this way prevents the point from snagging the quilt top and may help the basting process go more quickly. (Use an old spoon since it will likely get scratched by the needle.)

Square knot. The best knot for tying a quilt. To make a square knot, hold one "tail" in each hand. Wrap the left tail over the right tail, pull tightly, then wrap the new right tail over the new left tail and tighten the knot. Clip the thread or yarn to leave tails about ¾ to 1½ inches.

Stab stitch. Quilting that is done one stitch at a time by poking the needle straight down or straight up through the quilt.

Stencil. A cut-out pattern through which designs can be marked for quilting or painted for stenciling. Stencils often are made from lightweight cardboard or plastic.

Stenciling. A technique for painting on fabric by dabbing a special paintbrush over a cut-out stencil. Freezer paper, with the to-be-stenciled shape(s) cut away, can be ironed on the fabric. After applying paint, the freezer paper can be peeled away and reused. Stenciling is much faster than appliqué with similar results.

Stipple quilting. That which moves in close meandering lines to heavily quilt an area of a quilt. These quilting lines usually don't cross each other. Most often such quilting serves to contrast with unquilted areas that will be noticeably puffy by comparison.

Stitches per inch. The number of quilting stitches that can be worked per inch; they are counted on one side of the quilt, usually the top. Beginners might achieve only three or four stitches per inch; experienced quilters can sometimes get 15 or even 20 stitches per inch. The thickness of the batting is a significant determining factor in the size and spacing of quilting stitches.

Story quilts. Those that depict an event, whether real or imaginary.

Straight-grain binding. Strips cut on either crosswise or lengthwise grain. Straight grain has very little (if any) stretch. Straight-grain strips can be cut in any length (if you are willing to purchase sufficient yardage). Often binding is cut from the same fabric as borders, and therefore, it will not require the purchase of any additional fabric if binding is cut alongside border strips.

String quilts. Those made from very narrow strips of fabric, often in random or varying widths. String quilts are associated with frugality, but the style certainly can be chosen for its graphic qualities.

String-quilt blocks often are made with a foundation fabric to stabilize the small pieces of fabric.

Strip piecing. A technique that became very popular in the 1980s for its speed. Strips of fabric are cut (usually with a rotary cutter) and joined to make bands; the bands are cut into units and the units are assembled to make blocks.

Strippie quilts. Those that have vertical bands of simple piecing that alternate with long sashing.

Stuffed quilting. See *Trapunto.*

Summer quilt (or spread). That which has no batting, making it lighter for sleeping in hot weather.

Surface knot. A knot made at the end of a length of quilting thread right on the surface of the quilt top. To make the knot rest on the surface, hold it under a finger as the thread tightens. Then insert the needle through the exact hole where it came out to pop the knot into the quilt batting. Take a 1-inch-long stitch through the batting, bring the needle back through the quilt top, then clip the thread at the surface to leave the knot and tail inside the quilt.

Template. The pattern around which seam lines or cutting lines are marked on the fabric. Templates can be the paper pattern, but more often they are made from see-through plastic, which will last indefinitely. Cardboard and sandpaper also are used to make templates. Templates for machine piecing include seam allowances; those for hand piecing do not. Mark the patch letter and grain line arrow on the template.

Tension. A term referring to the tightness of the two threads on a sewing machine and the resulting line of stitching. When the tension is balanced, the threads will lock between the fabrics and not on the surface of either piece. Usually an adjustment of the upper tension only will be sufficient to correct an imbalance; the bobbin tension usually can remain the same. Tension often must be adjusted for machine quilting. When adjusting tension, practice first on fabrics (with batting if simulating machine quilting) to check the adjustment before working on the quilt.

Thimble. A metal or leather device worn on the sewing finger to protect it. For hand quilting, it is preferable that the thimble have indentations to help guide the needle and prevent it from slipping.

Thread. The strand pulled through fabric to hold a quilt together. It is available in many qualities and virtually every color imaginable. Good thread is a joy to use; bad thread can be a nightmare. See also *Quilting thread.*

Thread color. For hand appliqué, the color of thread should match the fabric patch being applied (not the background). When binding a quilt, match the thread to the binding fabric.

For machine appliqué, the thread can match the patch or it can contrast for stronger definition of shapes. For piecing, the thread ideally should match one or both fabrics. When a choice is practical, match the darker fabric. If matching the fabric would require changing the thread in the sewing machine too many times to keep your patience intact, select a medium neutral color such as gray or beige because those colors blend well.

Throat plate. The surface of the sewing machine where the actual stitching happens. See also *Feed dogs.*

Throw. A small quilt that is used for cuddling up with a good book or in front of the television. A throw is the quilted version of an afghan.

Tint. A variation of a color that has had white added to it; a lighter version of a hue.

Top. The upper layer of a quilt, which has the design and is usually the side that is seen.

Topper. A quilt that is used on the top of a bed over a bedspread or larger quilt. Toppers also can be used as throws.

Traditional quilts. Those made from time-honored designs that typically use repeated blocks.

Transfer. To mark a design in some way other than free-hand drawing. Methods include using iron-on commercial transfers, ironing on a photocopy, tracing over a light box, and using a transfer pencil.

Trapunto. Insertion of stuffing or yarn between layers of a quilt (after quilting) to give high relief and texture. Trapunto shows up best on solid fabrics. Trapunto is easily accomplished by using a 6-inch-long yarn or trapunto needle to insert fluffy yarn from the backing side of the quilt.

Trimming behind patches. Cutting away the background fabric or underneath appliqué patches to leave only one layer of fabric. Leave ³⁄₁₆- to ¼-inch allowance on the back side. Such trimming sometimes cuts through previous stitching, in which case additional backstitches should be made to secure the patch.

Tufting. See *Tying*.

Turkey red. A color of cloth and type of dye that became known in the nineteenth century for its reliable colorfastness.

Turning under corners on appliqués. One useful method for achieving sharp corners is to blind stitch up to the corner, take an extra stitch at the point, and then turn under the second side. Use the point of the needle to tuck under the allowance. A second method is to trim the seam allowance at the point and fold it down, then turn under and baste the allowances.

Two-block quilt. One made from two block designs that alternate. Such quilts often use two blocks that share some major seams, thus creating a blended design.

Two-sided quilt. A term referring to a quilt that has piecing or appliqué on both sides of a quilt. Often one side is more elaborate than the other.

Tying. Fastening the layers of the quilt with yarn, pearl cotton, embroidery floss, or narrow ribbon with individual tied knots or bows. The tails for ties can be on the front of the quilt or the back. Square knots are normally used to tie quilts. See also *Methodist knotting (or tying)*.

Underneath hand. The hand that is held under a quilt while hand quilting and that feels the prick of the needle. Right-handers would use their left hand under the quilt; left-handers would hold the quilt with their right hand underneath. Some quiltmakers protect the pricked finger with tape or a thimble; other quilters prefer to build up a callous in order to feel and guide the needle.

Unit. A portion of a block or border, which is usually indicated by a piecing diagram, to guide the quiltmaker in construction.

Utility quilts. Those made for warmth and practical use without extravagance in materials or labor.

Value. A term used to express the lightness or darkness of a color.

Vertical row. A row of blocks, with or without sashing, that runs from the top of the quilt to the bottom. Most quilts are constructed in horizontal rows, but some designs are better suited to assembly in vertical rows or columns.

Walking foot. A sewing machine attachment that replaces the regular presser foot for machine quilting. A walking foot feeds a quilt more evenly than the regular presser foot does; it is well worth the investment for anyone doing much machine quilting.

Warp. The threads that are parallel to the fabric selvages; lengthwise grain. Warp threads have very little, if any, stretch.

Weft. The threads that are perpendicular to the fabric selvages; crosswise grain. Weft threads may have some stretch.

White-on-white quilts. Whole-cloth quilts that are white or off-white.

Whole-cloth quilts. Those made from one large (perhaps seamed) piece of fabric that is usually a solid color. Whole-cloth quilts feature the quilting as the primary design element.

Wool batting. Batting that is made from wool. It has natural lanolin (unless the fiber has been well washed) and good body. The newly developed wool battings are wonderful to quilt and can be quilted up to 3 inches apart.

Writing on fabric. Inscribing or signing a patch or a quilt with permanent ink. Select a marker intended for use on fabric and test it for permanence. Fabric can be stabilized by pressing freezer paper to the wrong side. Masking tape can be used to indicate lines on which to write. After writing, peel away the freezer paper and tape.

Wrong side of fabric. The back side, which for a print is usually lighter and more blurry than the right side. (Solid fabric does not have right and wrong sides.) Sometimes the wrong side of the fabric may be used as part of the quilt design, especially for colorwash or picture quilts.

X-ray film. A good material to use for making templates.

Yardage. A term referring to a quantity of fabric. Yardage requirements are listed with most quilt patterns; many quiltmakers choose to buy extra fabric to ensure having plenty for a project and to add to their collections. The cotton fabrics favored by quiltmakers are usually 44 to 45 inches wide before shrinking. Most quilt shops sell fabric in ⅛-yard increments. Many also sell pieces in half width; see also *Fat eighth; Fat quarter.*

Yarn needle. A long, thick needle with a big eye used for tying quilts and doing trapunto. Select a needle just big enough to accommodate the yarn since a too-big needle will leave holes in the quilt and will be difficult to pull through.

Yo-yo quilts. Decorative bedcovers that are made of circles of fabric without batting or lining. Each yo-yo is made from a fabric circle cut approximately twice the size of the finished yo-yo. The edge is turned under to the wrong side with a running stitch, then the thread is pulled to gather the circle. Finished yo-yos are joined with overcast stitches. Another name for yo-yos is Suffolk puffs.

Yukata. Japanese cotton fabric, used to make summer kimonos, that can be incorporated in quiltmaking. It is narrow in width (about 14 inches), and the design is identical on both sides of the fabric.

Zigzag stitch. A machine stitch used for appliqué that is more open than a satin stitch.

If you've enjoyed this book, here are other titles of interest from Rodale Press.

Quilts from America's Heartland

Step-by-Step Directions for 35 Traditional Quilts

by Marianne Fons and Liz Porter

This collection of 28 antique quilts and 7 original quilts is a blend of old favorites and a fresh look for traditional designs.

Hardcover, 256 pages
ISBN 0–87596–589–X

The Thimbleberries Book of Quilts

Quilts of All Sizes Plus Decorative Accessories for Your Home

by Lynette Jensen

More than 30 projects in traditional designs—all with the author's added creative twist—are included, along with a special section featuring innovative ways to display and decorate with quilts.

Hardcover, 256 pages
ISBN 0–87596–630–6

Patchwork Quilts Made Easy

Make a Quilt You Can Be Proud of in Just Three Days

by Jean Wells

Jean Wells shares secrets from her 25 years of quiltmaking in the instructions for more than 45 projects. Her beautiful designs include Nine Patch, Pinwheel, Basket, Log Cabin, Bear's Paw, Fans, and more.

Hardcover, 256 pages
ISBN 0–87596–628–4

More Quick Country Quilting

60 New Fast and Fun Projects from the Author of Quick Country Quilting

by Debbie Mumm

A wonderfully whimsical collection of country designs, from wall and crib quilts to rag dolls and pillows.

Hardcover, 256 pages
ISBN 0–87596–627–6

Quick Country Christmas Quilts

by Debbie Mumm

Deck your home and find something for everyone on your holiday gift list, from festive quilts and stockings to table runners and tree skirts. A special section features quick and easy gifts that can be made in a weekend. Plus, a three-month Christmas planner helps you get organized so you can enjoy the holidays.

Hardcover, 256 pages
ISBN 0–87596–653–5

Quick and Easy Quiltmaking

26 Projects Featuring Speedy Cutting and Piecing Methods

by Mary Hickey, Nancy J. Martin, Marsha McCloskey, and Sara Nephew

Four of the country's top quilting teachers share their creativity, expertise, and timesaving techniques in these 26 wonderful quilt projects.

Hardcover, 256 pages
ISBN 0–87596–576–8

America's Best Quilting Projects

This series is the answer for quilters who can't get to all the big, exciting quilt shows across the country. Each year 25 of the country's best quilt projects are showcased, with complete step-by-step directions.

Special Feature: Holidays and Celebrations

Edited by Mary Green

Hardcover, 176 pages
ISBN 0–87596–551–2

Special Feature: Scrap Quilts

Edited by Mary Green

Hardcover, 176 pages
ISBN 0–87596–604–7

Special Feature: Star Quilts

Edited by Karen Costello Soltys

Hardcover, 176 pages
ISBN 0–87596–642–X

The Classic American Quilt Collection

Based on America's rich quilting heritage, each volume in this series features 12 outstanding quilts with detailed directions and color photos and illustrations.

Log Cabin

Hardcover, 144 pages
ISBN 0–87596–629–2

Nine Patch

Hardcover, 128 pages
ISBN 0–87596–643–8

Baskets

Hardcover, 128 pages
ISBN 0–87596–644–6

Wedding Ring

Hardcover, 128 pages
ISBN 0–87596–683–7

One Patch

Hardcover, 128 pages
ISBN 0–87596–684–5

Quiltmaking Tips and Techniques

Over 1,000 Creative Ideas to Make Your Quiltmaking Quicker, Easier and a Lot More Fun

From 60 Top-Notch Quilters and the Editors of Quilter's Newsletter Magazine

There's something new, useful, fun, and inspiring on every page of this book that covers all of the important quiltmaking techniques.

Hardcover, 352 pages
ISBN 0–87596–588–1